DATE DUE

PETEY & PUSSY

JOHN KERSCHBAUM

The artist would like to thank Frances and Norah
for their love and support and for brightening his day, every day.

He would also like to thank John, Stephen, Mike, Bob, Jay, Jim, Sue,
Jamie, Liz, Pat, Alex, Jane and Barbara for their friendship and advice.

Fantagraphics Books: 7563 Lake City Way, Seattle, WA 98115

Book Designer: Jacob Covey
Editorial Liaison: Gary Groth
Publicist: Eric Reynolds
Publishers: Gary Groth & Kim Thompson

 Visit the publisher's website at www.fantagraphics.com. None of the work available at our website will be quite as twisted as this book, but come anyway. Please.

Visit the artist's websites at www.johnkerschbaum.com and www.fontanellepress.com.

Distributed in the U.S. by W.W. Norton and Company, Inc. (212-354-5500)
Distributed in Canada by the Canadian Manda Group (416-516-0911)
Distributed in the UK by Turnaround Distribution (208-829-3009)
Distributed to comics stores by Diamond Comics Distributors (1-800-452-6642)

ISBN: 978-1-56097-979-1. Printed in Singapore.

PETEY & PUSSY

JOHN KERSCHBAUM

FANTAGRAPHICS BOOKS

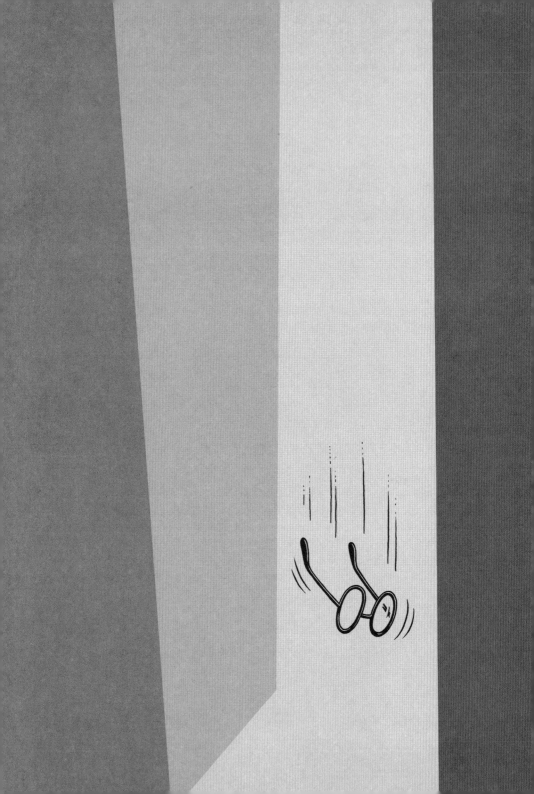

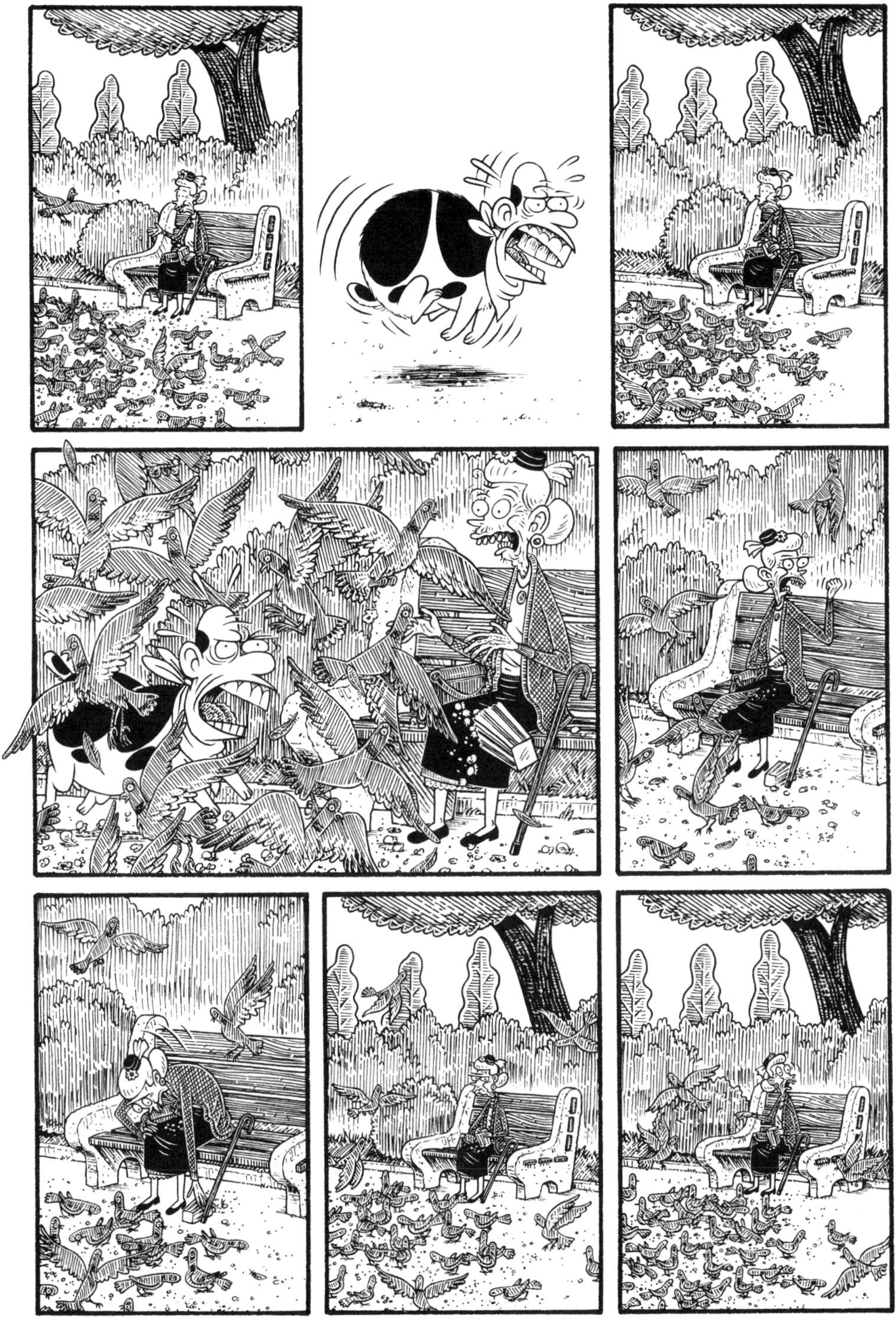

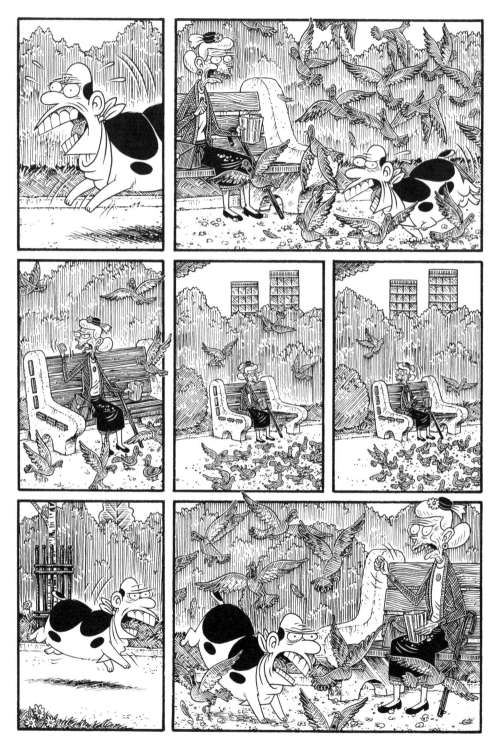

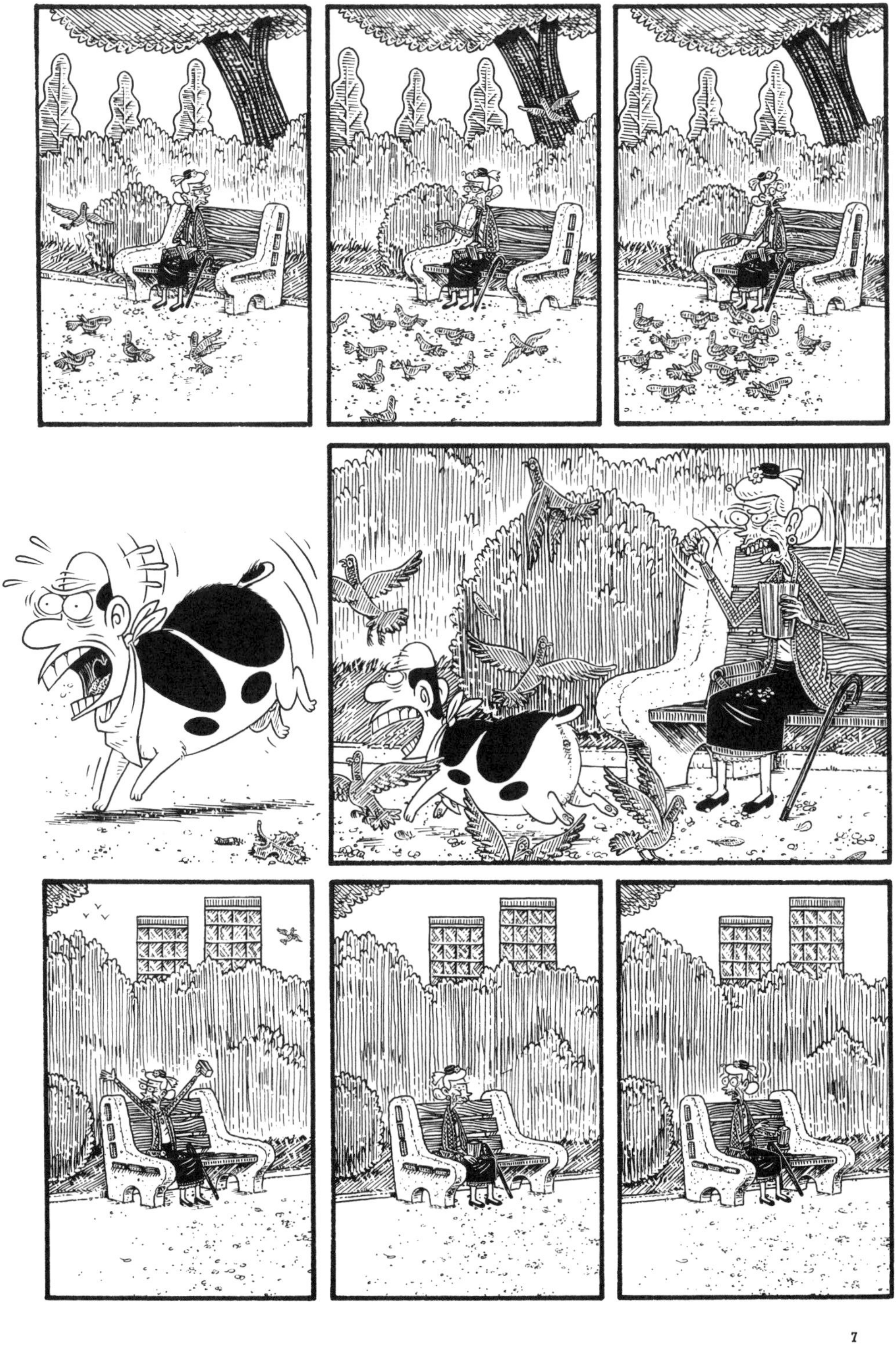

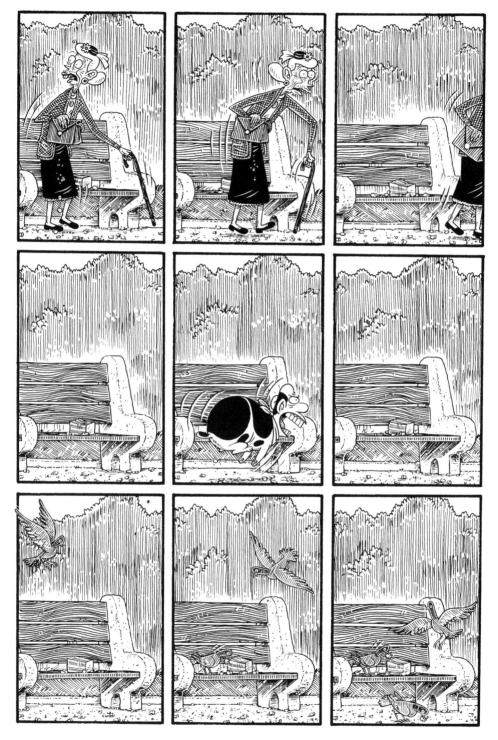

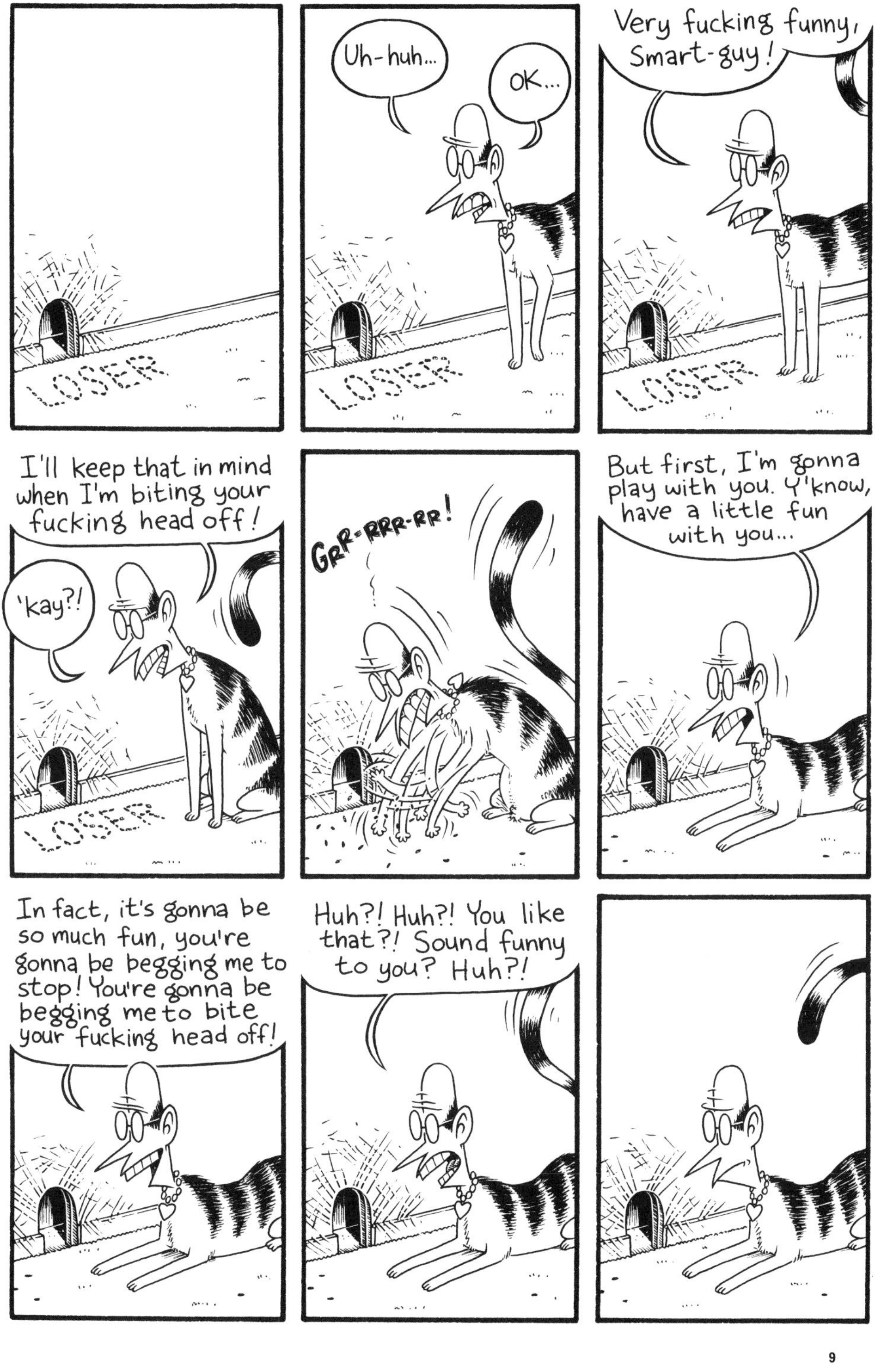
LOSER
Uh-huh...
OK...
LOSER
Very fucking funny, Smart-guy!
LOSER
I'll keep that in mind when I'm biting your fucking head off!
'kay?!
LOSER
GRR-RRR-RR!
But first, I'm gonna play with you. Y'know, have a little fun with you...
In fact, it's gonna be so much fun, you're gonna be begging me to stop! You're gonna be begging me to bite your fucking head off!
Huh?! Huh?! You like that?! Sound funny to you? Huh?!

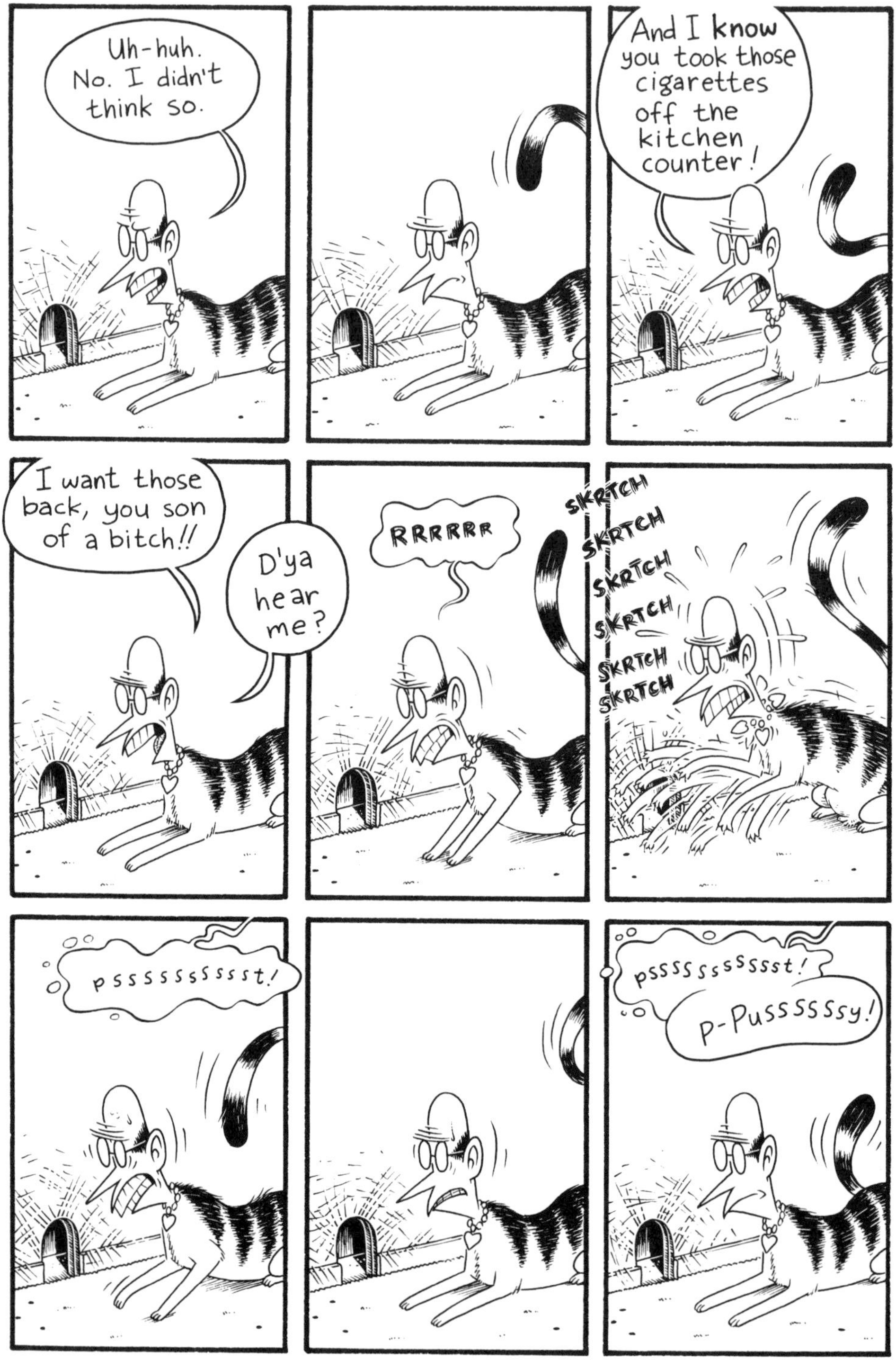
Uh-huh. No. I didn't think so.
And I know you took those cigarettes off the kitchen counter!
I want those back, you son of a bitch!!
D'ya hear me?
RRRRRR
SKRTCH SKRTCH SKRTCH SKRTCH SKRTCH SKRTCH
psssssssssst!
psssssssssst!
p-Pussssssy!

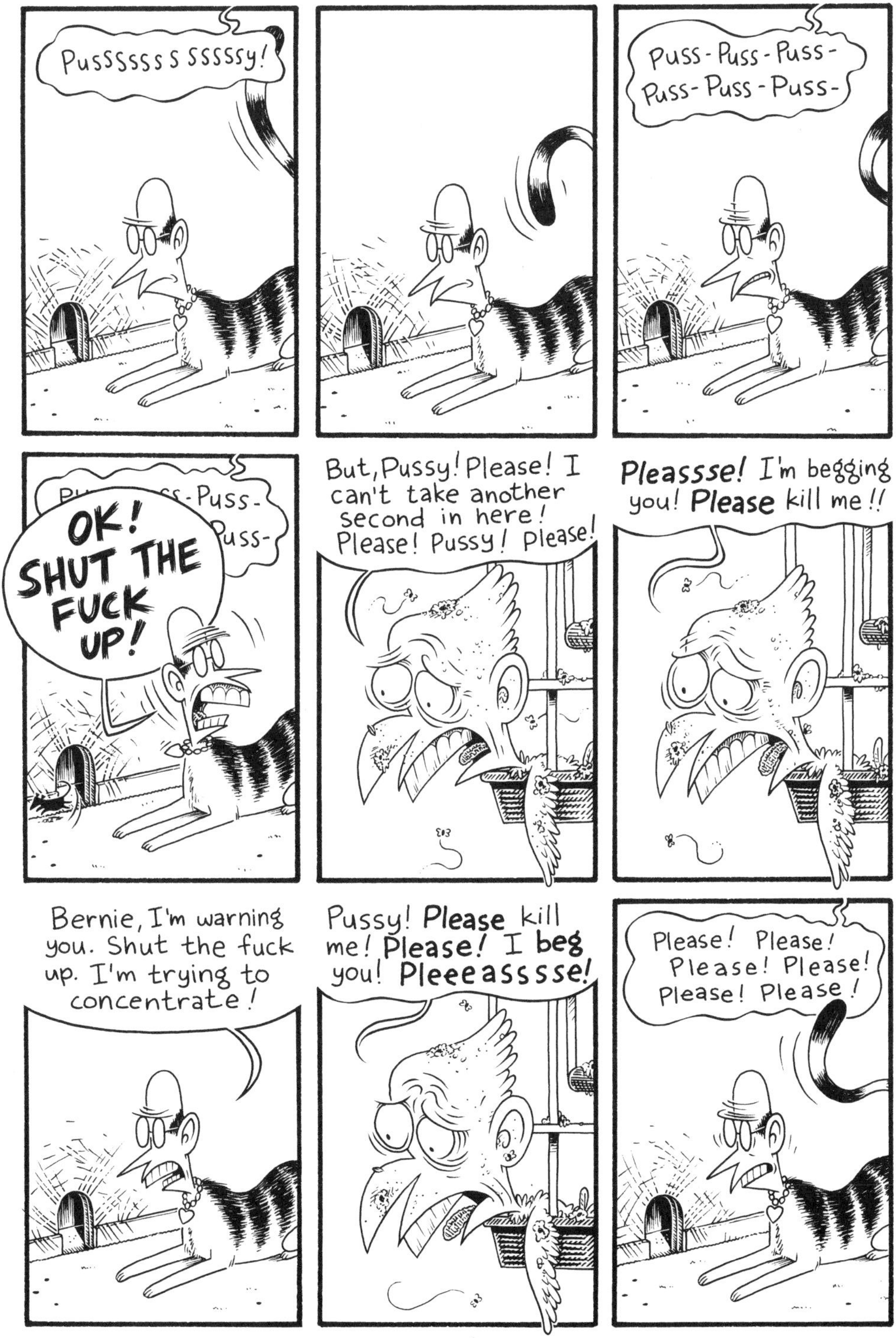
Pussssssss sssssy!
Puss-Puss-Puss-
Puss-Puss-Puss-
OK! SHUT THE FUCK UP!
But, Pussy! Please! I can't take another second in here! Please! Pussy! Please!
Pleassse! I'm begging you! Please kill me!!
Bernie, I'm warning you. Shut the fuck up. I'm trying to concentrate!
Pussy! Please kill me! Please! I beg you! Pleeeasssse!
Please! Please! Please! Please! Please! Please!

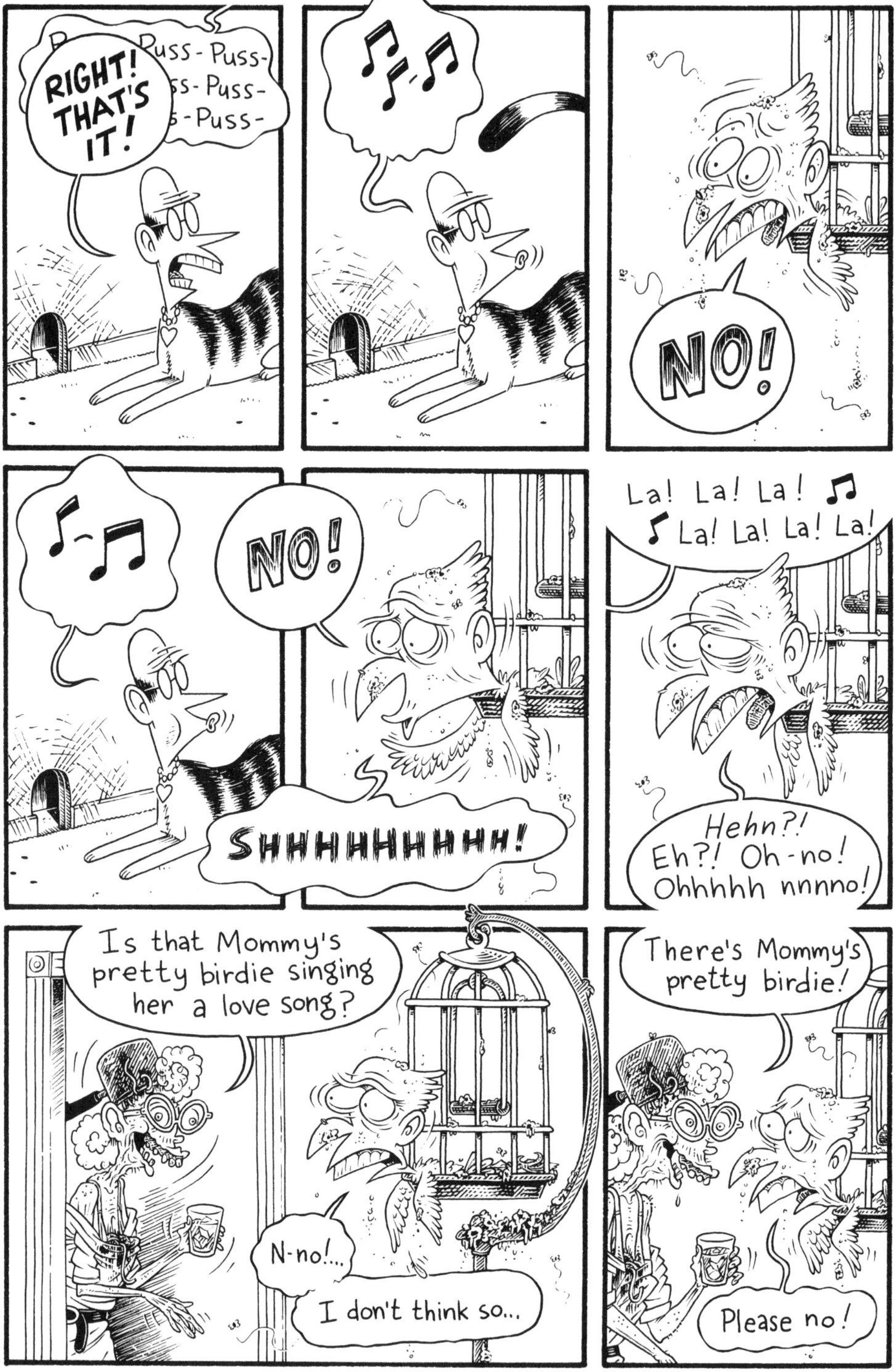
RIGHT! THAT'S IT!
uss - Puss-
ss - Puss-
s - Puss-
NO!
NO!
SHHHHHHHHH!
La! La! La! La! La! La! La!
Hehn?! Eh?! Oh-no! Ohhhhh nnnno!
Is that Mommy's pretty birdie singing her a love song?
N-no!...
I don't think so...
There's Mommy's pretty birdie!
Please no!

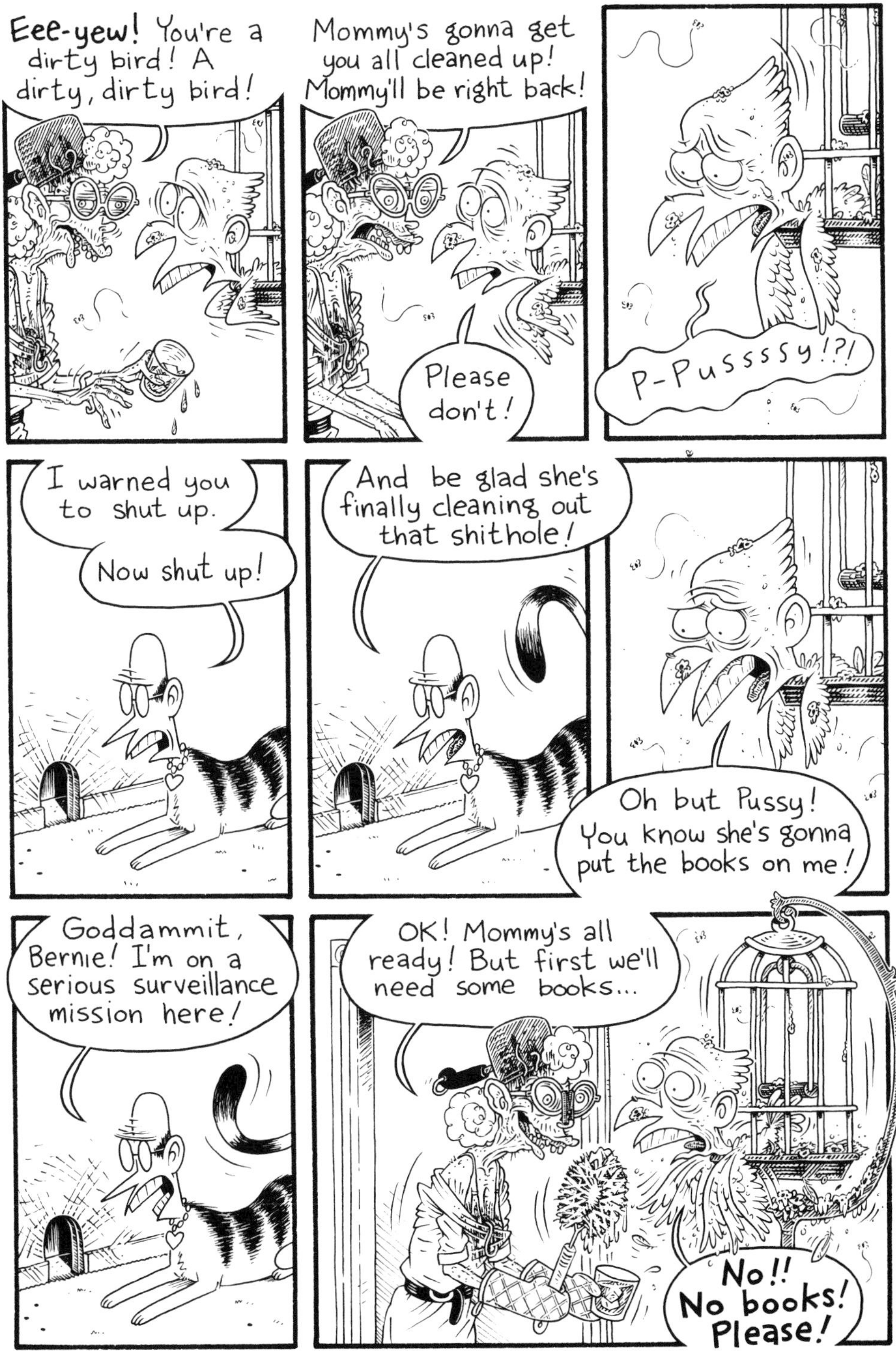
Eee-yew! You're a dirty bird! A dirty, dirty bird!
Mommy's gonna get you all cleaned up! Mommy'll be right back!
Please don't!
P-Pussssy!?!
I warned you to shut up.
Now shut up!
And be glad she's finally cleaning out that shithole!
Oh but Pussy! You know she's gonna put the books on me!
Goddammit, Bernie! I'm on a serious surveillance mission here!
OK! Mommy's all ready! But first we'll need some books...
No!! No books! Please!

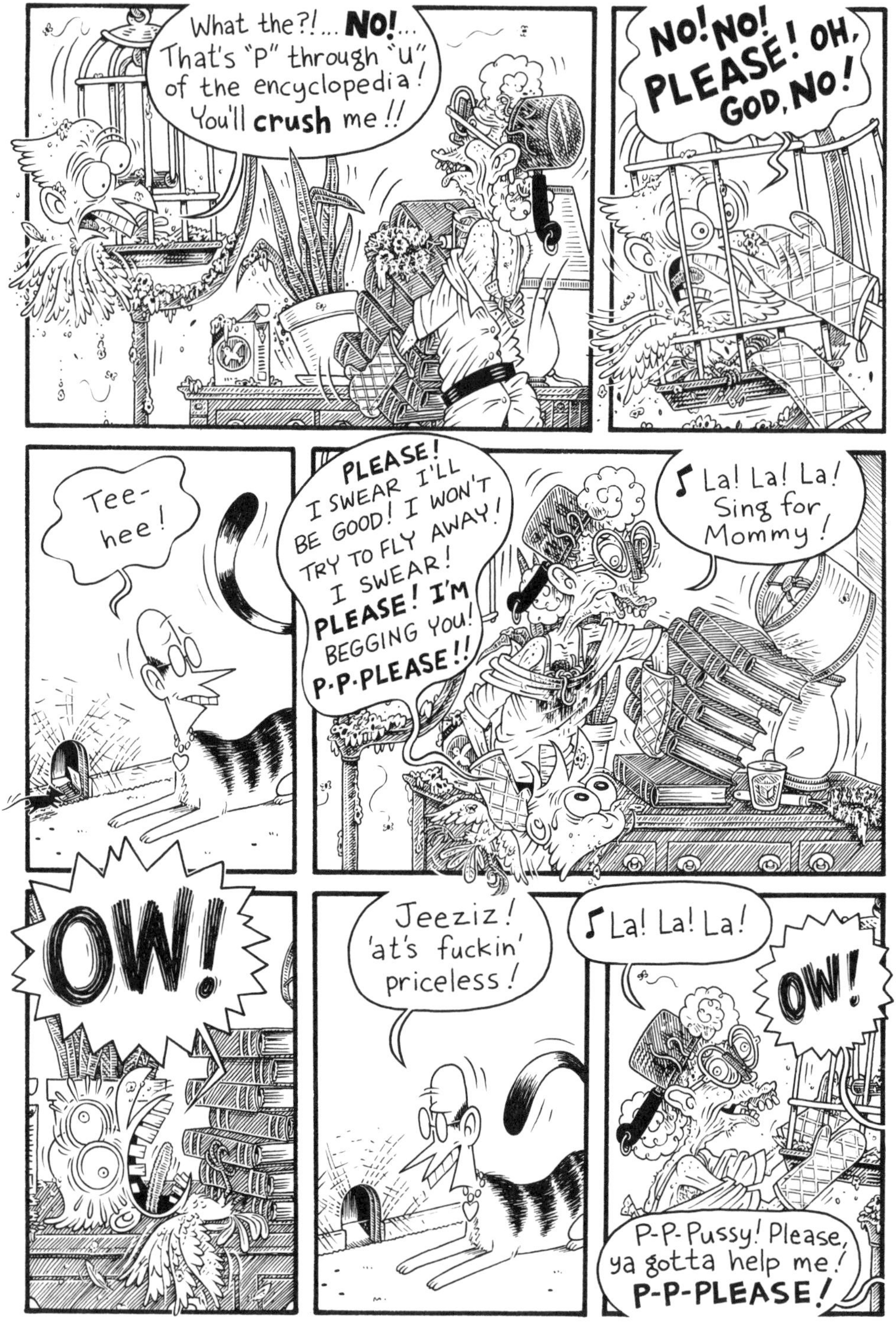
What the?!... NO!... That's "P" through "U" of the encyclopedia! You'll crush me!!
NO! NO! PLEASE! OH, GOD, NO!
Tee-hee!
PLEASE! I SWEAR I'LL BE GOOD! I WON'T TRY TO FLY AWAY! I SWEAR! PLEASE! I'M BEGGING YOU! P-P-PLEASE!!
La! La! La! Sing for Mommy!
OW!
Jeeziz! 'at's fuckin' priceless!
La! La! La!
OW!
P-P-Pussy! Please, ya gotta help me! P-P-PLEASE!

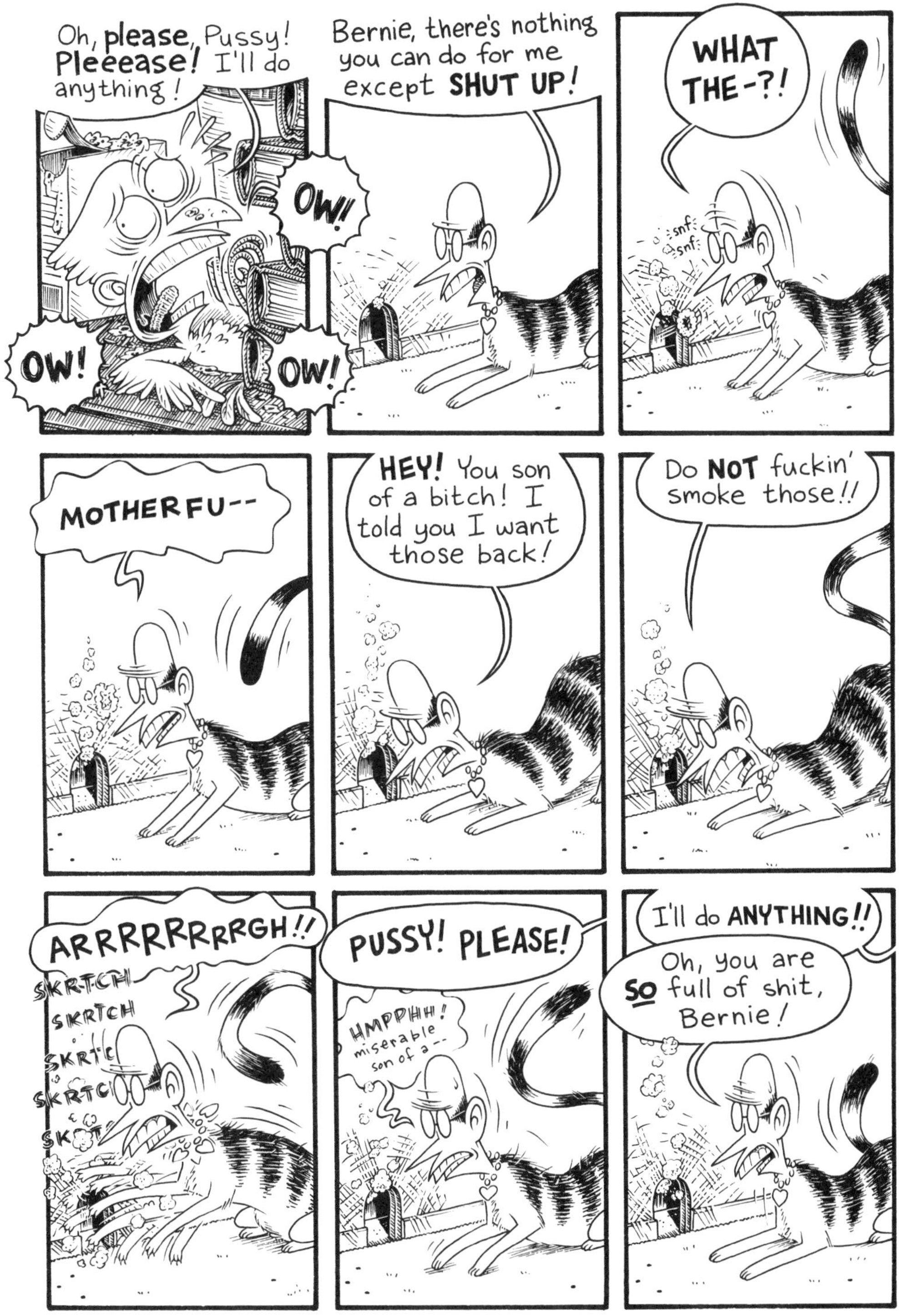
Oh, please, Pussy! Pleeease! I'll do anything!
OW!
OW!
OW!
Bernie, there's nothing you can do for me except SHUT UP!
WHAT THE-?!
snf snf
MOTHERFU--
HEY! You son of a bitch! I told you I want those back!
Do NOT fuckin' smoke those!!
ARRRRRRRGH!!
SKRTCH
SKRTCH
SKRTC
SKRTC
SK
PUSSY! PLEASE!
HMPPHH! miserable son of a--
I'll do ANYTHING!!
Oh, you are SO full of shit, Bernie!

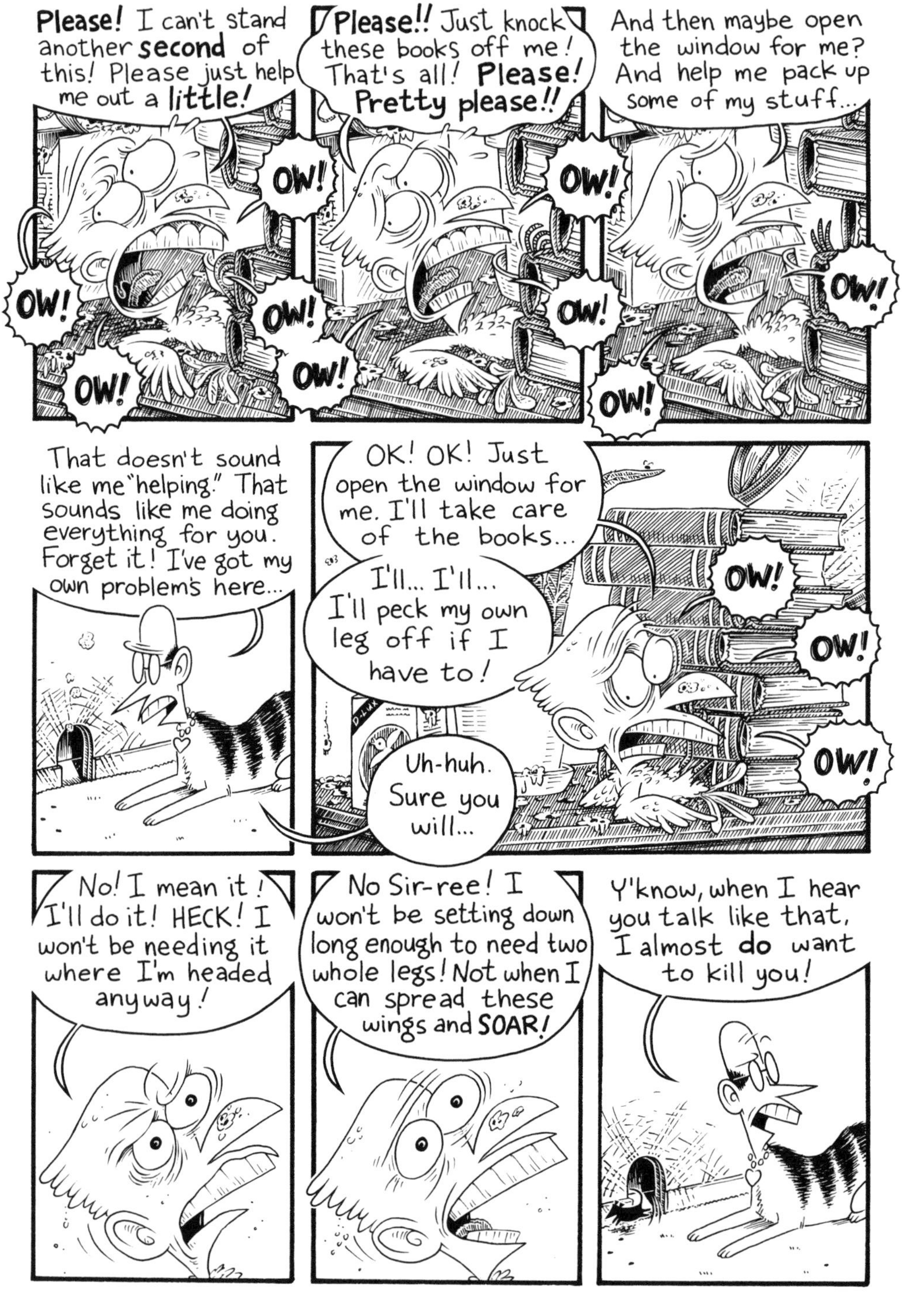
Please! I can't stand another second of this! Please just help me out a little!
OW!
OW!
OW!
OW!
Please!! Just knock these books off me! That's all! Please! Pretty please!!
OW!
OW!
OW!
And then maybe open the window for me? And help me pack up some of my stuff...
OW!
OW!
That doesn't sound like me "helping." That sounds like me doing everything for you. Forget it! I've got my own problem's here...
OK! OK! Just open the window for me. I'll take care of the books...
I'll... I'll... I'll peck my own leg off if I have to!
OW!
OW!
OW!
Uh-huh. Sure you will...
No! I mean it! I'll do it! HECK! I won't be needing it where I'm headed anyway!
No Sir-ree! I won't be setting down long enough to need two whole legs! Not when I can spread these wings and SOAR!
Y'know, when I hear you talk like that, I almost do want to kill you!

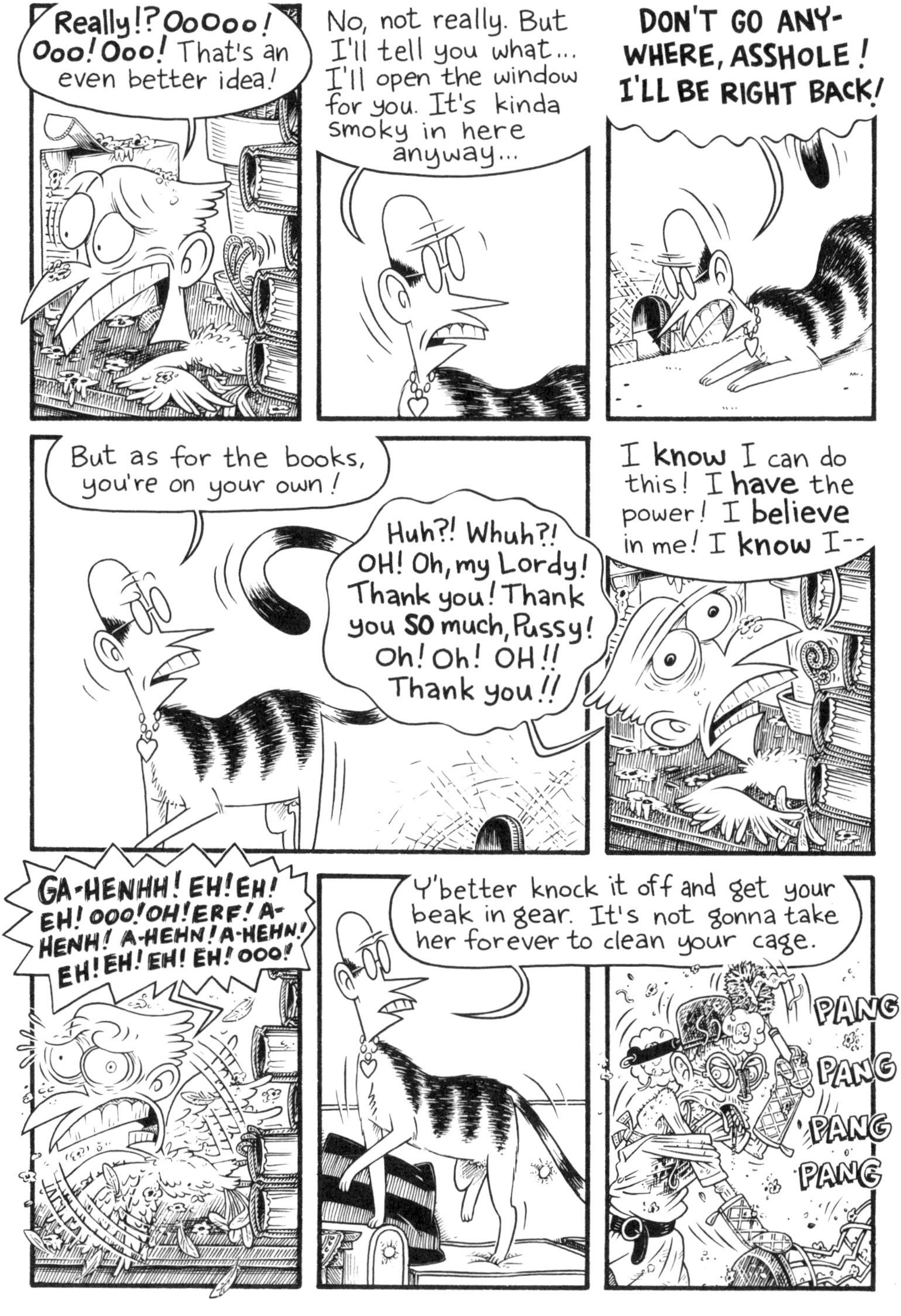
Really!? OoOoo! Ooo! Ooo! That's an even better idea!
No, not really. But I'll tell you what... I'll open the window for you. It's kinda smoky in here anyway...
DON'T GO ANYWHERE, ASSHOLE! I'LL BE RIGHT BACK!
But as for the books, you're on your own!
Huh?! Whuh?! OH! Oh, my Lordy! Thank you! Thank you SO much, Pussy! Oh! Oh! OH!! Thank you!!
I know I can do this! I have the power! I believe in me! I know I--
GA-HENHH! EH! EH! EH! OOO! OH! ERF! A-HENH! A-HEHN! A-HEHN! EH! EH! EH! EH! OOO!
Y'better knock it off and get your beak in gear. It's not gonna take her forever to clean your cage.
PANG
PANG
PANG
PANG

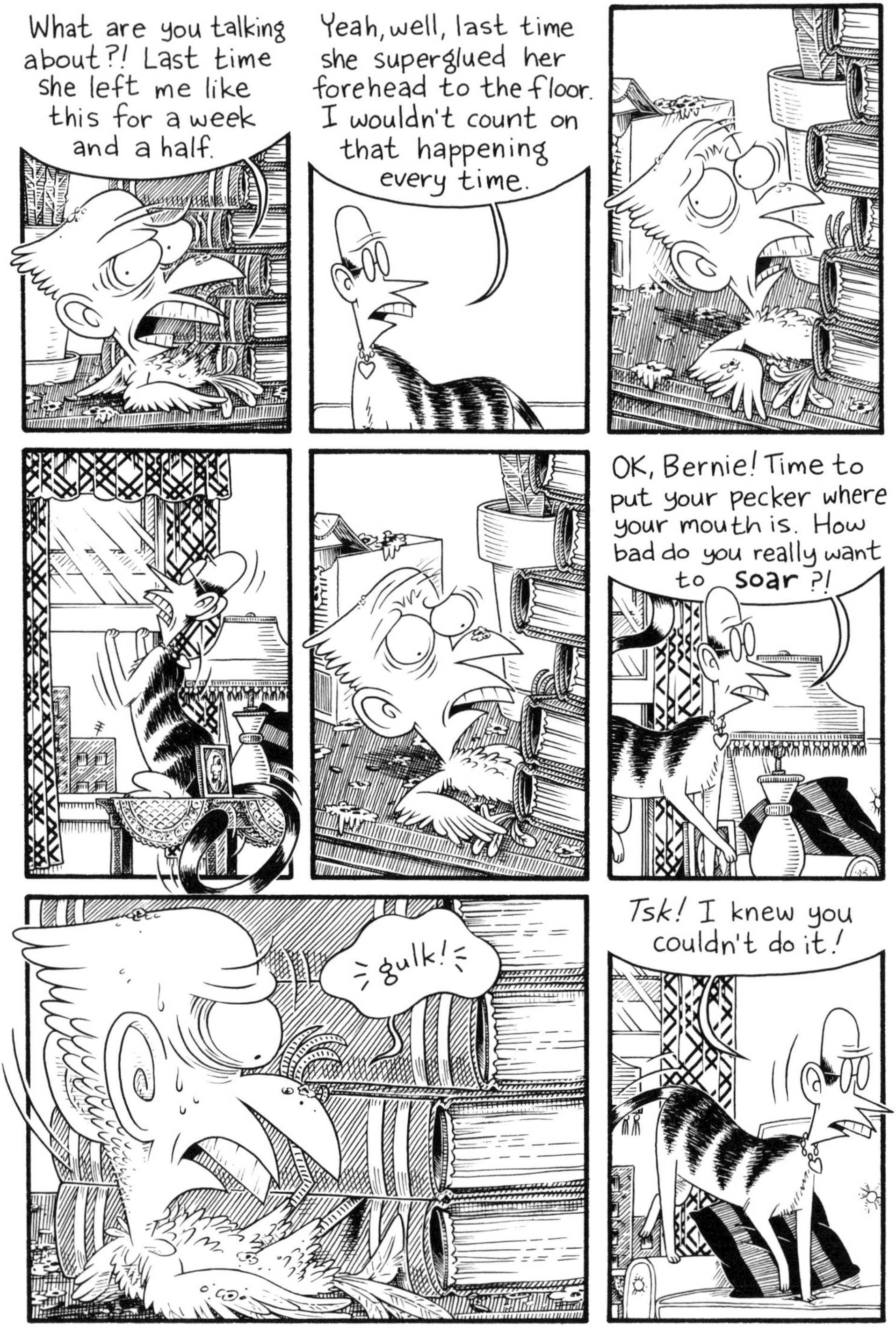
What are you talking about?! Last time she left me like this for a week and a half.
Yeah, well, last time she superglued her forehead to the floor. I wouldn't count on that happening every time.
OK, Bernie! Time to put your pecker where your mouth is. How bad do you really want to **soar**?!
gulk!
Tsk! I knew you couldn't do it!

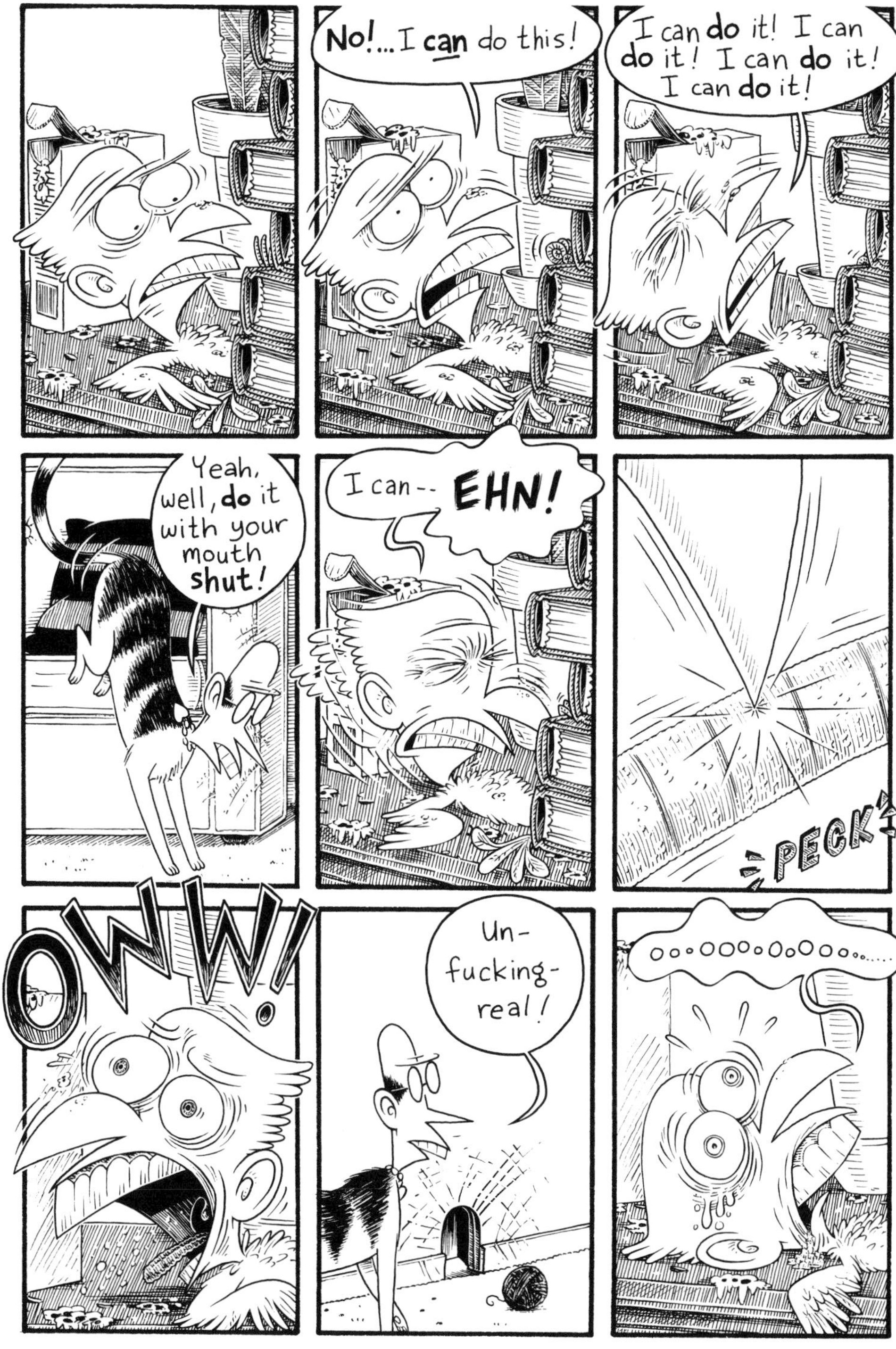

No!...I can do this!
I can do it! I can do it! I can do it! I can do it!
Yeah, well, do it with your mouth shut!
I can--
EHN!
PECK
OWW!
Un-fucking-real!
ooo0OOoOoOOoo.....

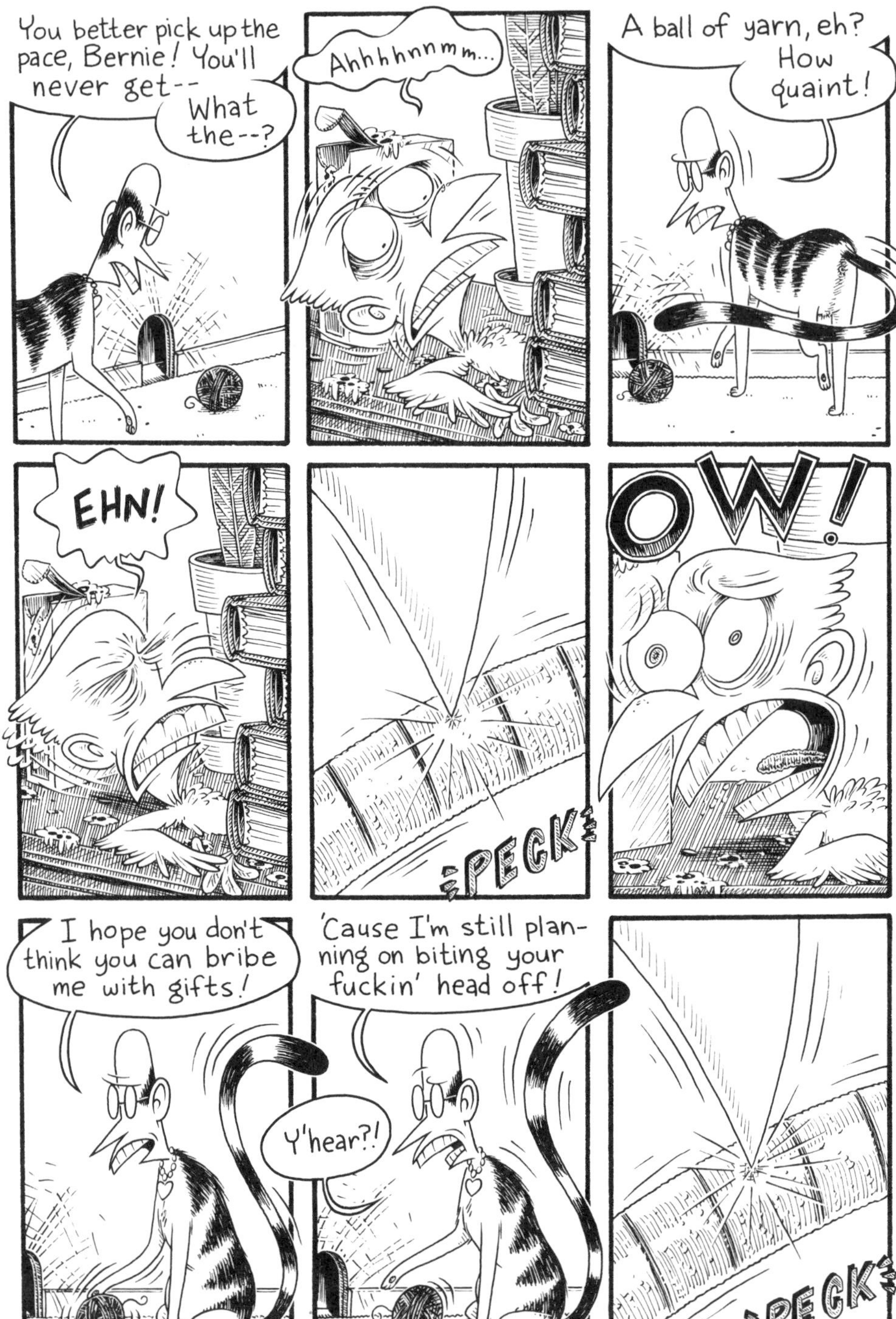
You better pick up the pace, Bernie! You'll never get--
What the--?
Ahhhhnnmm...
A ball of yarn, eh?
How quaint!
EHN!
PECK
OW!
I hope you don't think you can bribe me with gifts!
'Cause I'm still planning on biting your fuckin' head off!
Y'hear?!
PECK

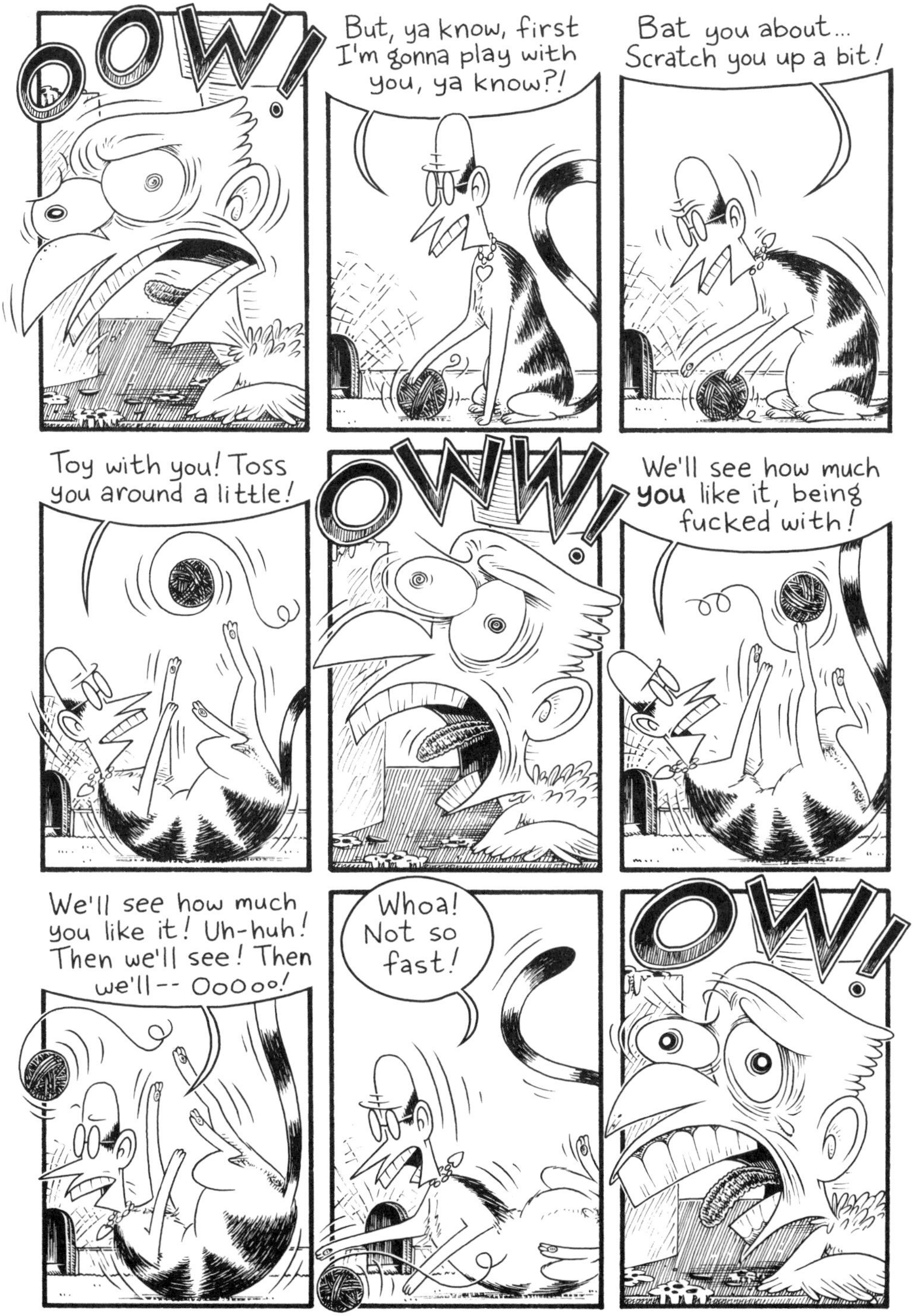
OOW!
But, ya know, first I'm gonna play with you, ya know?!
Bat you about... Scratch you up a bit!
Toy with you! Toss you around a little!
OWW!
We'll see how much **you** like it, being fucked with!
We'll see how much you like it! Uh-huh! Then we'll see! Then we'll-- Ooooo!
Whoa! Not so fast!
OW!

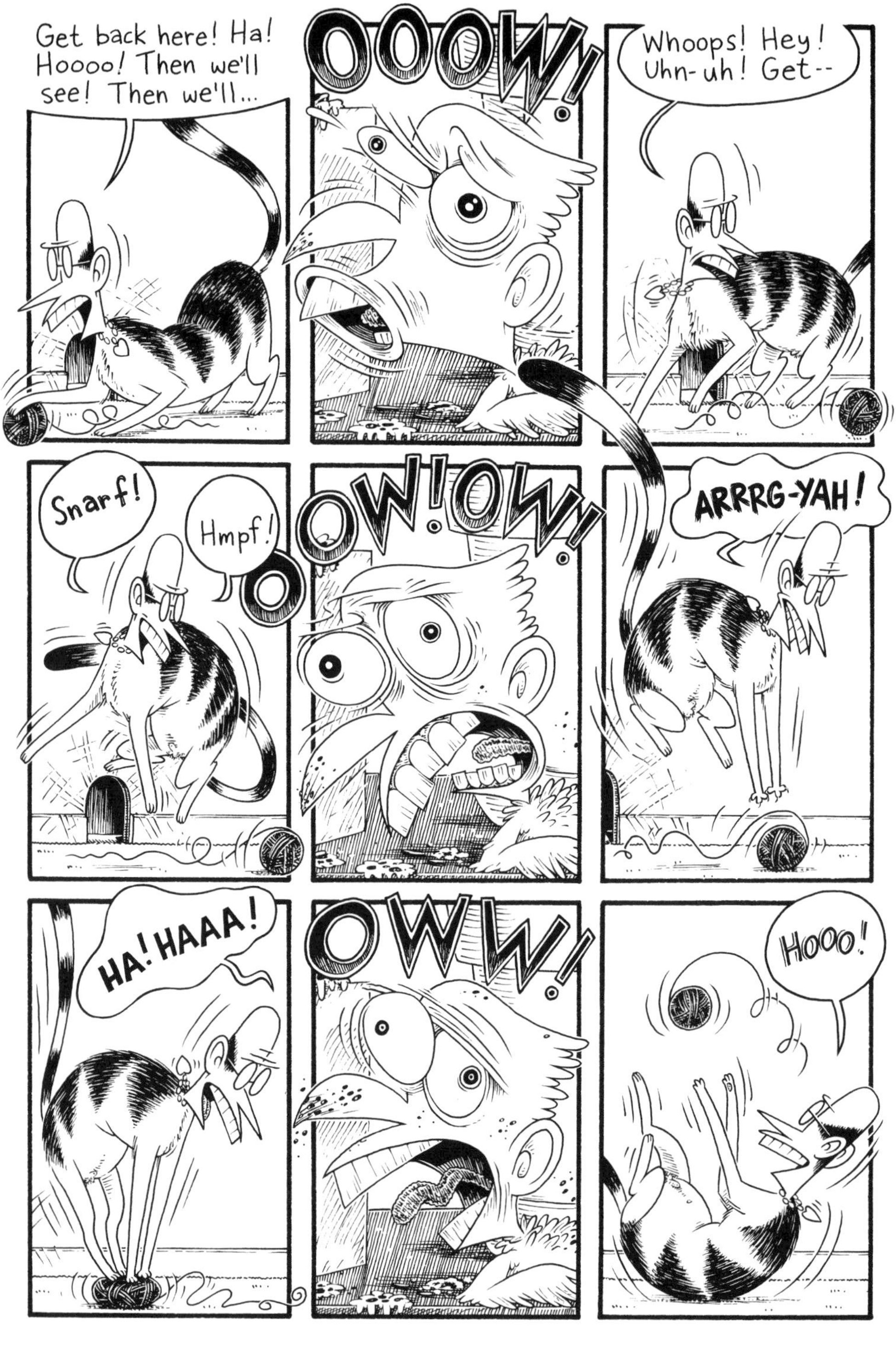
Get back here! Ha! Hoooo! Then we'll see! Then we'll...
OOOW!
Whoops! Hey! Uhn-uh! Get--
Snarf!
Hmpf!
OOW!OW!
ARRRG-YAH!
HA! HAAA!
OWW!
HOOO!

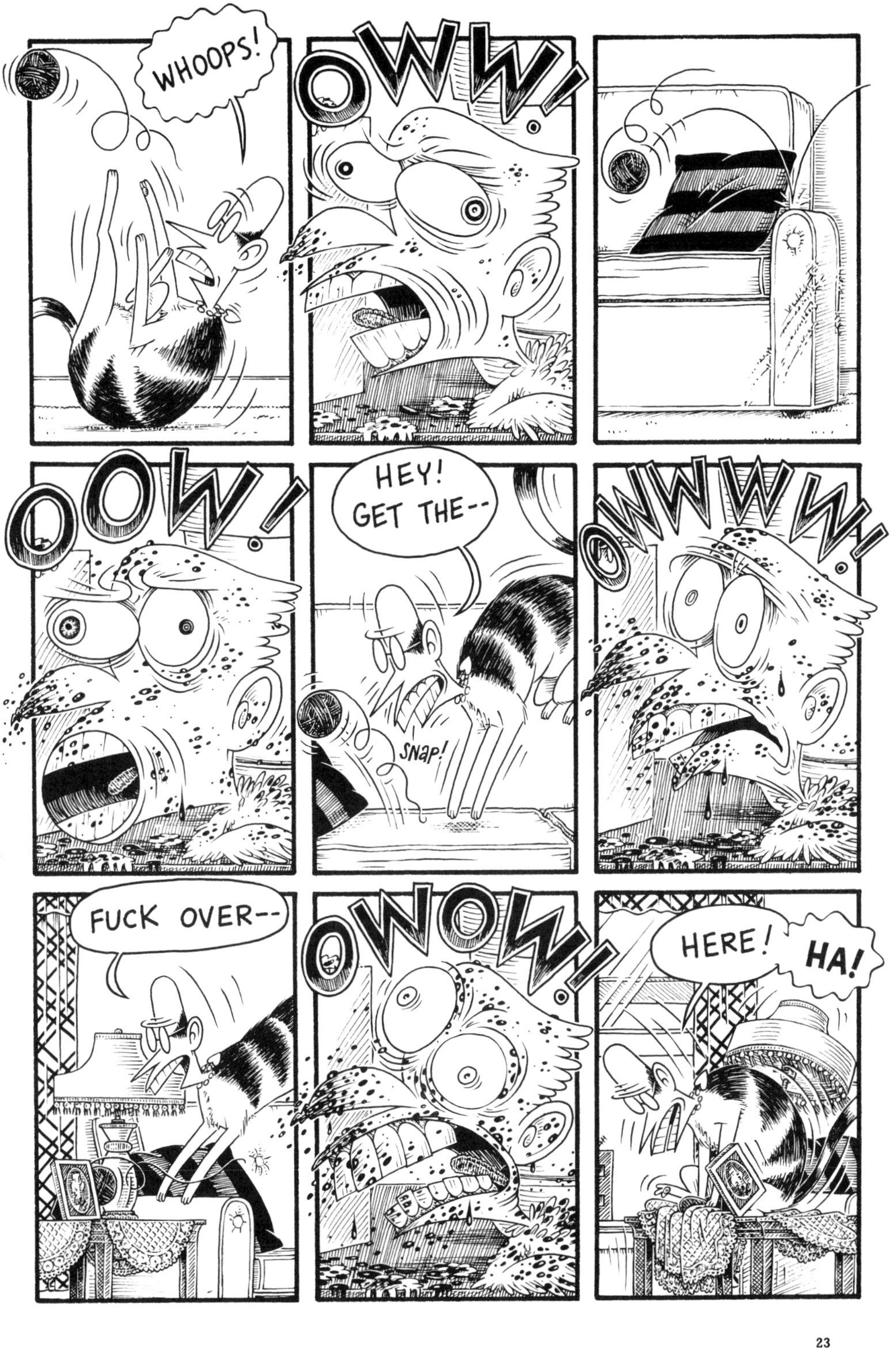

WHOOPS!
OWW!
OOW!
HEY! GET THE--
SNAP!
OWWWW!
FUCK OVER--
OWOW!
HERE!
HA!

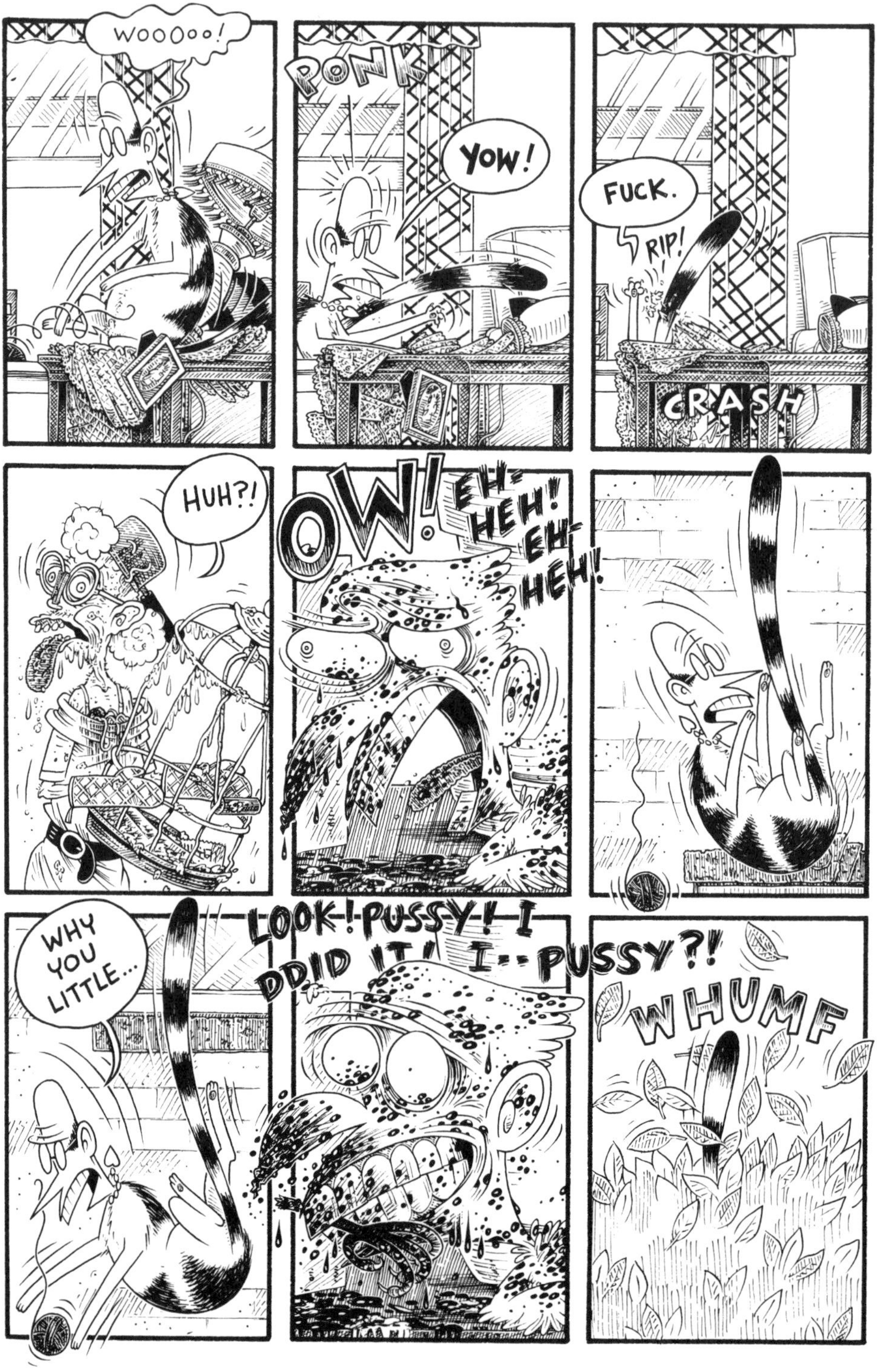
WOOOoo!
PONK
YOW!
FUCK.
RIP!
CRASH
HUH?!
OW!
EH-HEH! EH-HEH!
WHY YOU LITTLE...
LOOK! PUSSY! I DDID IT! I-- PUSSY?!
WHUMF

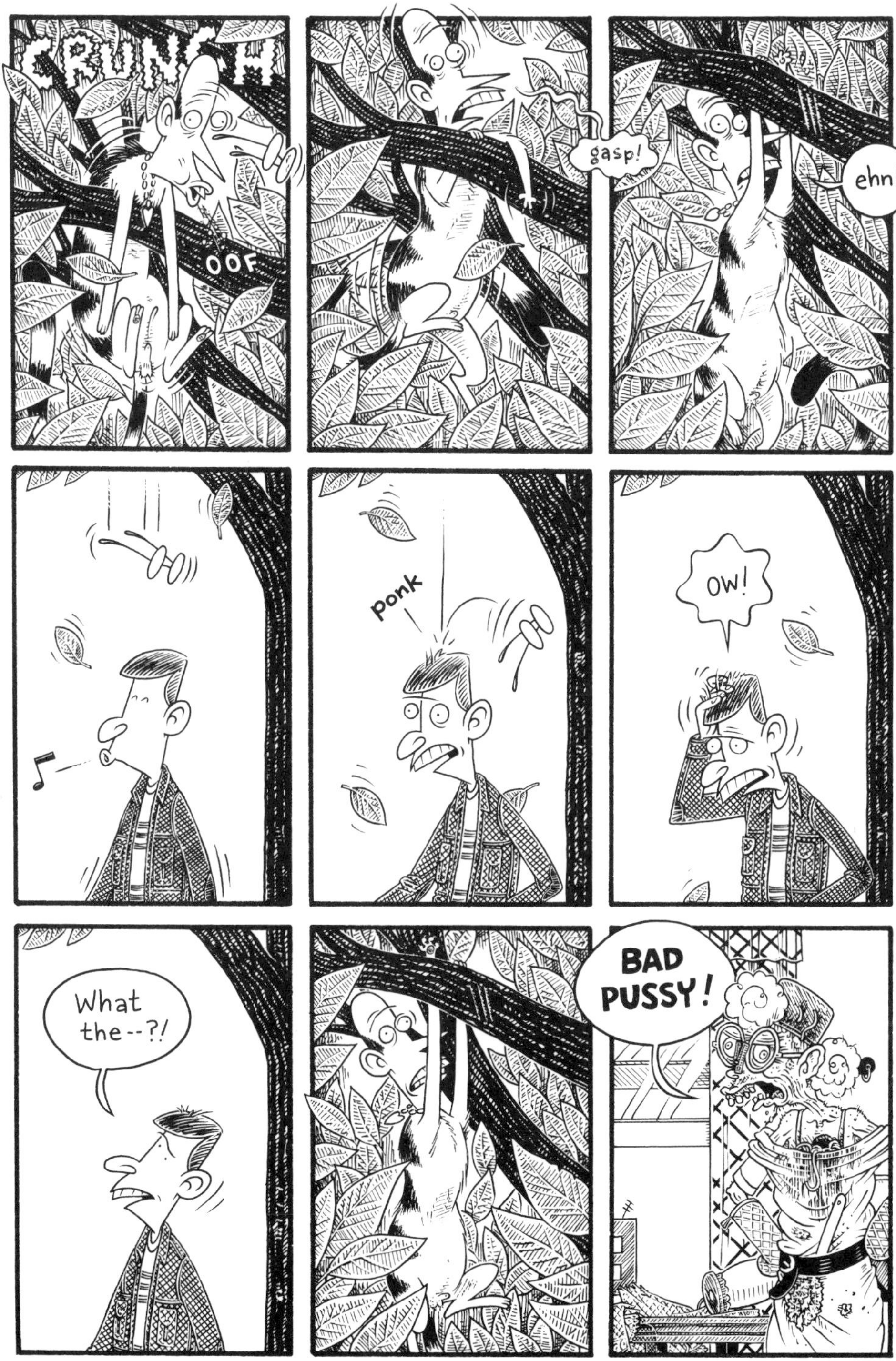

CRUNCH
OOF
gasp!
ehn!
ponk
OW!
What the--?!
BAD PUSSY!

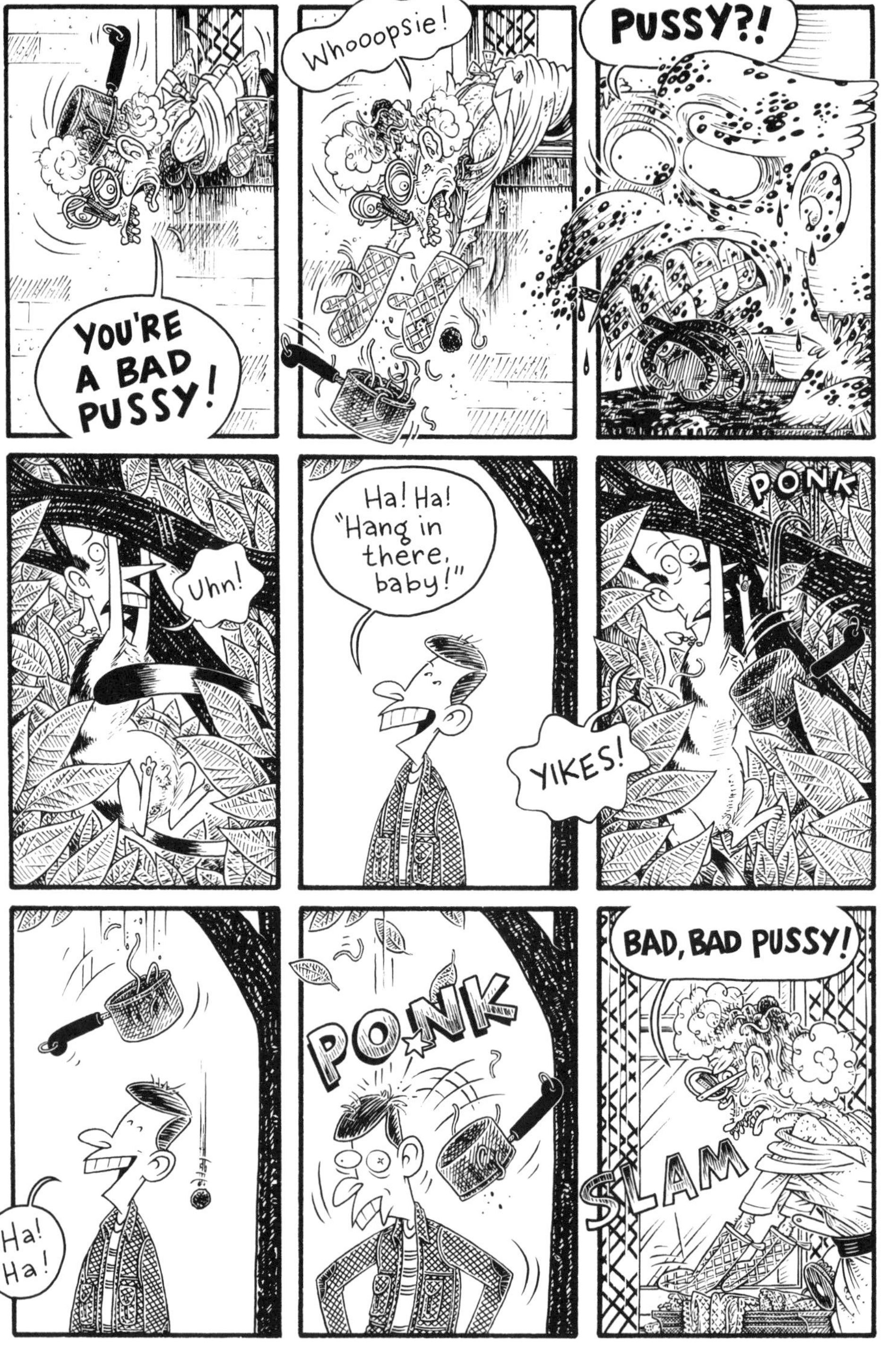
YOU'RE A BAD PUSSY!
Whooopsie!
PUSSY?!
Uhn!
Ha! Ha! "Hang in there, baby!"
PONK
YIKES!
Ha! Ha!
PONK
BAD, BAD PUSSY!
SLAM

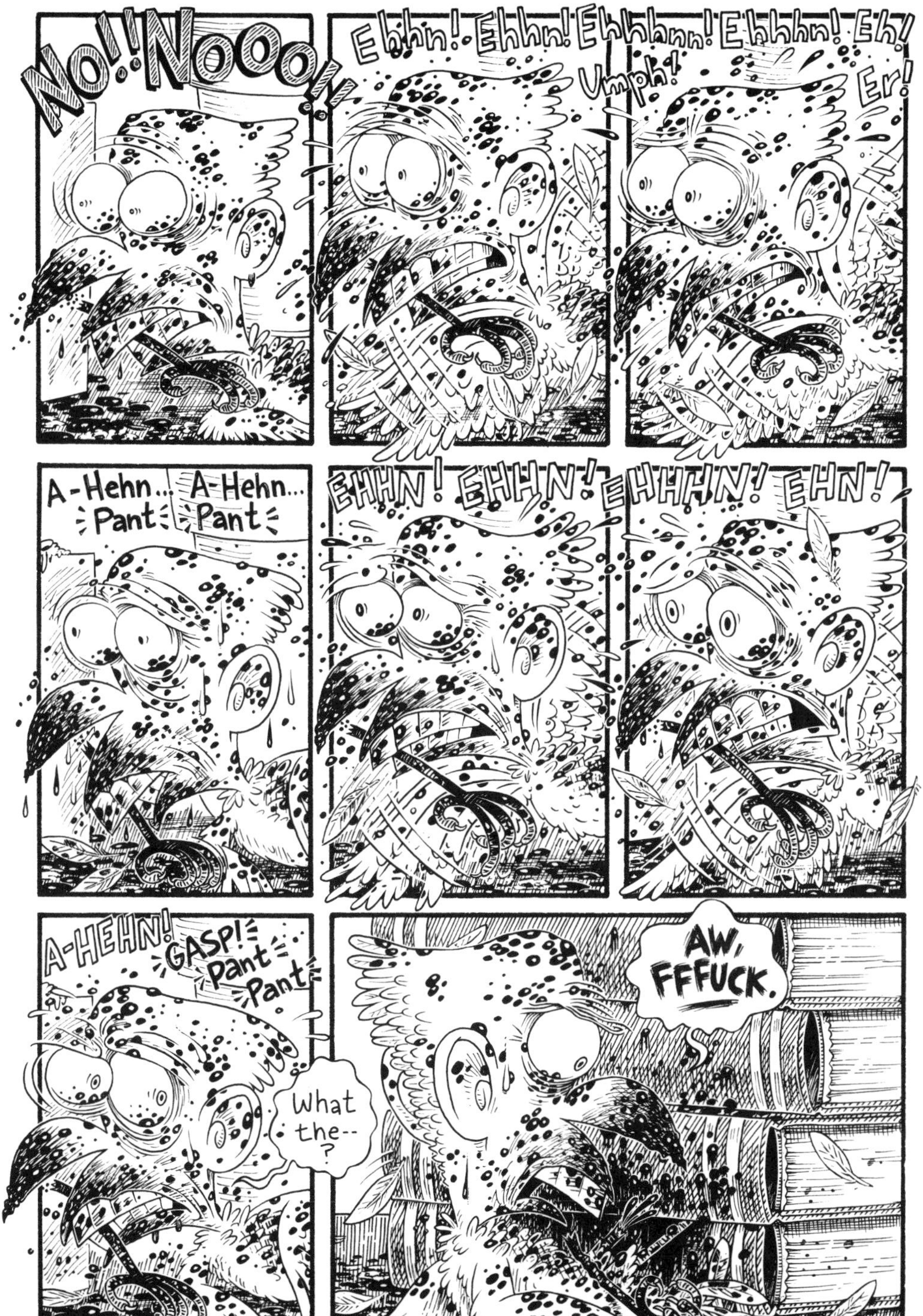
NO!! NOOOO!!
Ehhn! Ehhn! Ehhhnn! Ehhhn! Eh!
Umph!
Er!
A-Hehn... Pant
A-Hehn... Pant
EHHN! EHHN! EHHHN! EHN!
A-HEHN! GASP! Pant Pant
What the--?
AW, FFFUCK.

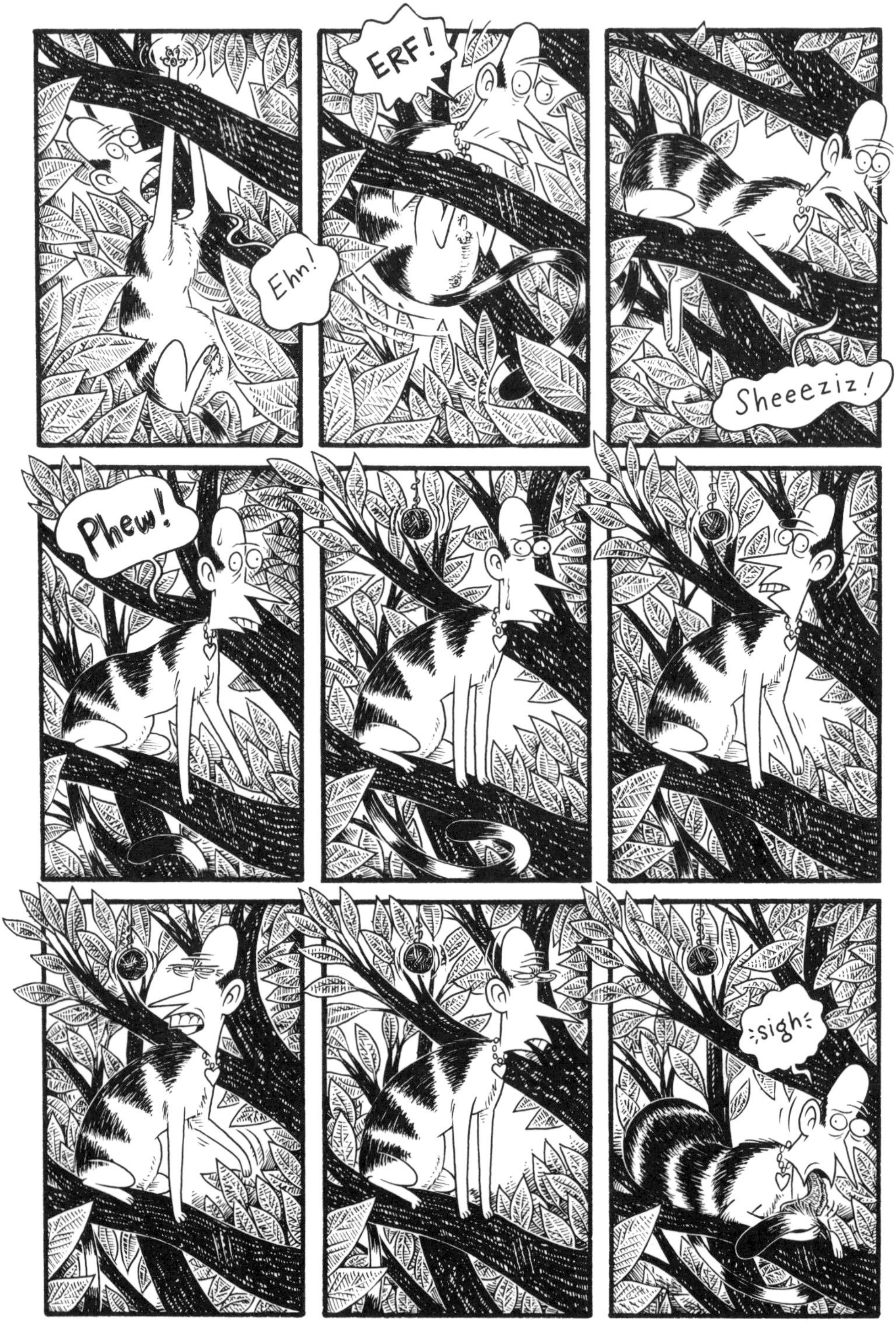

Ehn!
ERF!
Sheeeziz!
Phew!
sigh

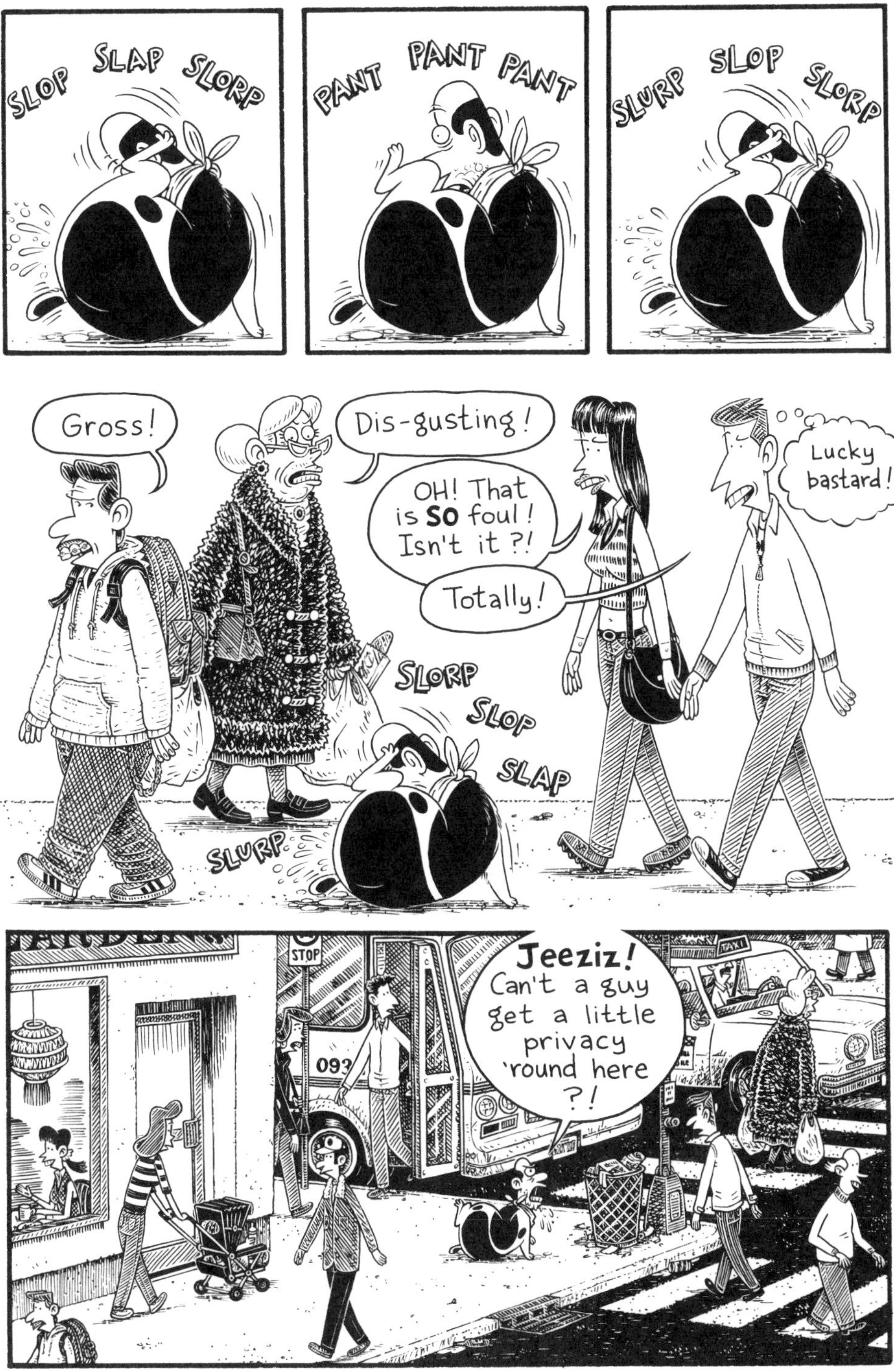
SLOP SLAP SLORP
PANT PANT PANT
SLURP SLOP SLORP
Gross!
Dis-gusting!
OH! That is **SO** foul! Isn't it?!
Totally!
Lucky bastard!
SLORP
SLOP
SLAP
SLURP
STOP
TAXI
Jeeziz! Can't a guy get a little privacy 'round here?!

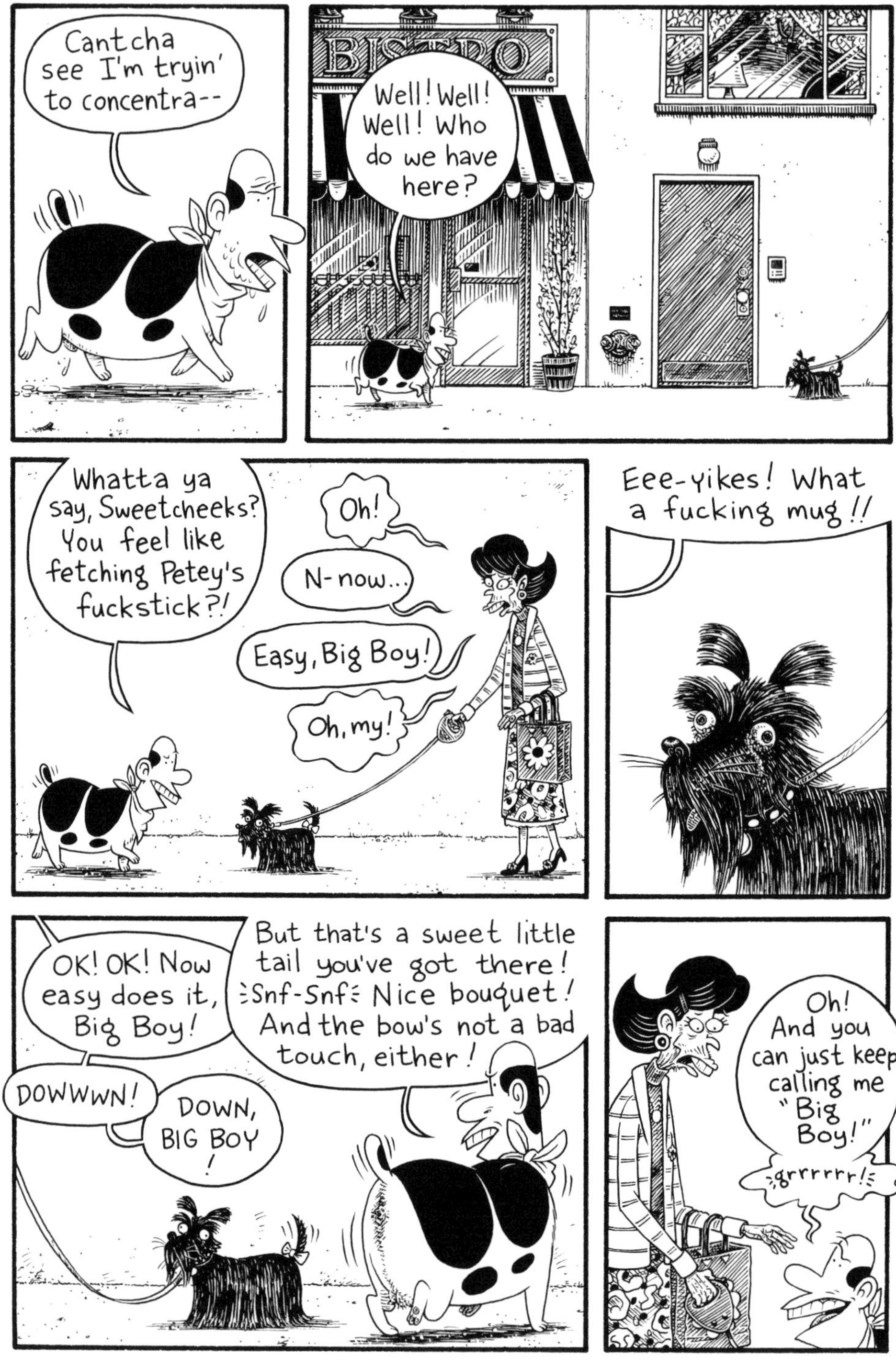
Cantcha see I'm tryin' to concentra--
BISTRO
Well! Well! Well! Who do we have here?
Whatta ya say, Sweetcheeks? You feel like fetching Petey's fuckstick?!
Oh!
N-now...
Easy, Big Boy!
Oh, my!
Eee-yikes! What a fucking mug!!
OK! OK! Now easy does it, Big Boy!
DOWWWN!
DOWN, BIG BOY!
But that's a sweet little tail you've got there! Snf-Snf Nice bouquet! And the bow's not a bad touch, either!
Oh! And you can just keep calling me "Big Boy!"
grrrrrr!

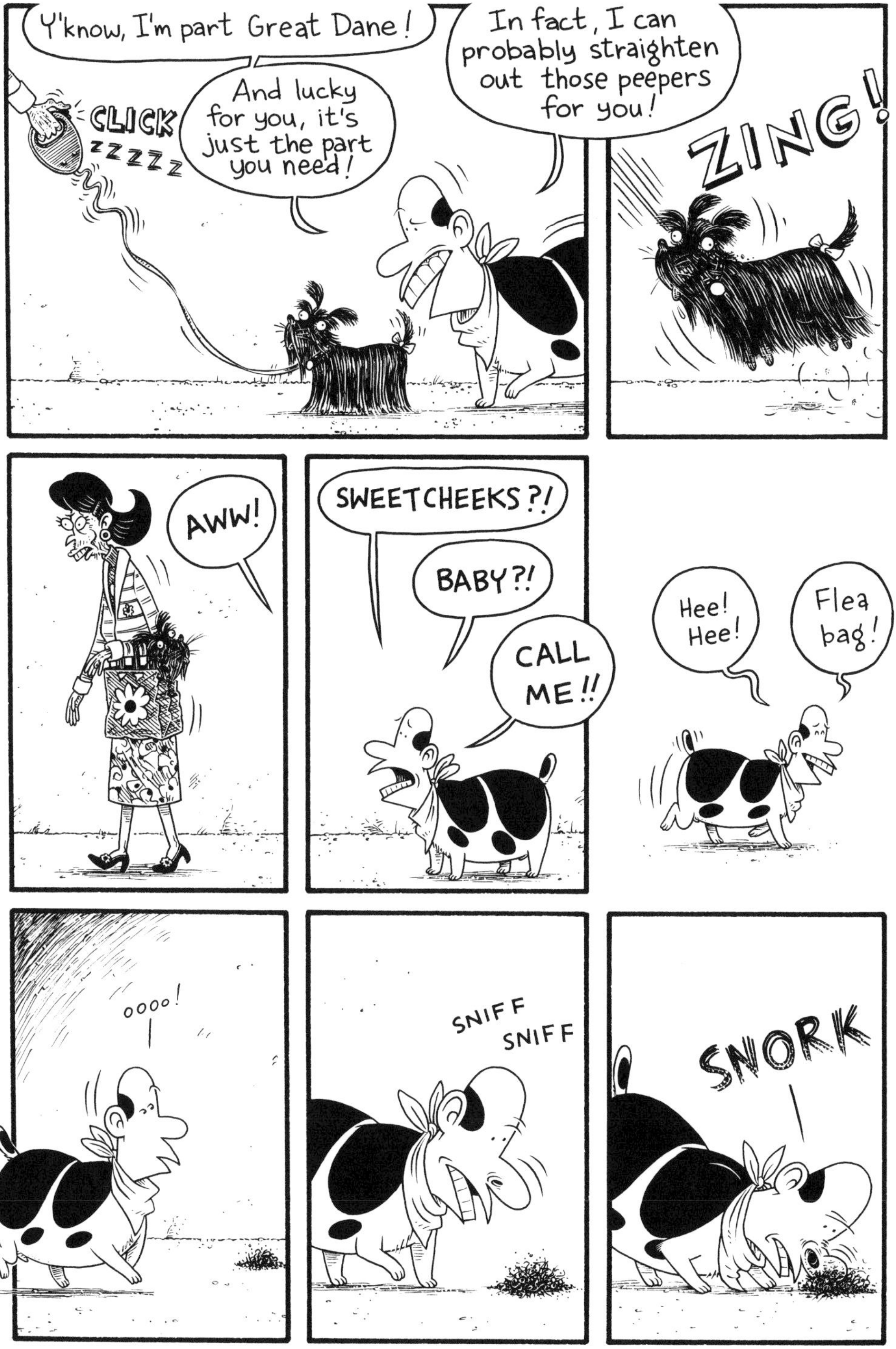
Y'know, I'm part Great Dane!
CLICK
ZZZZZ
And lucky for you, it's just the part you need!
In fact, I can probably straighten out those peepers for you!
ZING!
AWW!
SWEETCHEEKS?!
BABY?!
CALL ME!!
Hee! Hee!
Flea bag!
oooo!
SNIFF SNIFF
SNORK

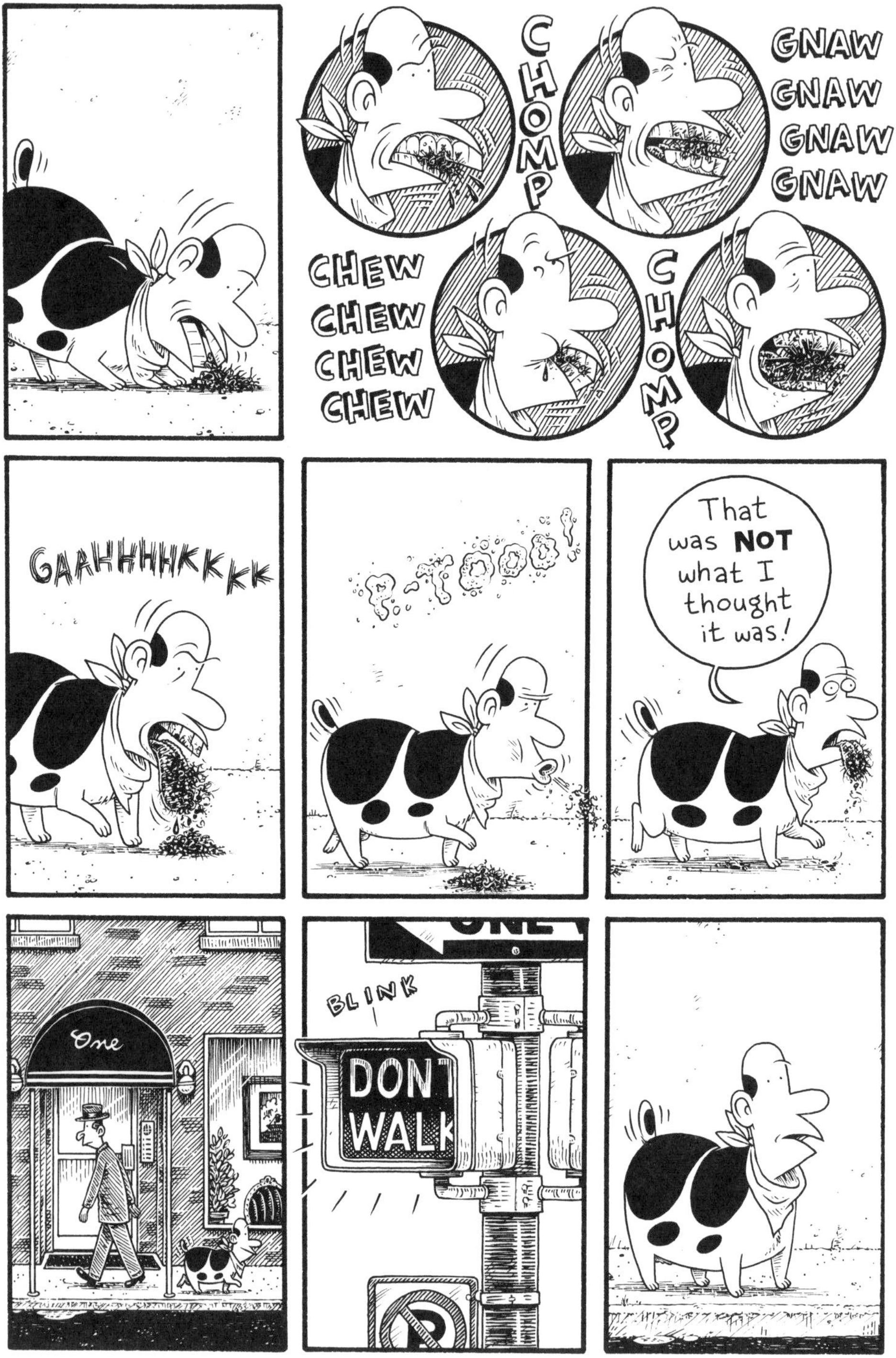
CHOMP
GNAW
GNAW
GNAW
GNAW
CHEW
CHEW
CHEW
CHEW
CHOMP
GAAHHHHKKKK
P-TOOO!
That was NOT what I thought it was!
One
BLINK
DON'T WALK

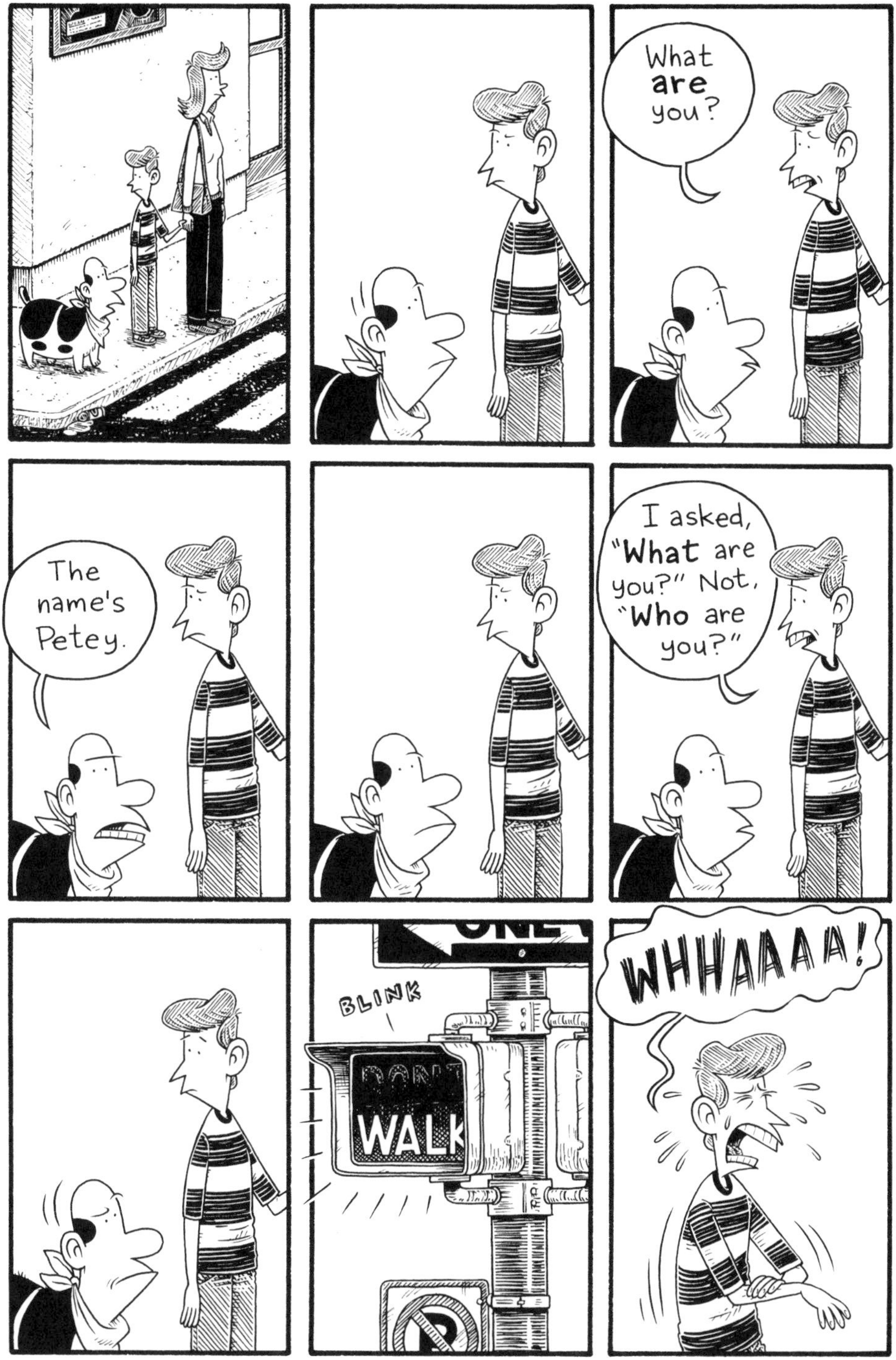
What **are** you?
The name's Petey.
I asked, "**What** are you?" Not, "**Who** are you?"
BLINK
WALK
WHHAAAA!

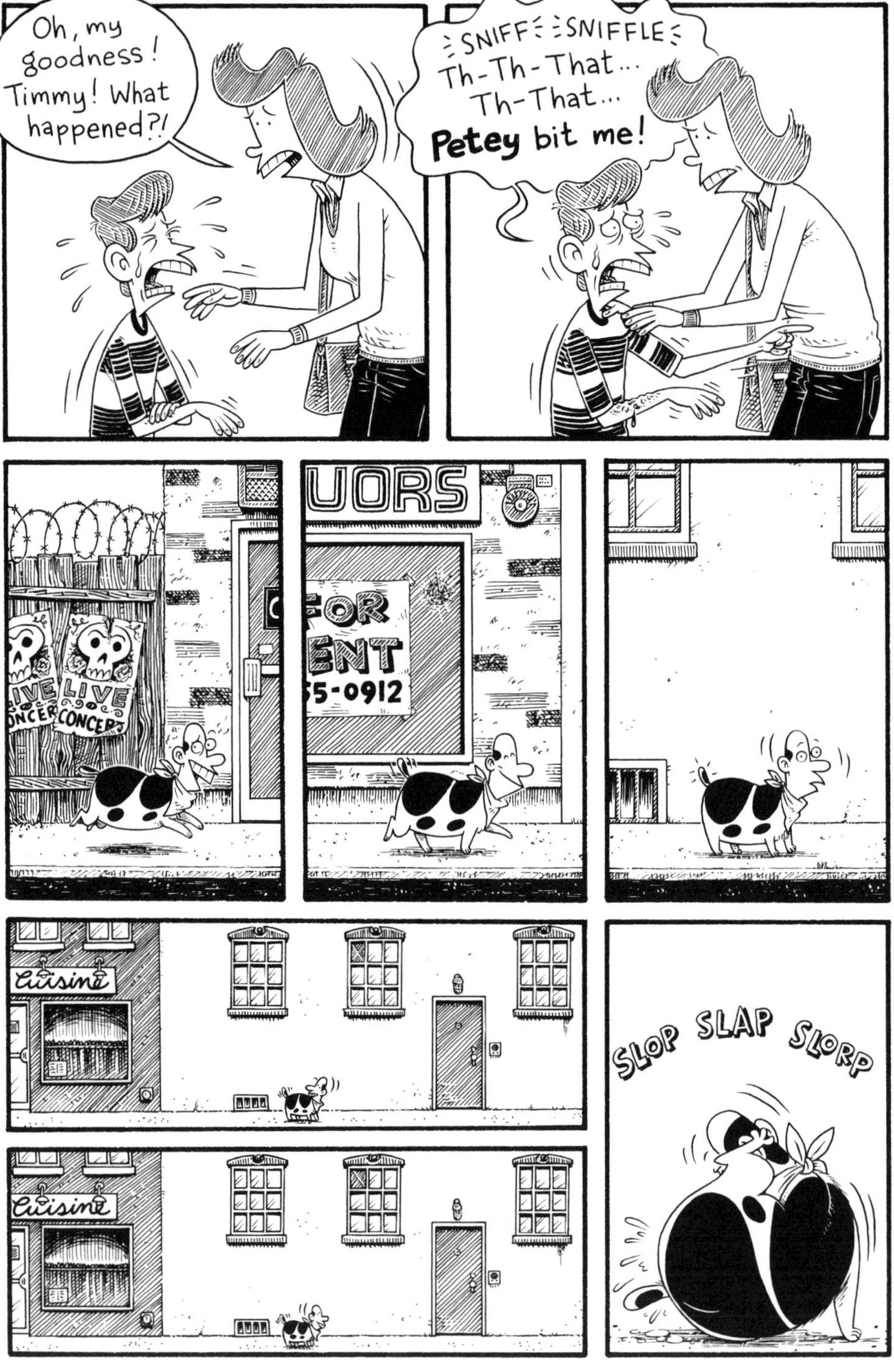

Oh, my goodness! Timmy! What happened?!
SNIFF SNIFFLE
Th-Th-That... Th-That... **Petey** bit me!
UORS
FOR ENT 55-0912
LIVE CONCER
LIVE CONCER
Cuisine
Cuisine
SLOP SLAP SLORP

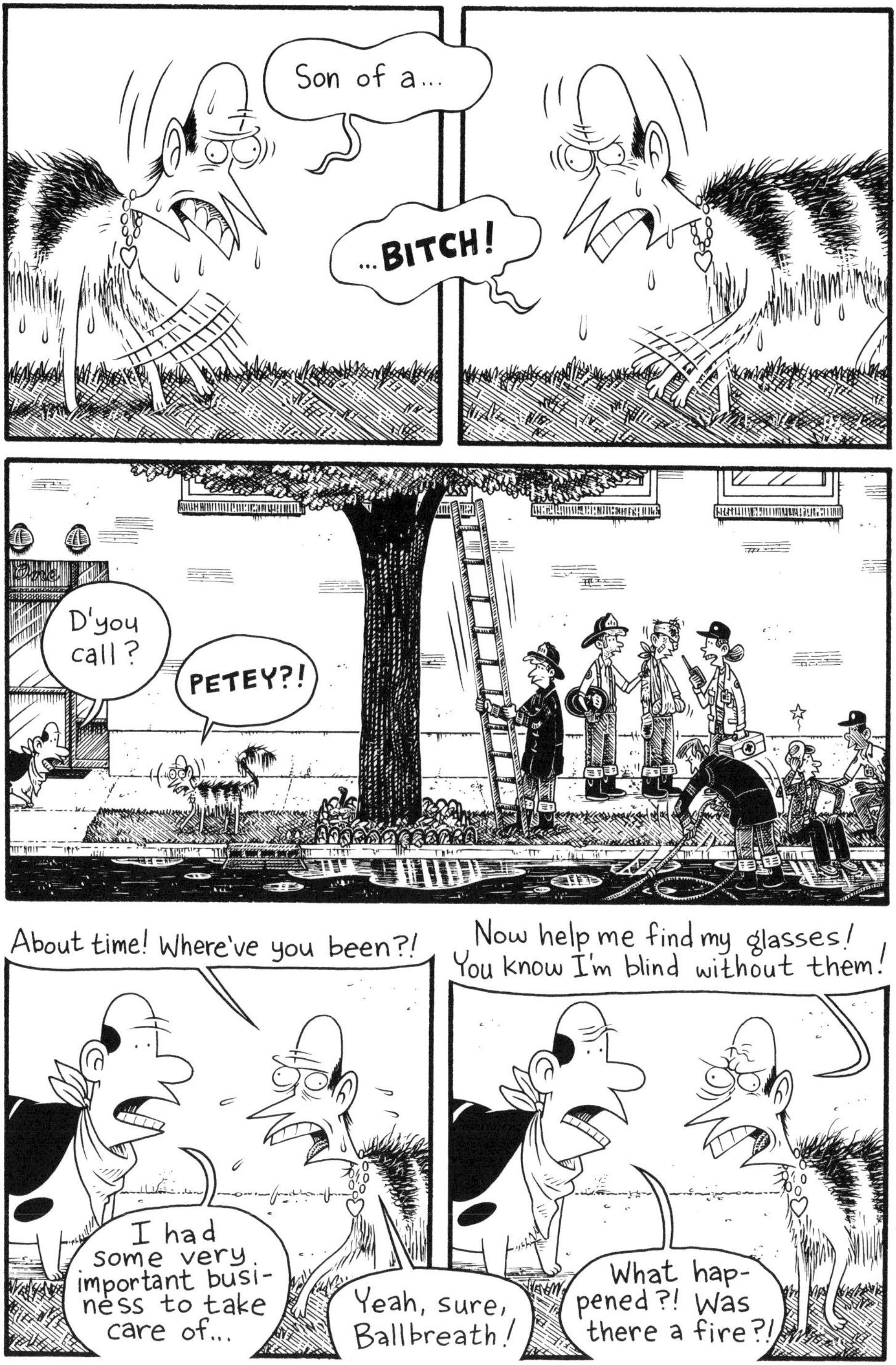
Son of a...
...BITCH!
D'you call?
PETEY?!
About time! Where've you been?!
I had some very important business to take care of...
Yeah, sure, Ballbreath!
Now help me find my glasses! You know I'm blind without them!
What happened?! Was there a fire?!

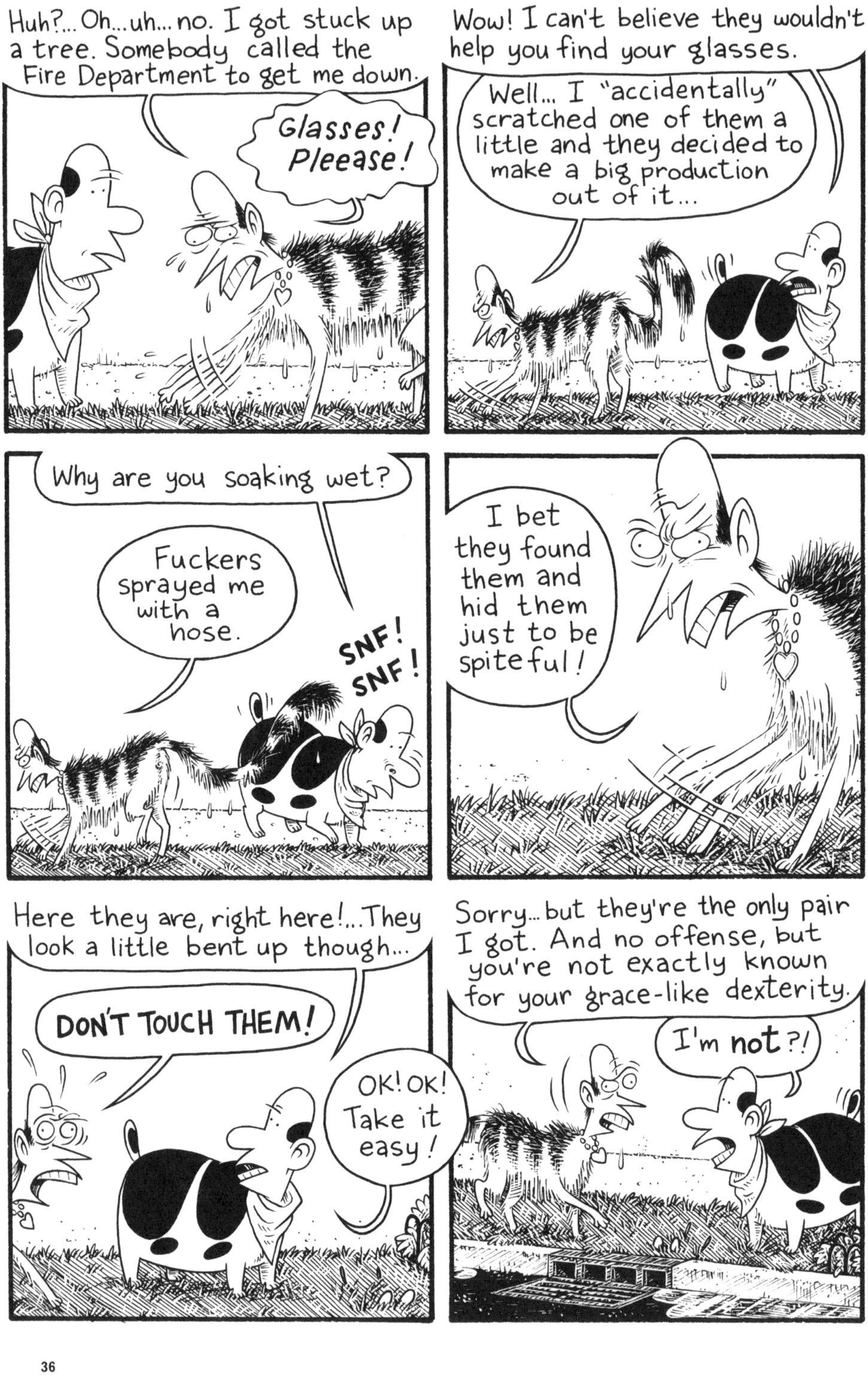
Huh?... Oh...uh... no. I got stuck up a tree. Somebody called the Fire Department to get me down.
Glasses! Pleease!
Wow! I can't believe they wouldn't help you find your glasses.
Well... I "accidentally" scratched one of them a little and they decided to make a big production out of it...
Why are you soaking wet?
Fuckers sprayed me with a hose.
SNF! SNF!
I bet they found them and hid them just to be spiteful!
Here they are, right here!... They look a little bent up though...
DON'T TOUCH THEM!
OK! OK! Take it easy!
Sorry... but they're the only pair I got. And no offense, but you're not exactly known for your grace-like dexterity.
I'm not?!

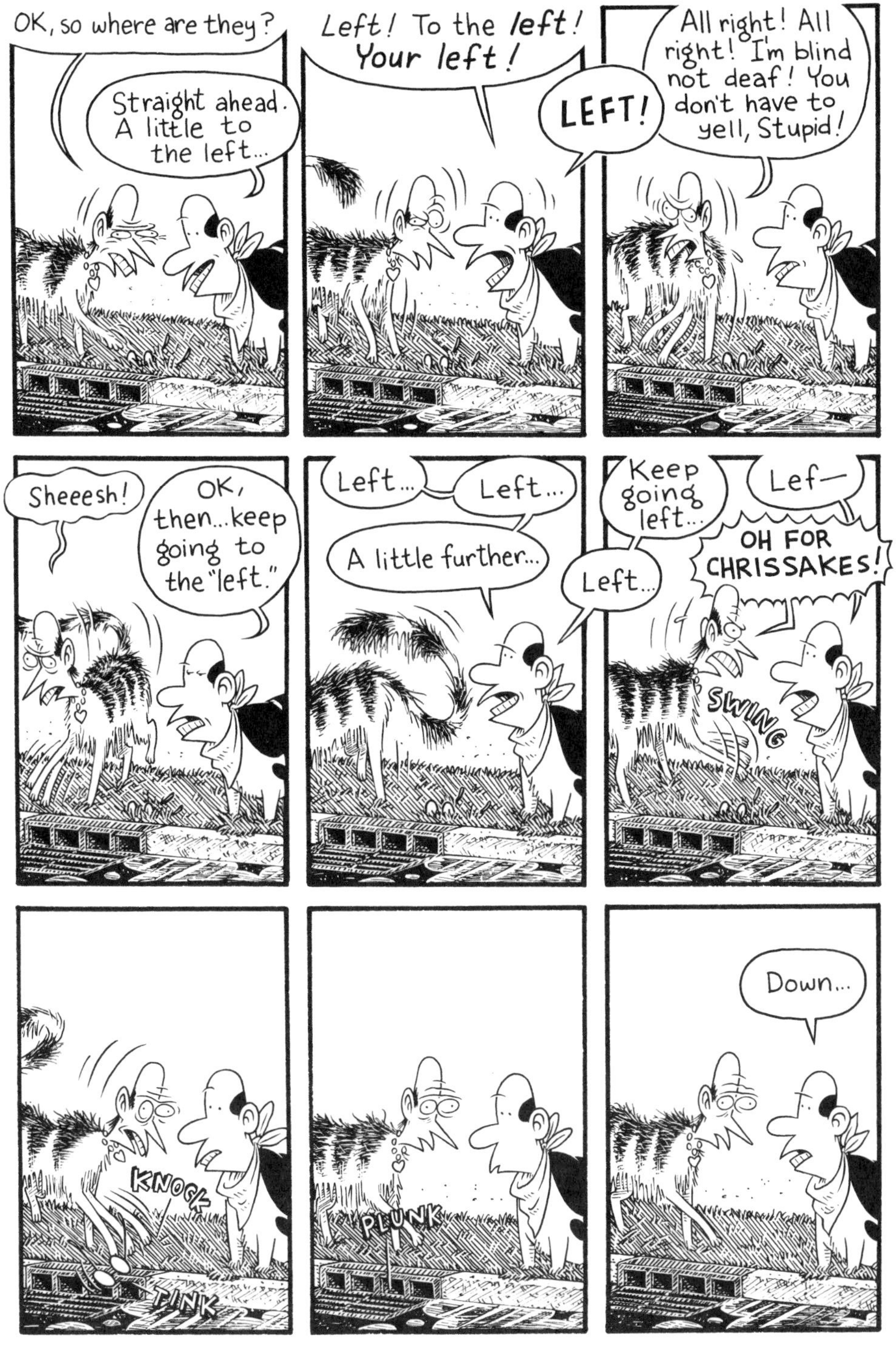
OK, so where are they?
Straight ahead. A little to the left...
Left! To the *left*! *Your left*!
LEFT!
All right! All right! I'm blind not deaf! You don't have to yell, Stupid!
Sheeesh!
OK, then...keep going to the "left."
Left...
Left...
A little further...
Left...
Keep going left...
Lef—
OH FOR CHRISSAKES!
SWING
KNOCK
TINK
PLUNK
Down...

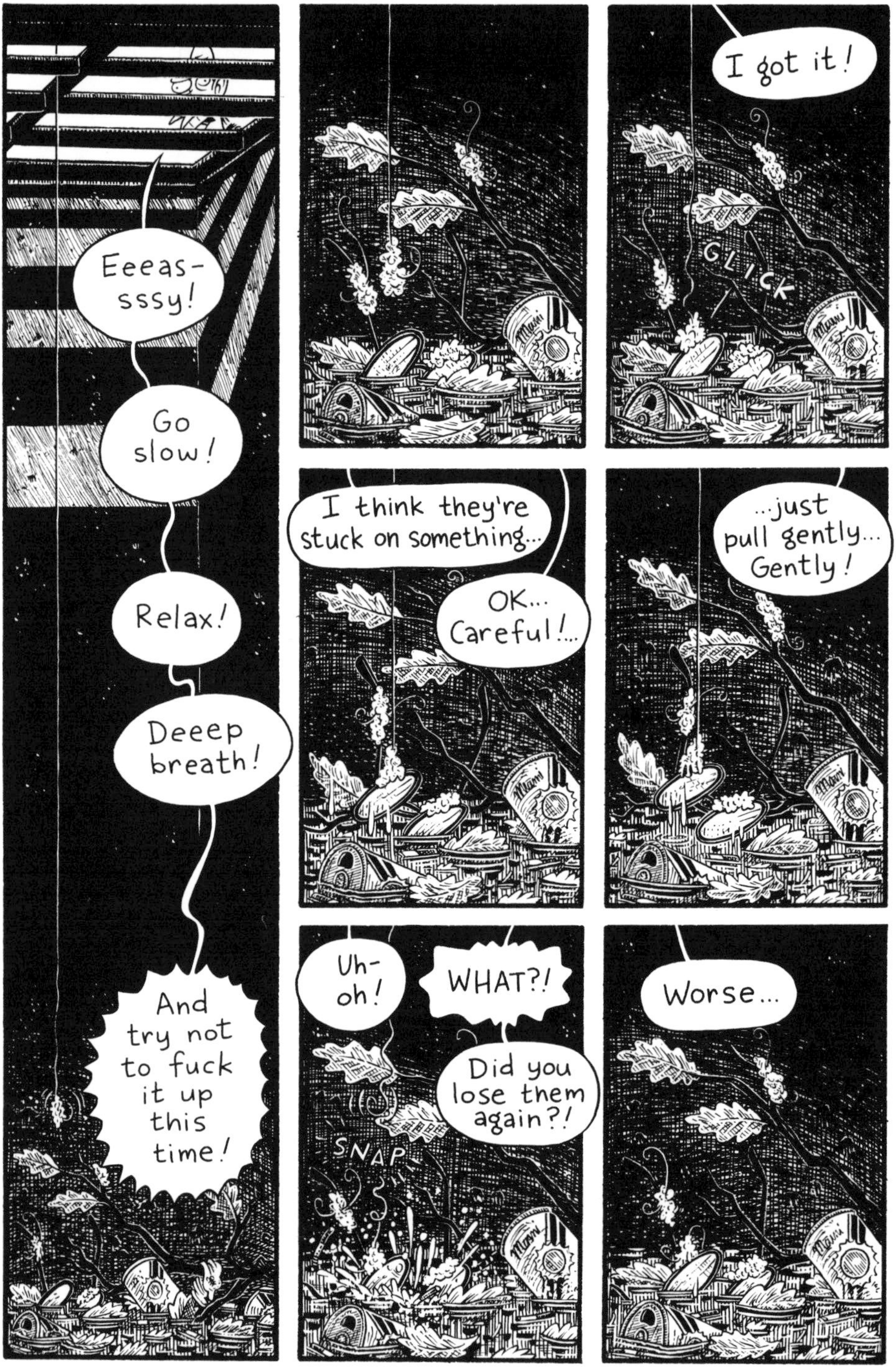
Eeeas-
sssy!
Go
slow!
Relax!
Deeep
breath!
And
try not
to fuck
it up
this
time!
I got it!
GLICK
I think they're
stuck on something...
OK...
Careful!...
...just
pull gently...
Gently!
Uh-
oh!
WHAT?!
Did you
lose them
again?!
SNAP
Worse...

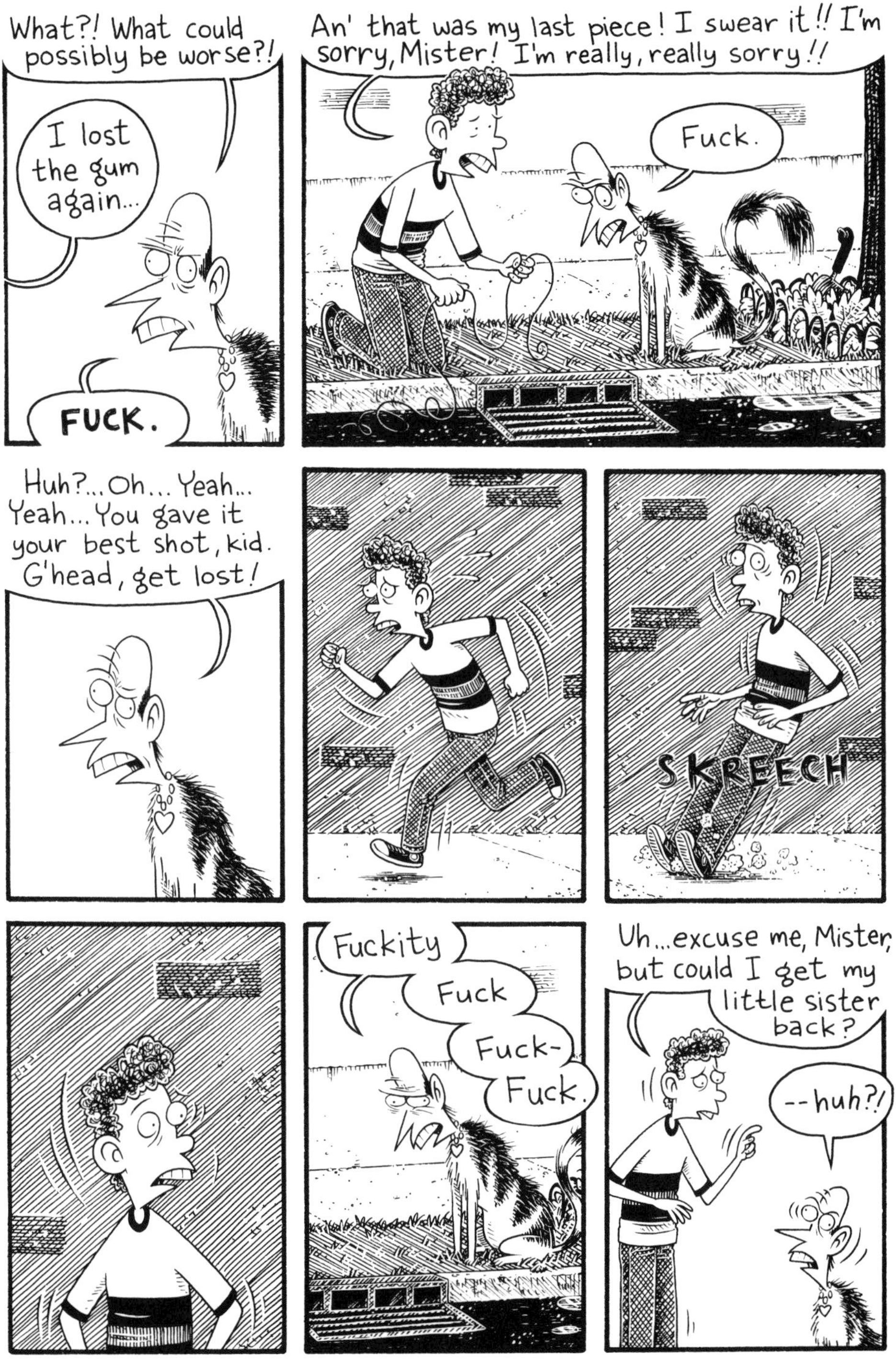
What?! What could possibly be worse?!
I lost the gum again...
FUCK.
An' that was my last piece! I swear it!! I'm sorry, Mister! I'm really, really sorry!!
Fuck.
Huh?...Oh... Yeah... Yeah... You gave it your best shot, kid. G'head, get lost!
SKREECH
Fuckity
Fuck
Fuck-
Fuck.
Uh...excuse me, Mister, but could I get my little sister back?
--huh?!

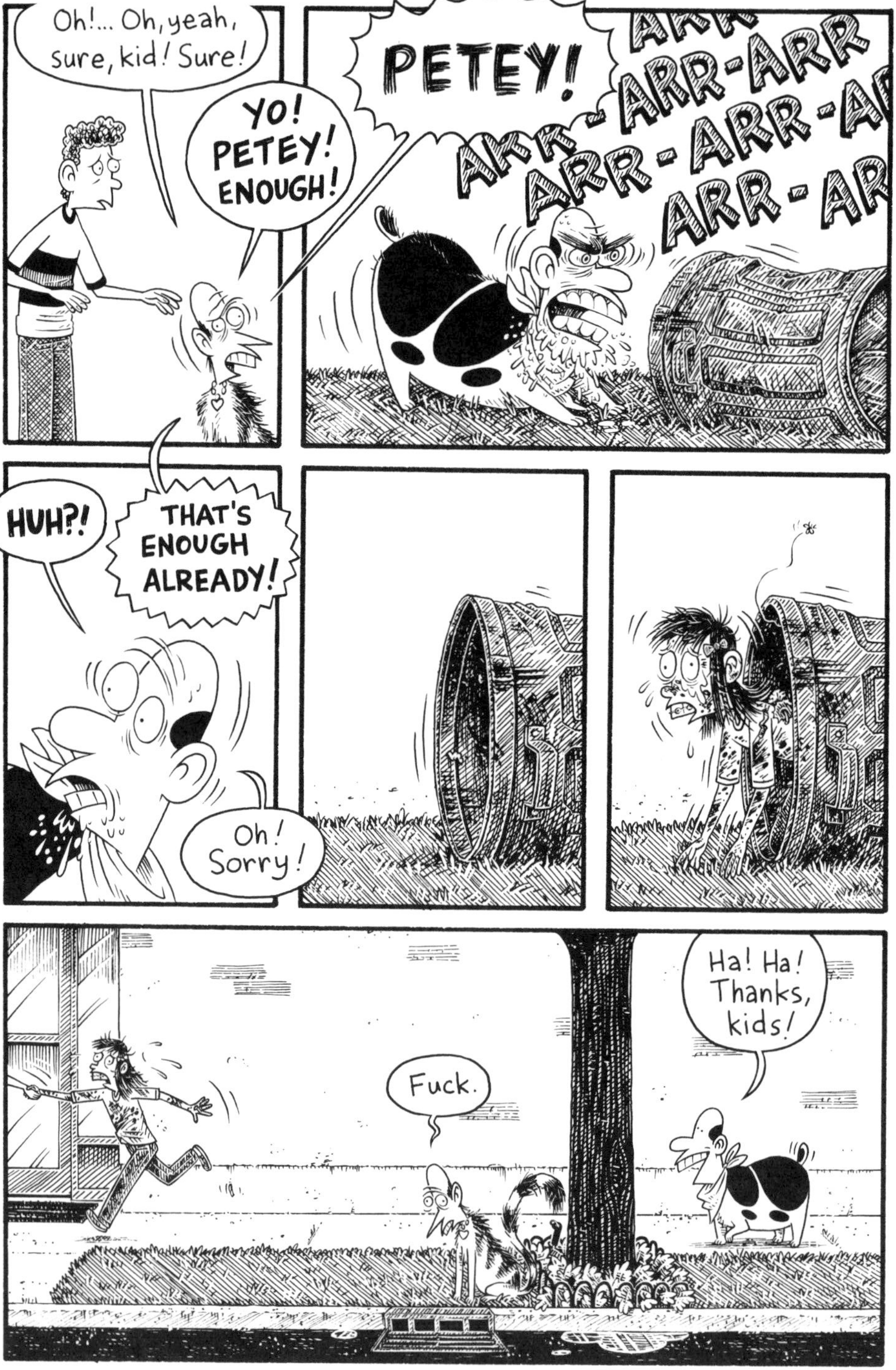
Oh!... Oh, yeah, sure, kid! Sure!
YO! PETEY! ENOUGH!
PETEY!
ARR-ARR-ARR
ARR-ARR-ARR
ARR-ARR-ARR
ARR-AR
HUH?!
THAT'S ENOUGH ALREADY!
Oh! Sorry!
Fuck.
Ha! Ha! Thanks, kids!

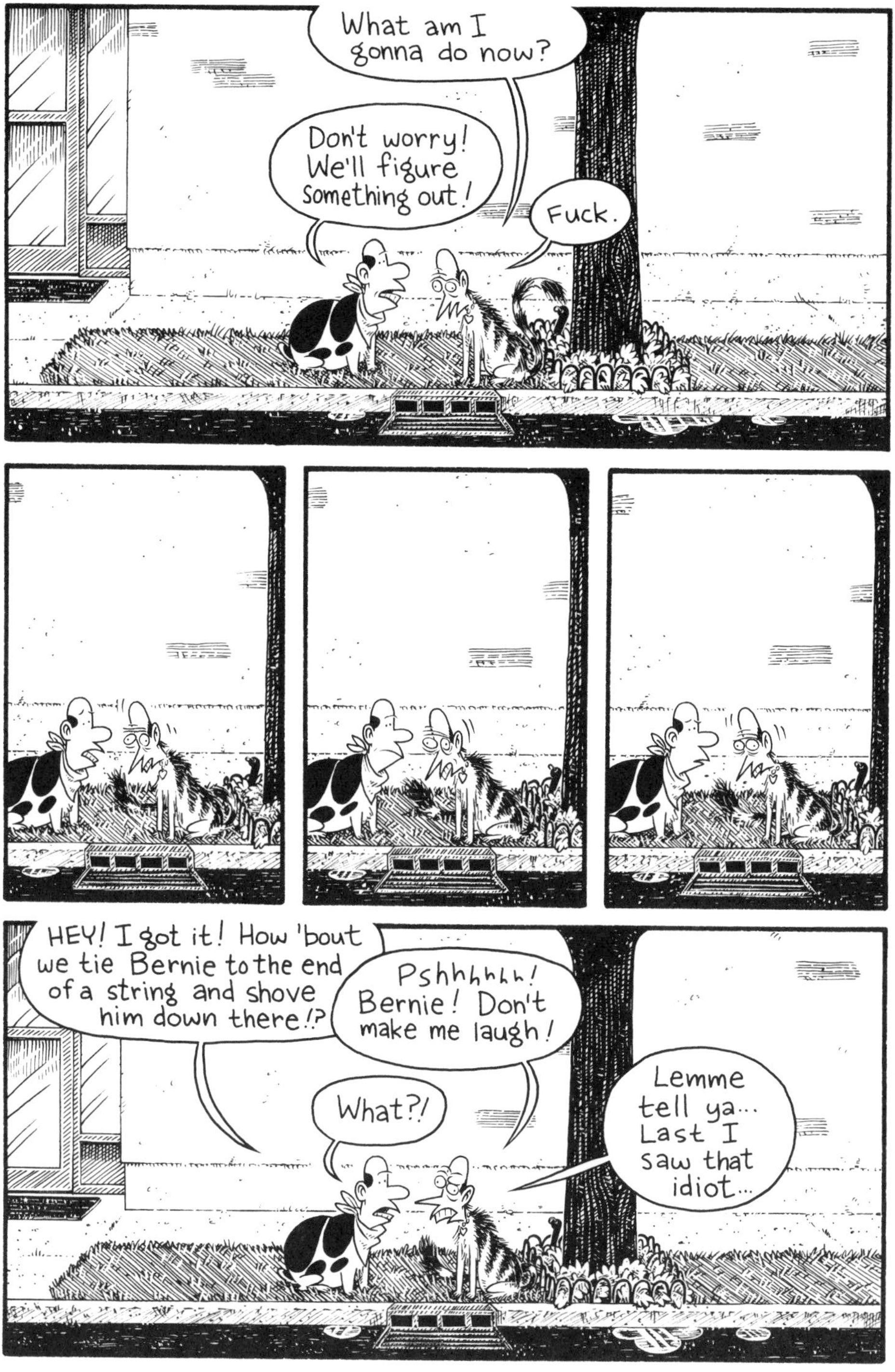
What am I gonna do now?
Don't worry! We'll figure something out!
Fuck.
HEY! I got it! How 'bout we tie Bernie to the end of a string and shove him down there!?
Pshhhhhh! Bernie! Don't make me laugh!
What?!
Lemme tell ya... Last I saw that idiot...

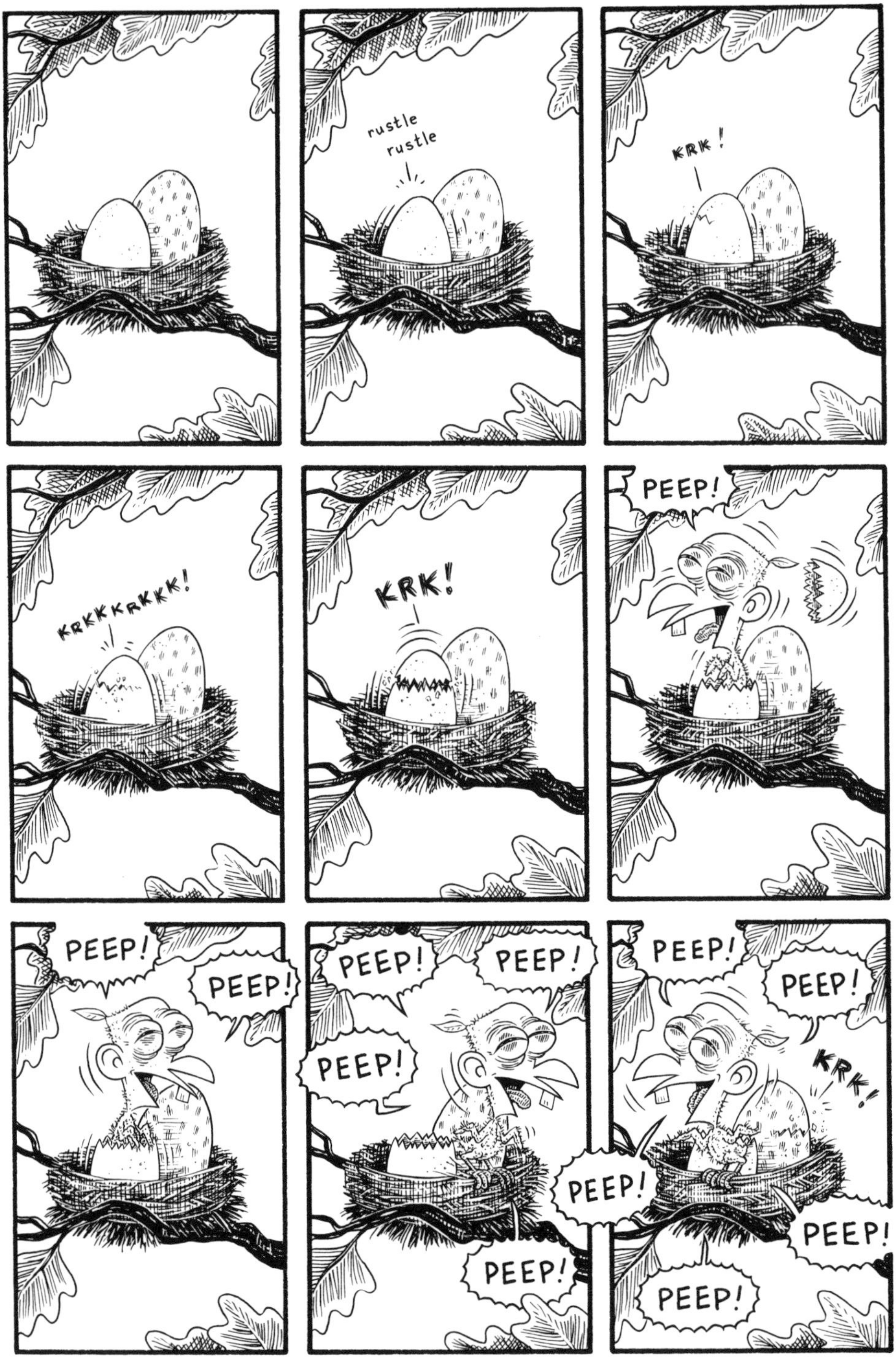
rustle
rustle
KRK!
KRKKKRKKK!
KRK!
PEEP!
PEEP!
PEEP!
PEEP!
PEEP!
PEEP!
PEEP!
PEEP!
PEEP!
PEEP!
KRK!
PEEP!
PEEP!
PEEP!

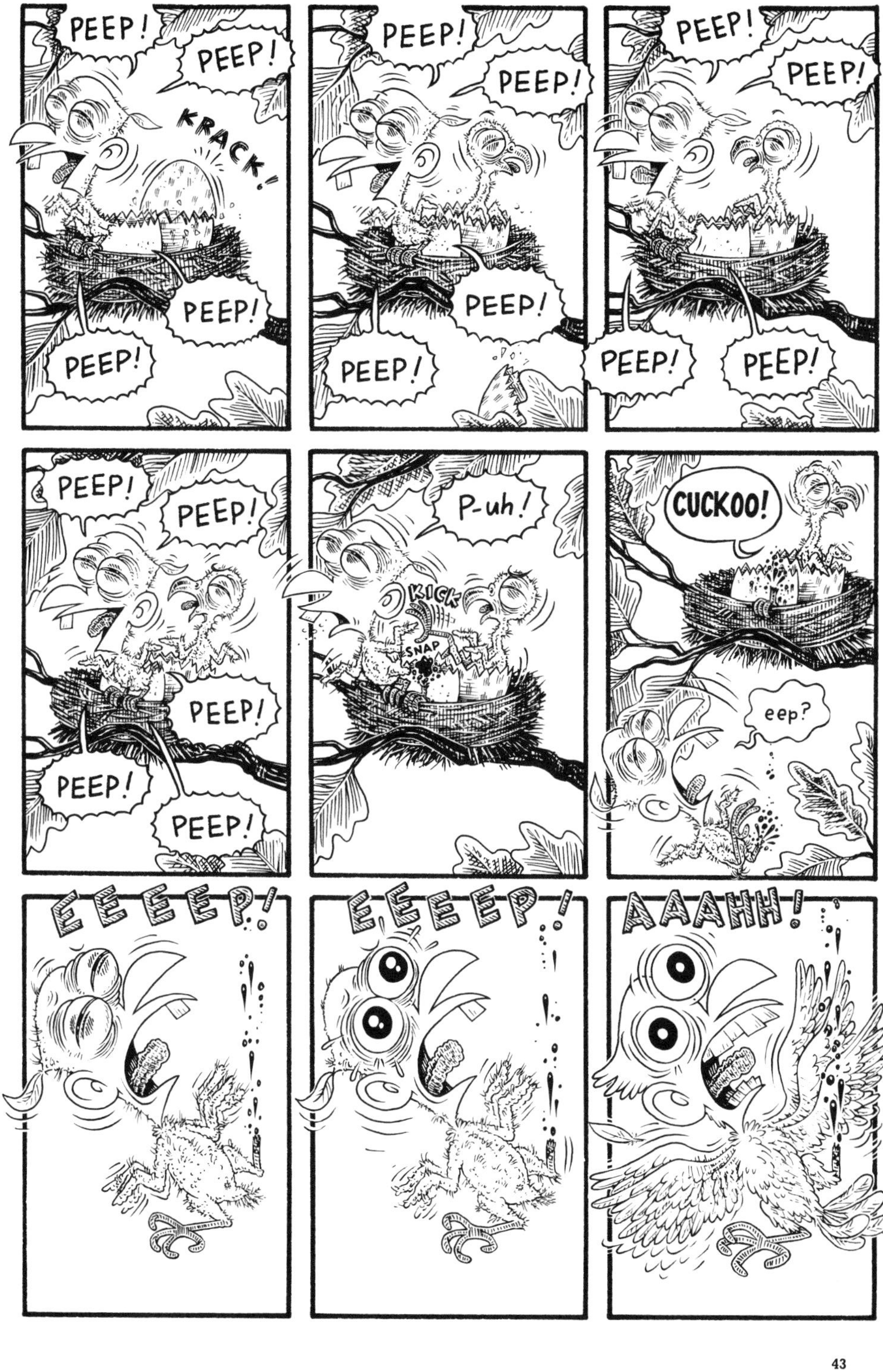
PEEP!
PEEP!
KRACK!
PEEP!
PEEP!
PEEP!
PEEP!
PEEP!
PEEP!
PEEP!
PEEP!
PEEP!
PEEP!
PEEP!
PEEP!
PEEP!
PEEP!
P-uh!
KICK
SNAP
CUCKOO!
eep?
EEEEP!
EEEEP!
AAAHH!

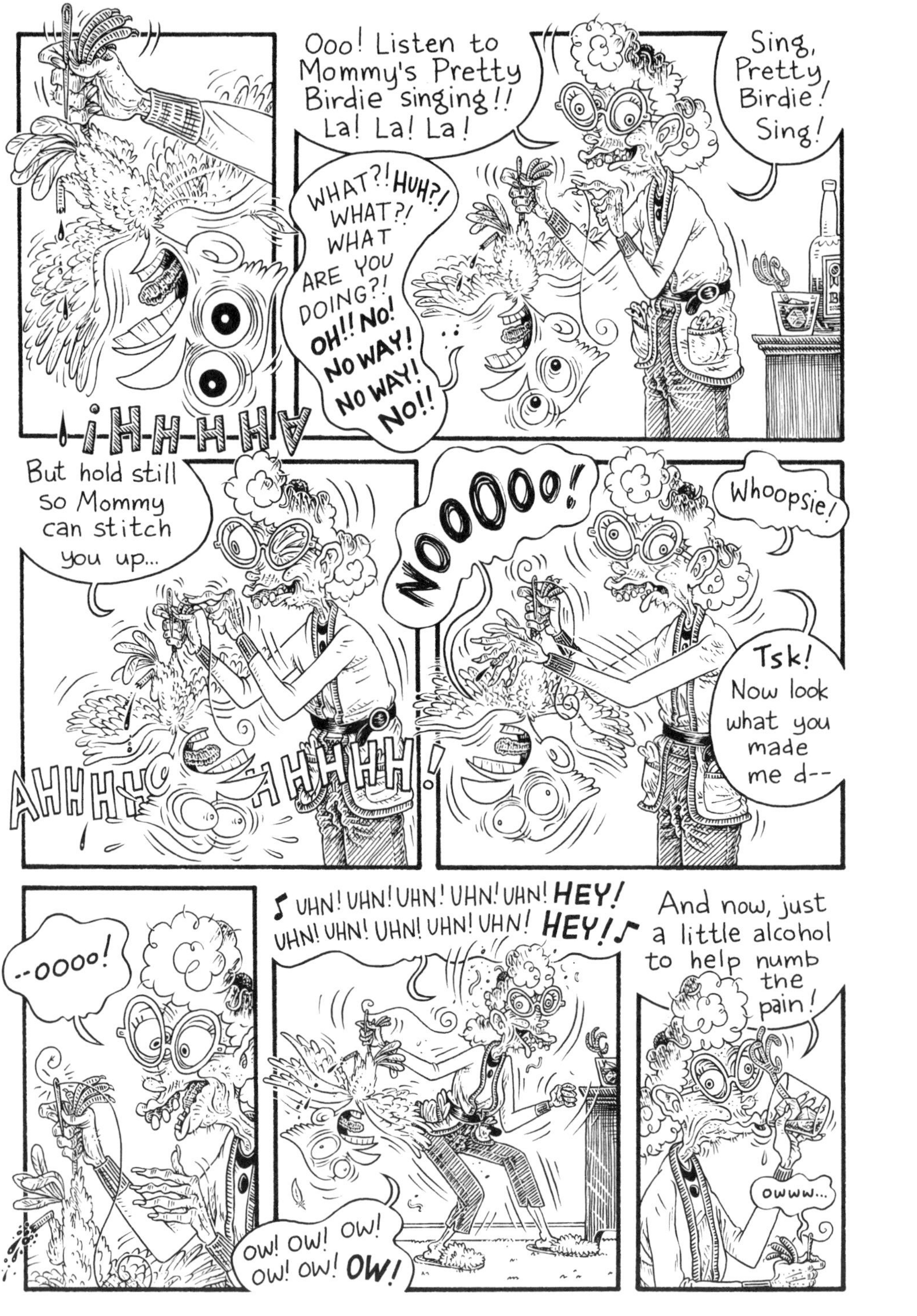

AHHHHH!
Ooo! Listen to Mommy's Pretty Birdie singing!! La! La! La!
Sing, Pretty Birdie! Sing!
WHAT?! HUH?! WHAT?! WHAT ARE YOU DOING?! OH!! NO! NO WAY! NO WAY! NO!!
But hold still so Mommy can stitch you up...
AHHHHHHHHHHH!
NOOOOO!
Whoopsie!
Tsk! Now look what you made me d--
--oooo!
♪ UHN! UHN! UHN! UHN! UHN! HEY! UHN! UHN! UHN! UHN! UHN! HEY! ♪
OW! OW! OW! OW! OW! OW!
And now, just a little alcohol to help numb the pain!
owww...

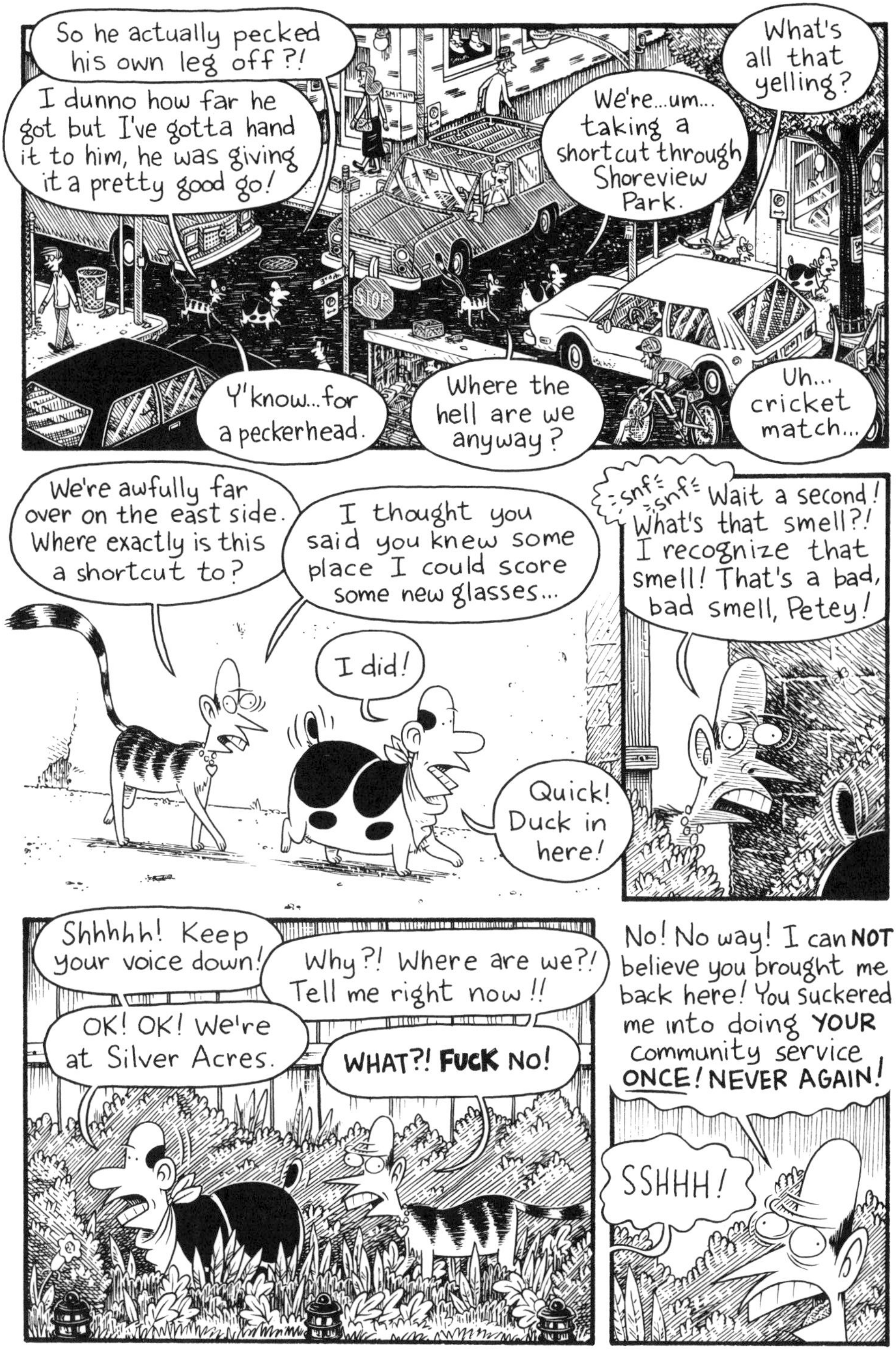
So he actually pecked his own leg off?!
I dunno how far he got but I've gotta hand it to him, he was giving it a pretty good go!
Y'know...for a peckerhead.
Where the hell are we anyway?
We're...um... taking a shortcut through Shoreview Park.
What's all that yelling?
Uh... cricket match...
We're awfully far over on the east side. Where exactly is this a shortcut to?
I thought you said you knew some place I could score some new glasses...
I did!
Quick! Duck in here!
snf snf Wait a second! What's that smell?! I recognize that smell! That's a bad, bad smell, Petey!
Shhhhh! Keep your voice down!
Why?! Where are we?! Tell me right now!!
OK! OK! We're at Silver Acres.
WHAT?! FUCK NO!
No! No way! I can NOT believe you brought me back here! You suckered me into doing YOUR community service ONCE! NEVER AGAIN!
SSHHH!

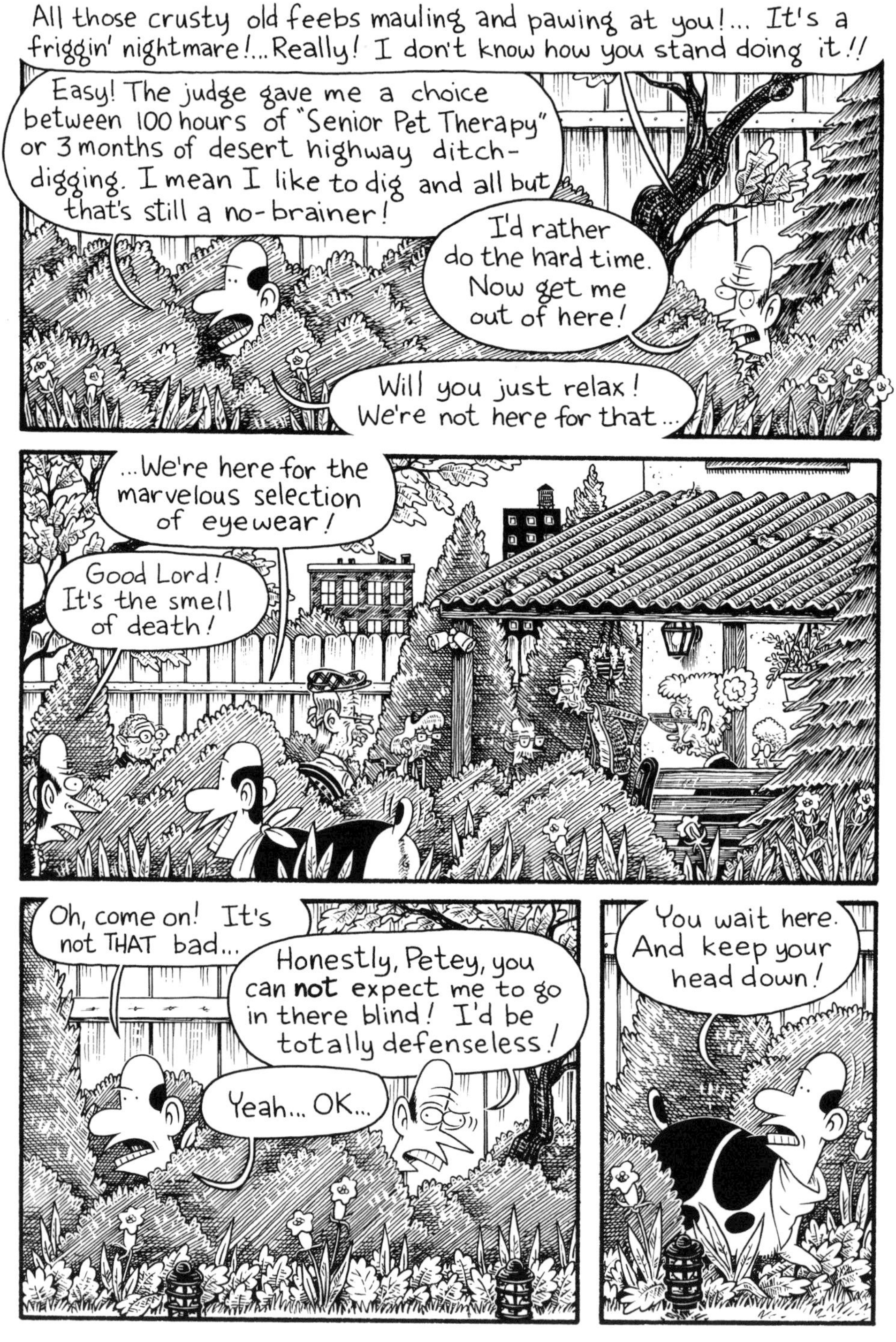
All those crusty old feebs mauling and pawing at you!... It's a friggin' nightmare!... Really! I don't know how you stand doing it!!
Easy! The judge gave me a choice between 100 hours of "Senior Pet Therapy" or 3 months of desert highway ditch-digging. I mean I like to dig and all but that's still a no-brainer!
I'd rather do the hard time. Now get me out of here!
Will you just relax! We're not here for that...
...We're here for the marvelous selection of eyewear!
Good Lord! It's the smell of death!
Oh, come on! It's not THAT bad...
Honestly, Petey, you can **not** expect me to go in there blind! I'd be totally defenseless!
Yeah... OK...
You wait here. And keep your head down!

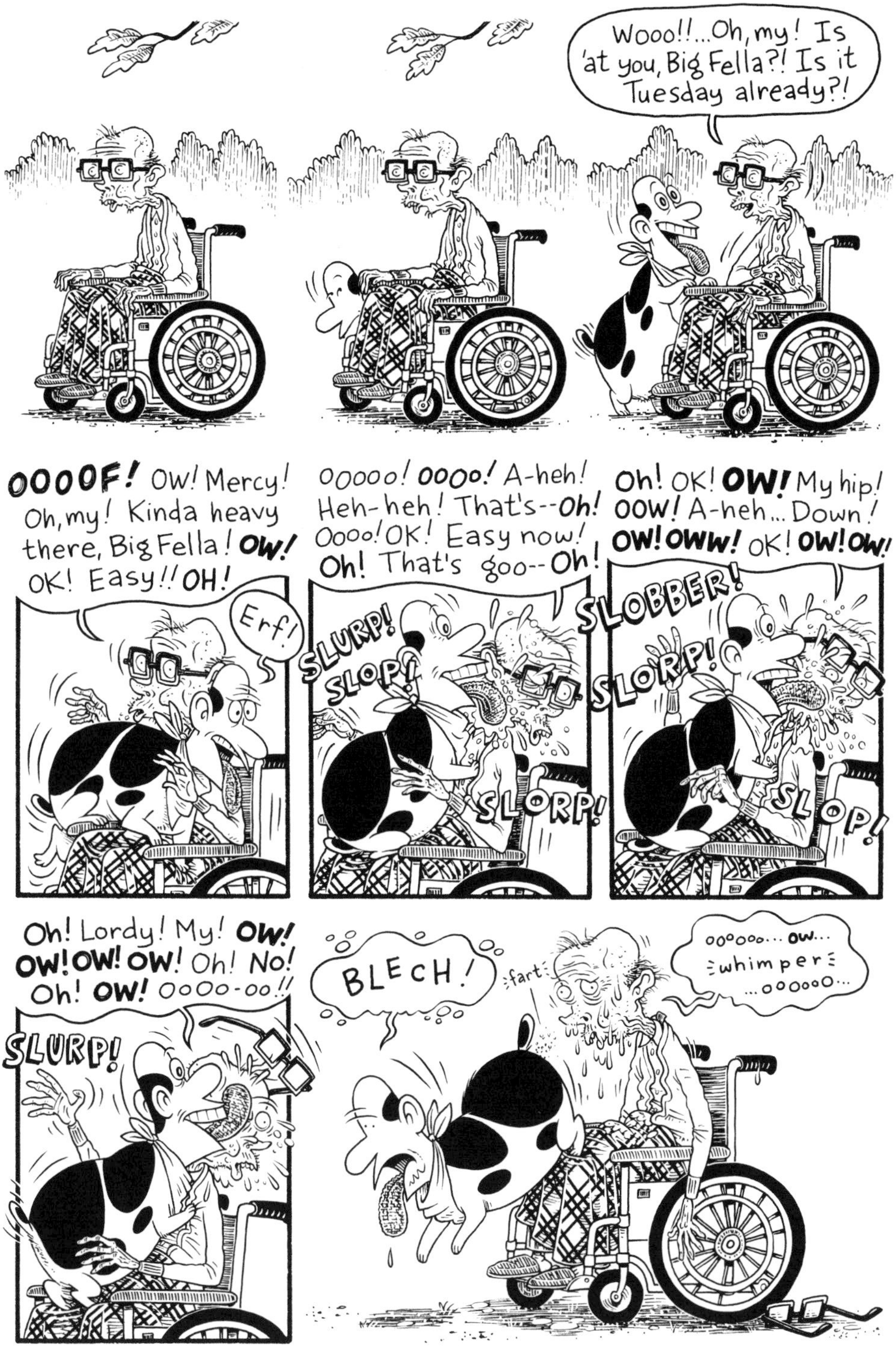
Wooo!!...Oh, my! Is 'at you, Big Fella?! Is it Tuesday already?!
OOOOF! OW! Mercy! Oh, my! Kinda heavy there, Big Fella! OW! OK! Easy!! OH!
Erf!
OOOOO! OOOO! A-heh! Heh-heh! That's--Oh! Oooo! OK! Easy now! Oh! That's goo--Oh!
SLURP!
SLOP!
SLORP!
Oh! OK! OW! My hip! OOW! A-heh... Down! OW! OWW! OK! OW! OW!
SLOBBER!
SLORP!
SLOP!
Oh! Lordy! My! OW! OW! OW! OW! Oh! No! Oh! OW! OOOO-OO!!
SLURP!
BLECH!
fart
OOOOOO... OW... whimper ...OOOOOO...

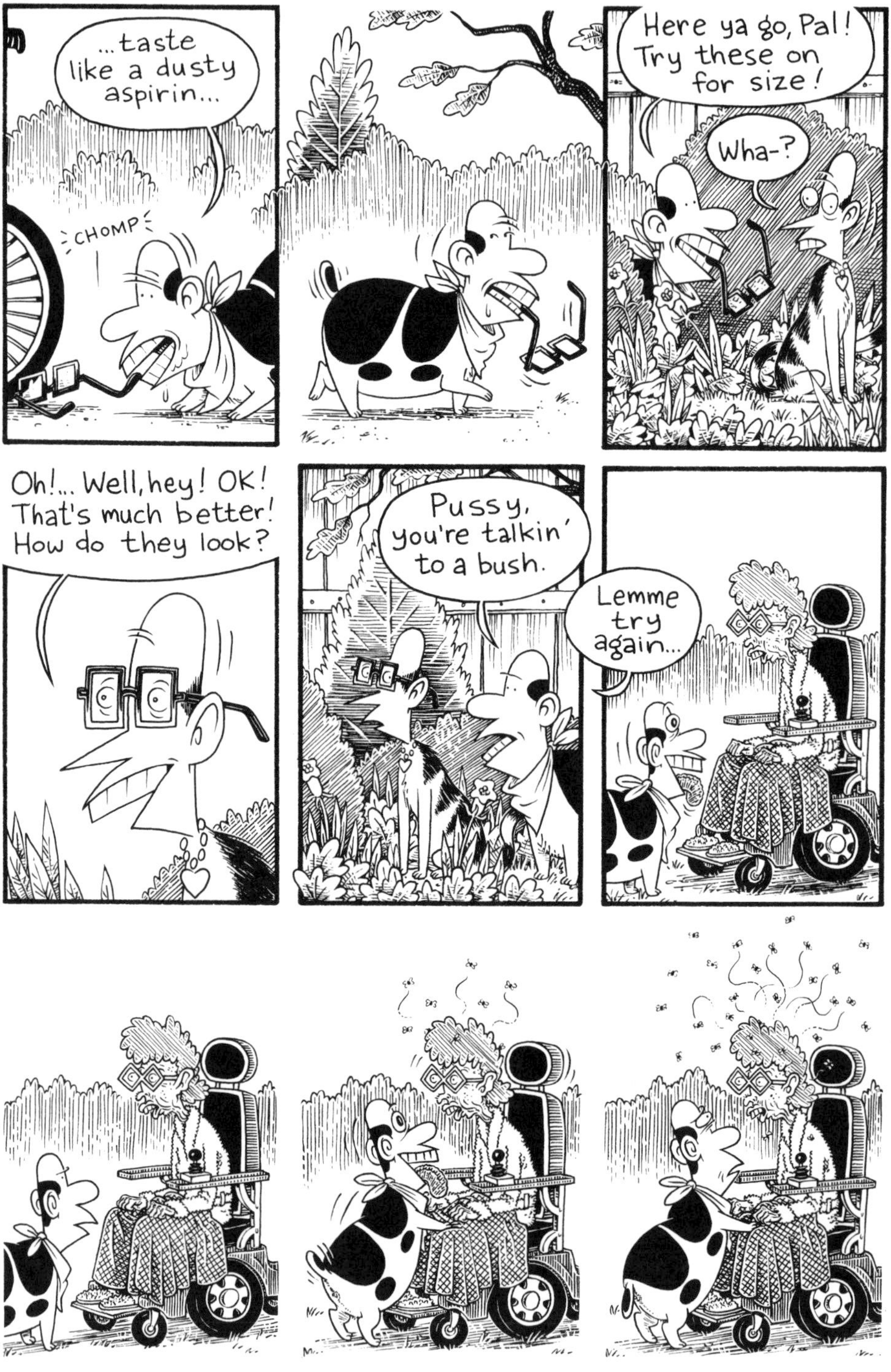
...taste like a dusty aspirin...
CHOMP
Here ya go, Pal! Try these on for size!
Wha-?
Oh!... Well, hey! OK! That's much better! How do they look?
Pussy, you're talkin' to a bush.
Lemme try again...

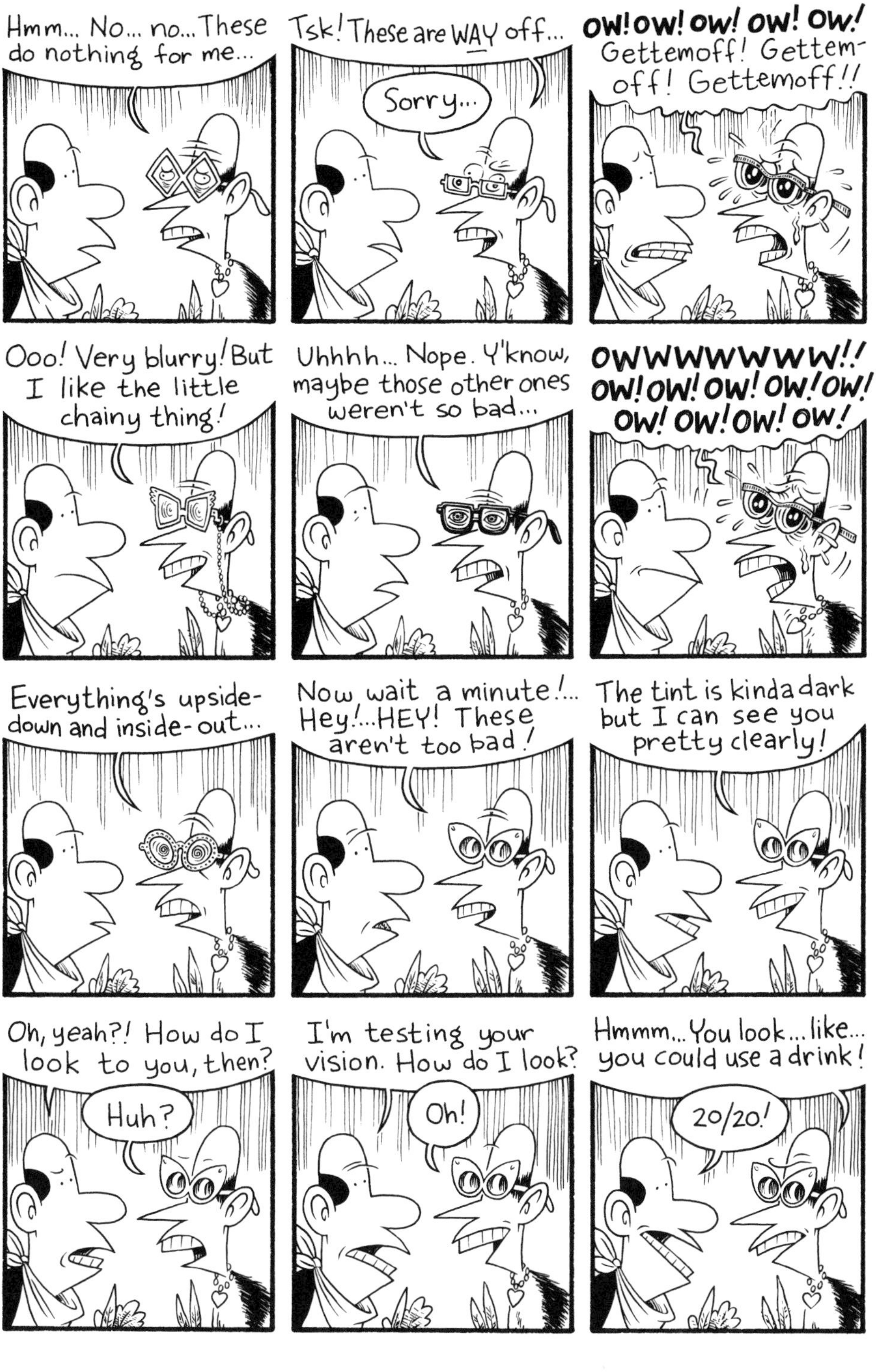

Hmm... No... no... These do nothing for me...
Tsk! These are WAY off...
Sorry...
OW! OW! OW! OW! OW! Gettemoff! Gettem-off! Gettemoff!!
Ooo! Very blurry! But I like the little chainy thing!
Uhhhh... Nope. Y'know, maybe those other ones weren't so bad...
OWWWWWWW!! OW! OW! OW! OW! OW! OW! OW! OW! OW!
Everything's upside-down and inside-out...
Now wait a minute!... Hey!...HEY! These aren't too bad!
The tint is kinda dark but I can see you pretty clearly!
Oh, yeah?! How do I look to you, then?
Huh?
I'm testing your vision. How do I look?
Oh!
Hmmm... You look... like... you could use a drink!
20/20!

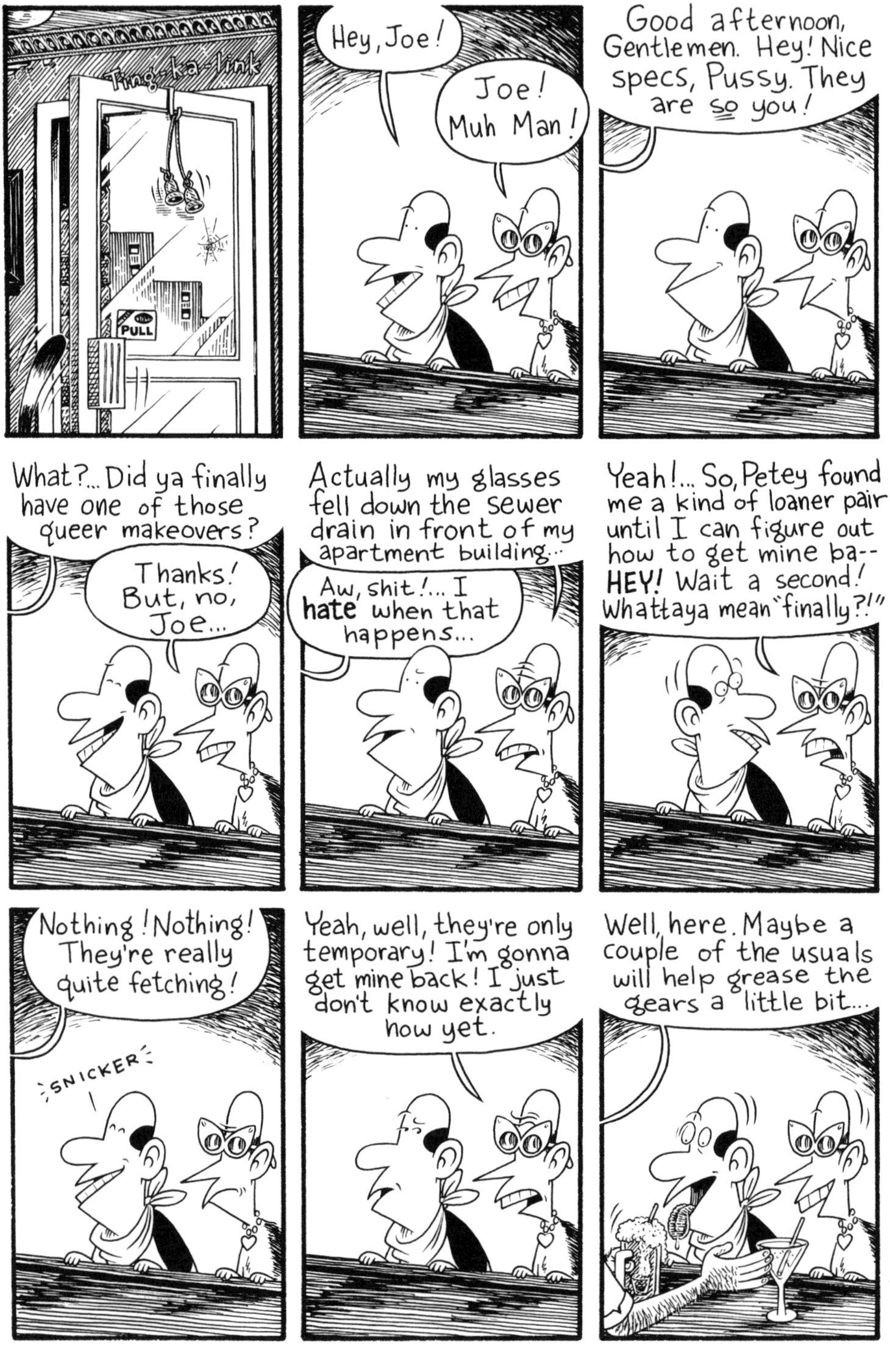
Ting-ka-link
PULL
Hey, Joe!
Joe! Muh Man!
Good afternoon, Gentlemen. Hey! Nice specs, Pussy. They are so you!
What?... Did ya finally have one of those queer makeovers?
Thanks! But, no, Joe...
Actually my glasses fell down the sewer drain in front of my apartment building...
Aw, shit!... I hate when that happens...
Yeah!... So, Petey found me a kind of loaner pair until I can figure out how to get mine ba-- HEY! Wait a second! Whattaya mean "finally?!"
Nothing! Nothing! They're really quite fetching!
SNICKER
Yeah, well, they're only temporary! I'm gonna get mine back! I just don't know exactly how yet.
Well, here. Maybe a couple of the usuals will help grease the gears a little bit...

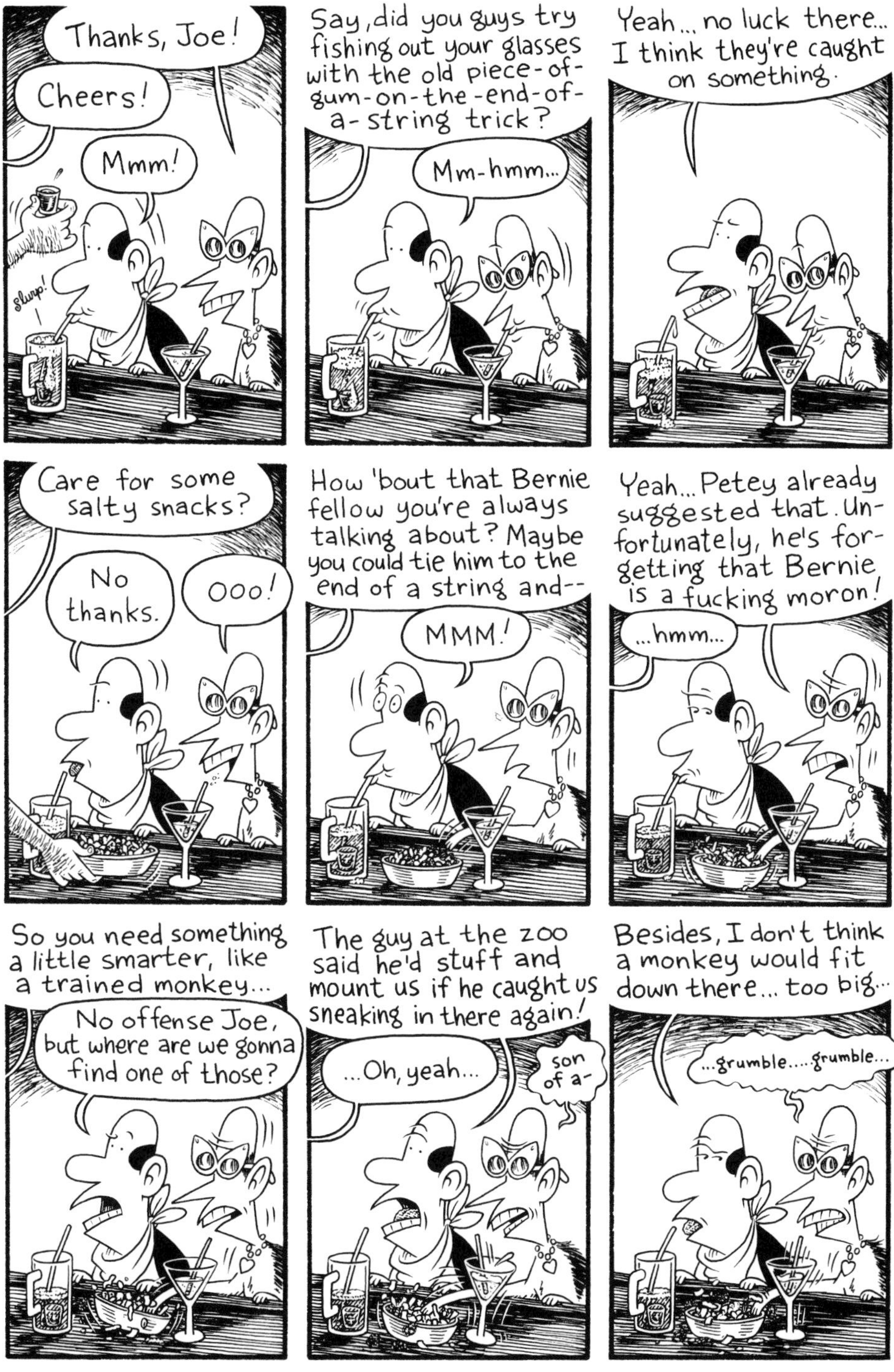

Thanks, Joe!
Cheers!
Mmm!
slurp!
Say, did you guys try fishing out your glasses with the old piece-of-gum-on-the-end-of-a-string trick?
Mm-hmm...
Yeah... no luck there... I think they're caught on something.
Care for some salty snacks?
No thanks.
Ooo!
How 'bout that Bernie fellow you're always talking about? Maybe you could tie him to the end of a string and--
MMM!
Yeah... Petey already suggested that. Unfortunately, he's forgetting that Bernie is a fucking moron!
...hmm...
So you need something a little smarter, like a trained monkey...
No offense Joe, but where are we gonna find one of those?
The guy at the zoo said he'd stuff and mount us if he caught us sneaking in there again!
...Oh, yeah...
son of a-
Besides, I don't think a monkey would fit down there... too big...
...grumble.....grumble...

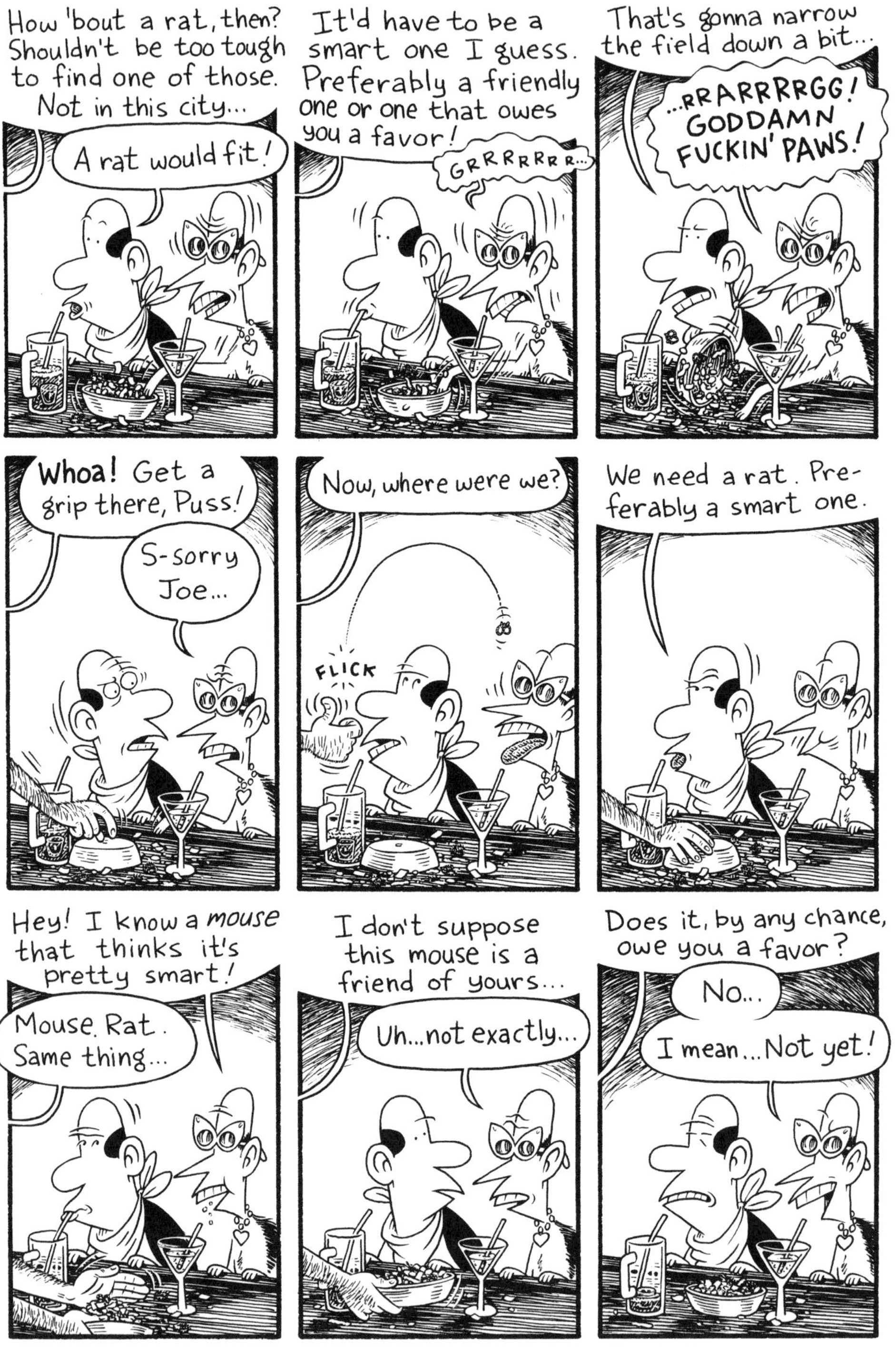
How 'bout a rat, then? Shouldn't be too tough to find one of those. Not in this city...
A rat would fit!
It'd have to be a smart one I guess. Preferably a friendly one or one that owes you a favor!
GRRRRRRR...
That's gonna narrow the field down a bit...
...RRARRRRGG! GODDAMN FUCKIN' PAWS!
Whoa! Get a grip there, Puss!
S-sorry Joe...
Now, where were we?
FLICK
We need a rat. Preferably a smart one.
Hey! I know a mouse that thinks it's pretty smart!
Mouse. Rat. Same thing...
I don't suppose this mouse is a friend of yours...
Uh...not exactly...
Does it, by any chance, owe you a favor?
No...
I mean... Not yet!

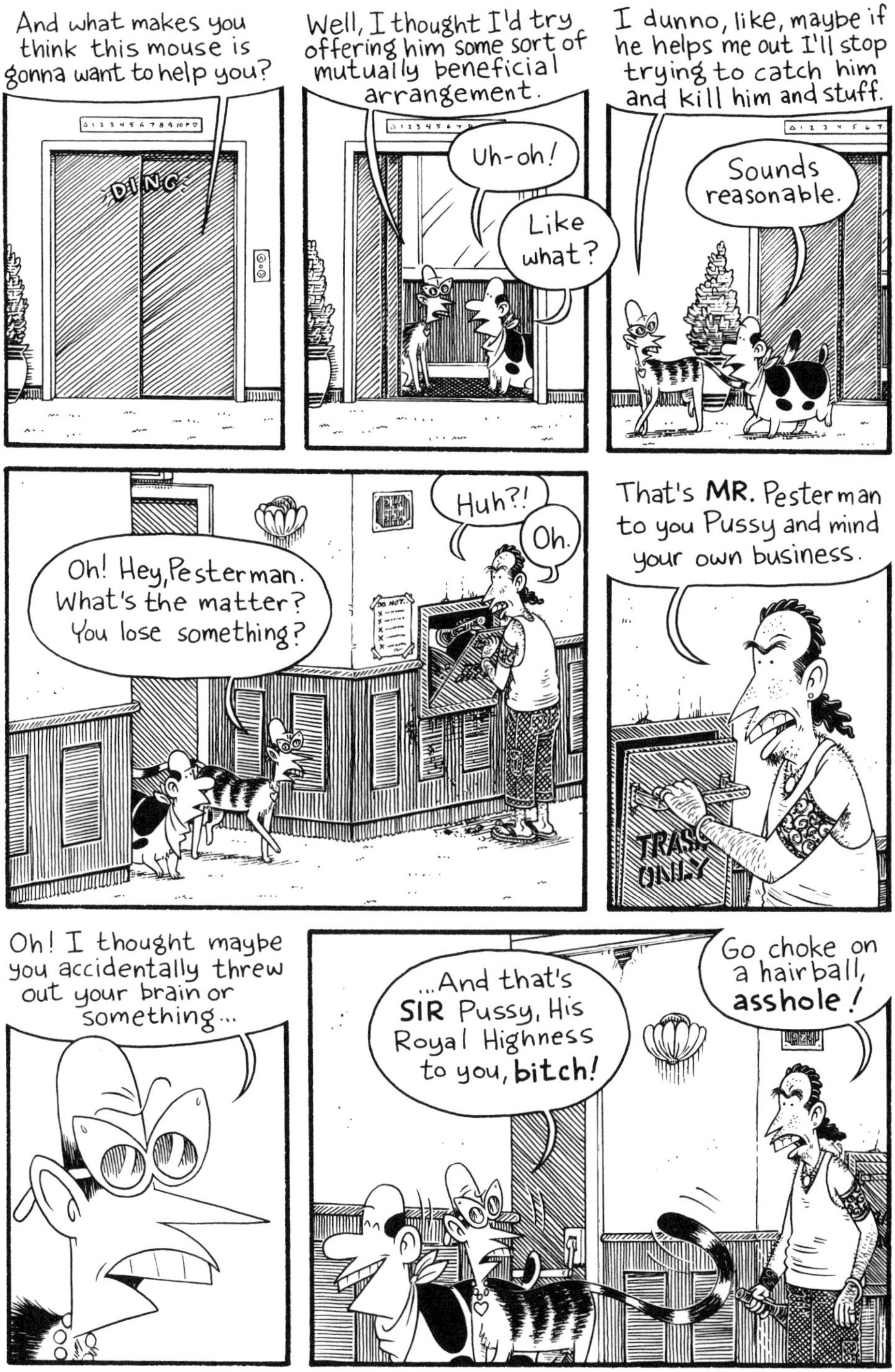

And what makes you think this mouse is gonna want to help you?
DING
Well, I thought I'd try offering him some sort of mutually beneficial arrangement.
Uh-oh!
Like what?
I dunno, like, maybe if he helps me out I'll stop trying to catch him and kill him and stuff.
Sounds reasonable.
Huh?!
Oh.
Oh! Hey, Pesterman. What's the matter? You lose something?
That's **MR.** Pesterman to you Pussy and mind your own business.
TRASH ONLY
Oh! I thought maybe you accidentally threw out your brain or something...
...And that's **SIR** Pussy, His Royal Highness to you, **bitch**!
Go choke on a hairball, **asshole**!

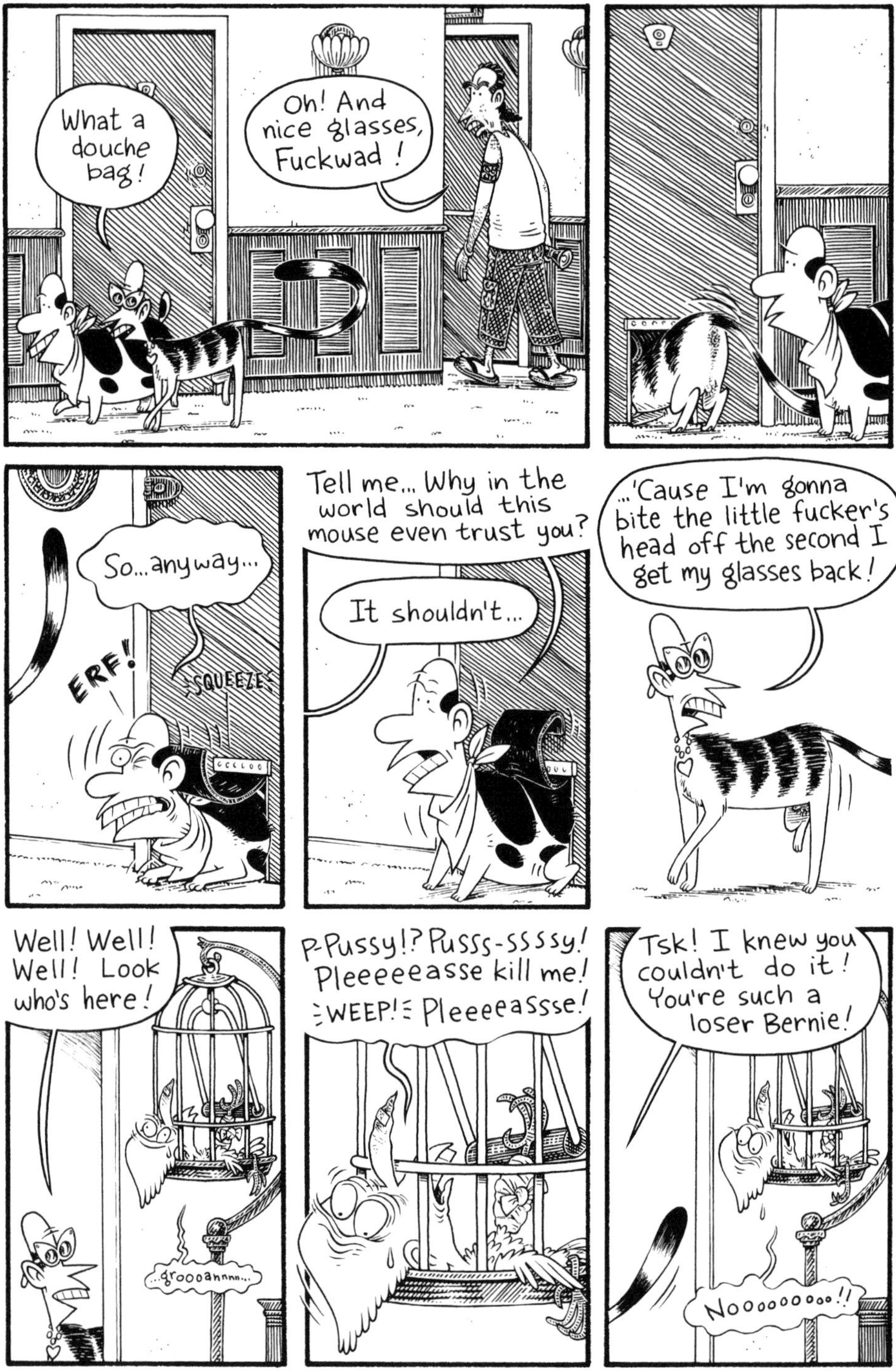
What a douche bag!
Oh! And nice glasses, Fuckwad!
So...anyway...
ERF!
SQUEEZE
Tell me... Why in the world should this mouse even trust you?
It shouldn't...
...'Cause I'm gonna bite the little fucker's head off the second I get my glasses back!
Well! Well! Well! Look who's here!
...groooannnn...
P-Pussy!? Pusss-sssssy! Pleeeeeasse kill me!
WEEP! Pleeeeassse!
Tsk! I knew you couldn't do it! You're such a loser Bernie!
Nooooooooo!!

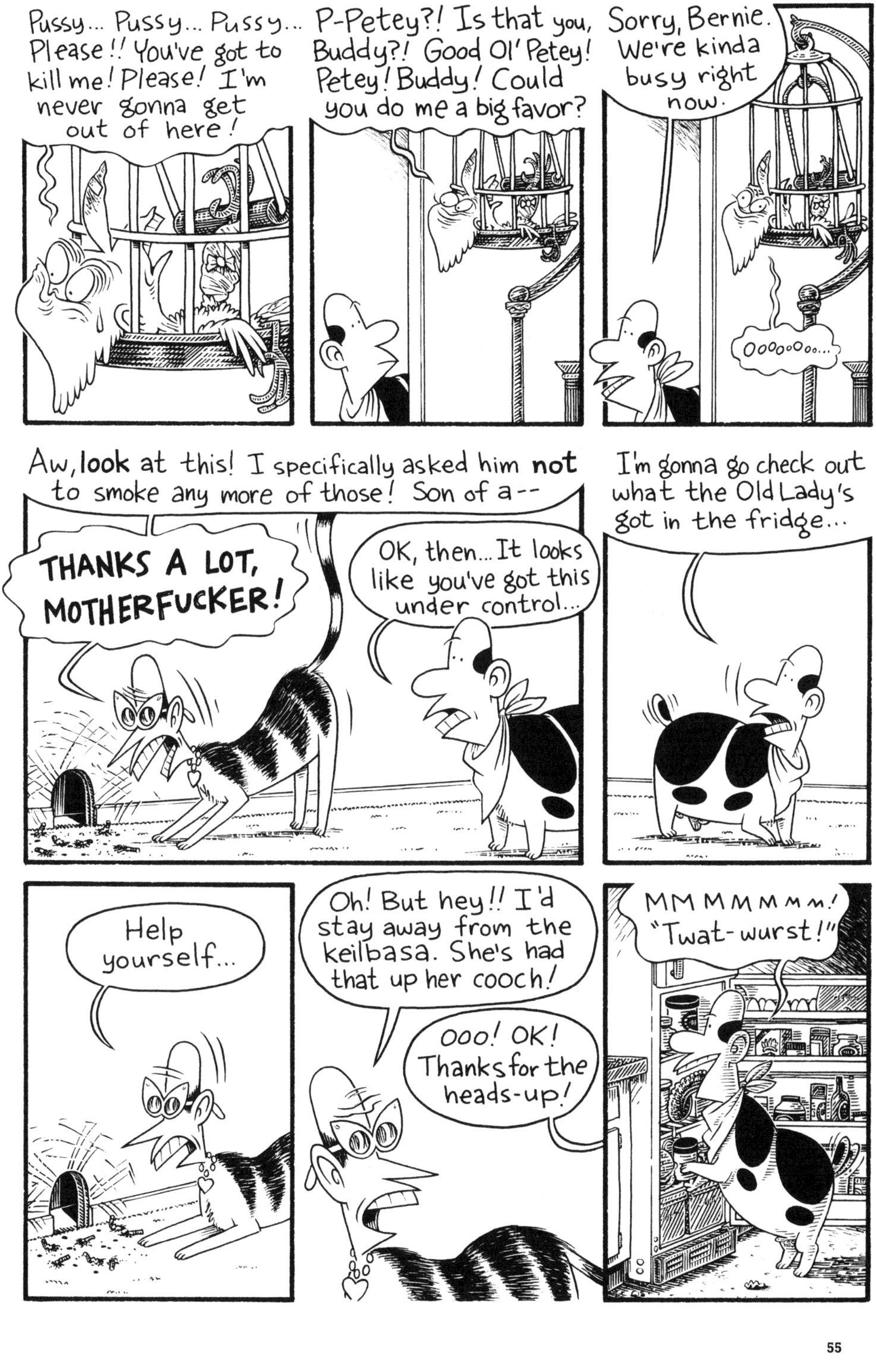
Pussy... Pussy... Pussy... Please!! You've got to kill me! Please! I'm never gonna get out of here!
P-Petey?! Is that you, Buddy?! Good Ol' Petey! Petey! Buddy! Could you do me a big favor?
Sorry, Bernie. We're kinda busy right now.
Ooooooo...
Aw, look at this! I specifically asked him not to smoke any more of those! Son of a--
THANKS A LOT, MOTHERFUCKER!
OK, then... It looks like you've got this under control...
I'm gonna go check out what the Old Lady's got in the fridge...
Help yourself...
Oh! But hey!! I'd stay away from the keilbasa. She's had that up her cooch!
Ooo! OK! Thanks for the heads-up!
MMMMMMM! "Twat-wurst!"

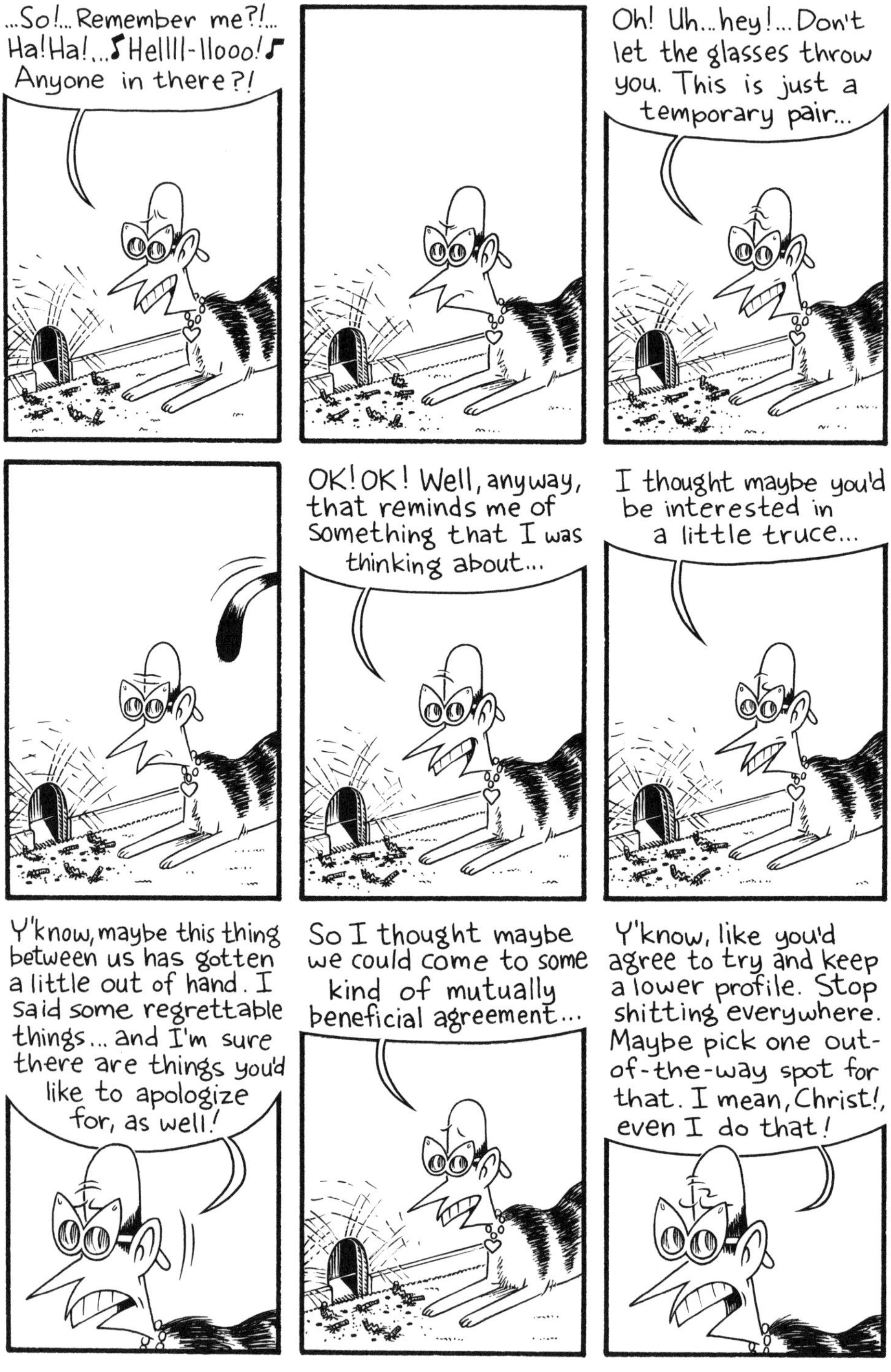
...So!...Remember me?!... Ha!Ha!...♪Hellll-llooo!♪ Anyone in there?!
Oh! Uh...hey!...Don't let the glasses throw you. This is just a temporary pair...
OK! OK! Well, anyway, that reminds me of Something that I was thinking about...
I thought maybe you'd be interested in a little truce...
Y'know, maybe this thing between us has gotten a little out of hand. I said some regrettable things... and I'm sure there are things you'd like to apologize for, as well!
So I thought maybe we could come to some kind of mutually beneficial agreement...
Y'know, like you'd agree to try and keep a lower profile. Stop shitting everywhere. Maybe pick one out-of-the-way spot for that. I mean, Christ!, even I do that!

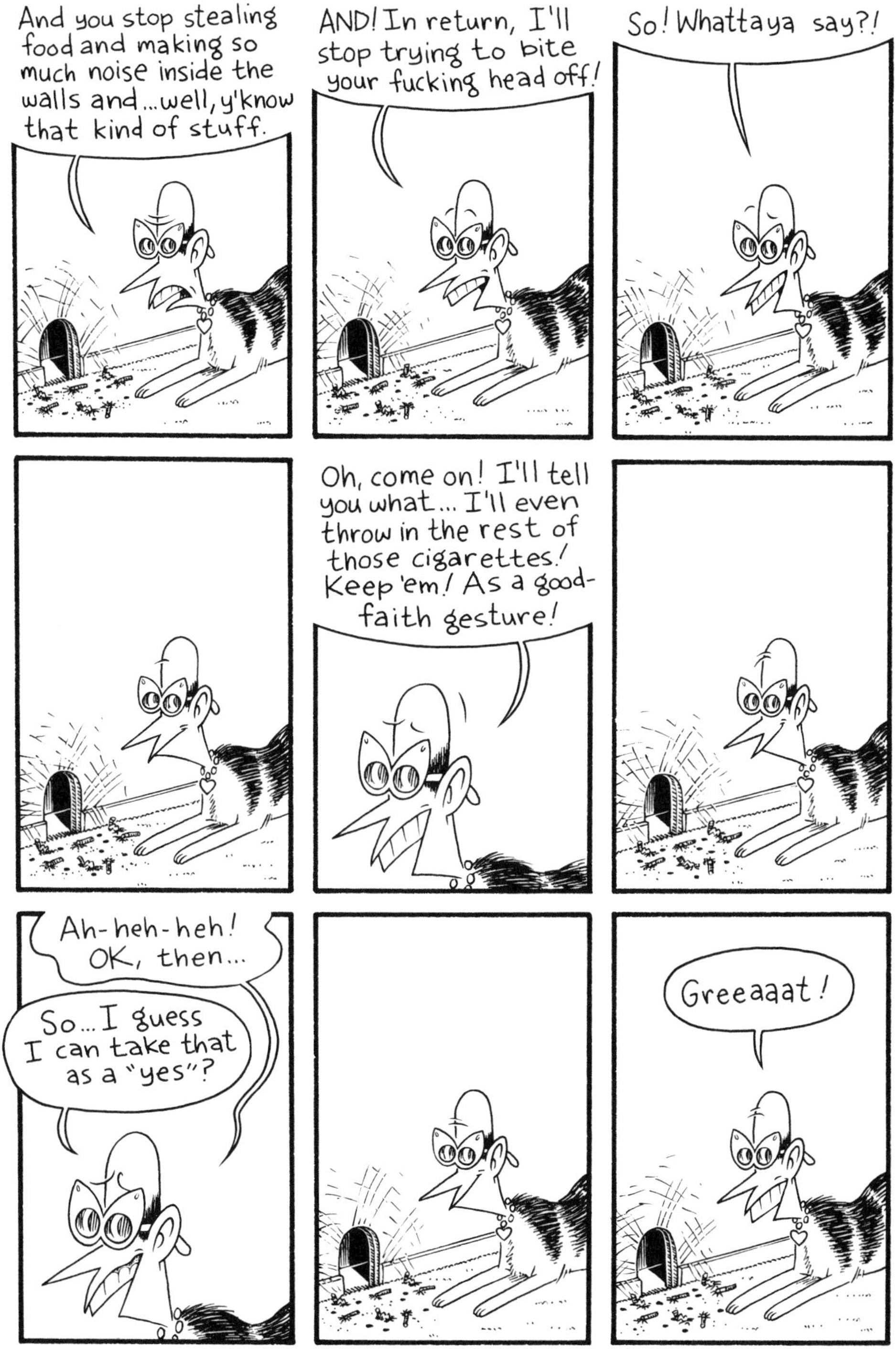
And you stop stealing food and making so much noise inside the walls and...well, y'know that kind of stuff.
AND! In return, I'll stop trying to bite your fucking head off!
So! Whattaya say?!
Oh, come on! I'll tell you what... I'll even throw in the rest of those cigarettes! Keep 'em! As a good-faith gesture!
Ah-heh-heh! OK, then...
So... I guess I can take that as a "yes"?
Greeaaat!

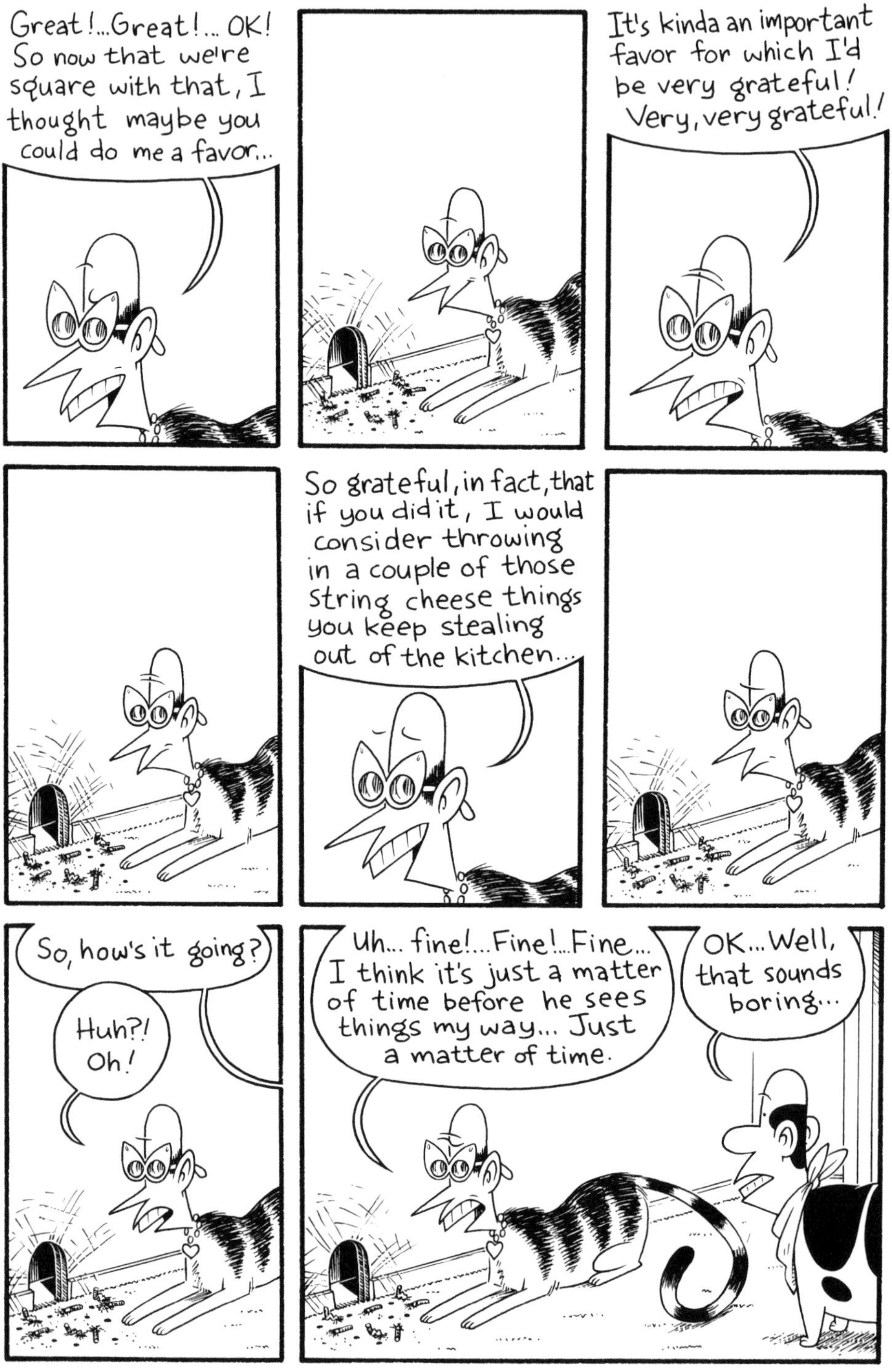
Great!...Great!... OK! So now that we're square with that, I thought maybe you could do me a favor...
It's kinda an important favor for which I'd be very grateful! Very, very grateful!
So grateful, in fact, that if you did it, I would consider throwing in a couple of those string cheese things you keep stealing out of the kitchen...
So, how's it going?
Huh?! Oh!
Uh... fine!...Fine!...Fine... I think it's just a matter of time before he sees things my way... Just a matter of time.
OK...Well, that sounds boring...

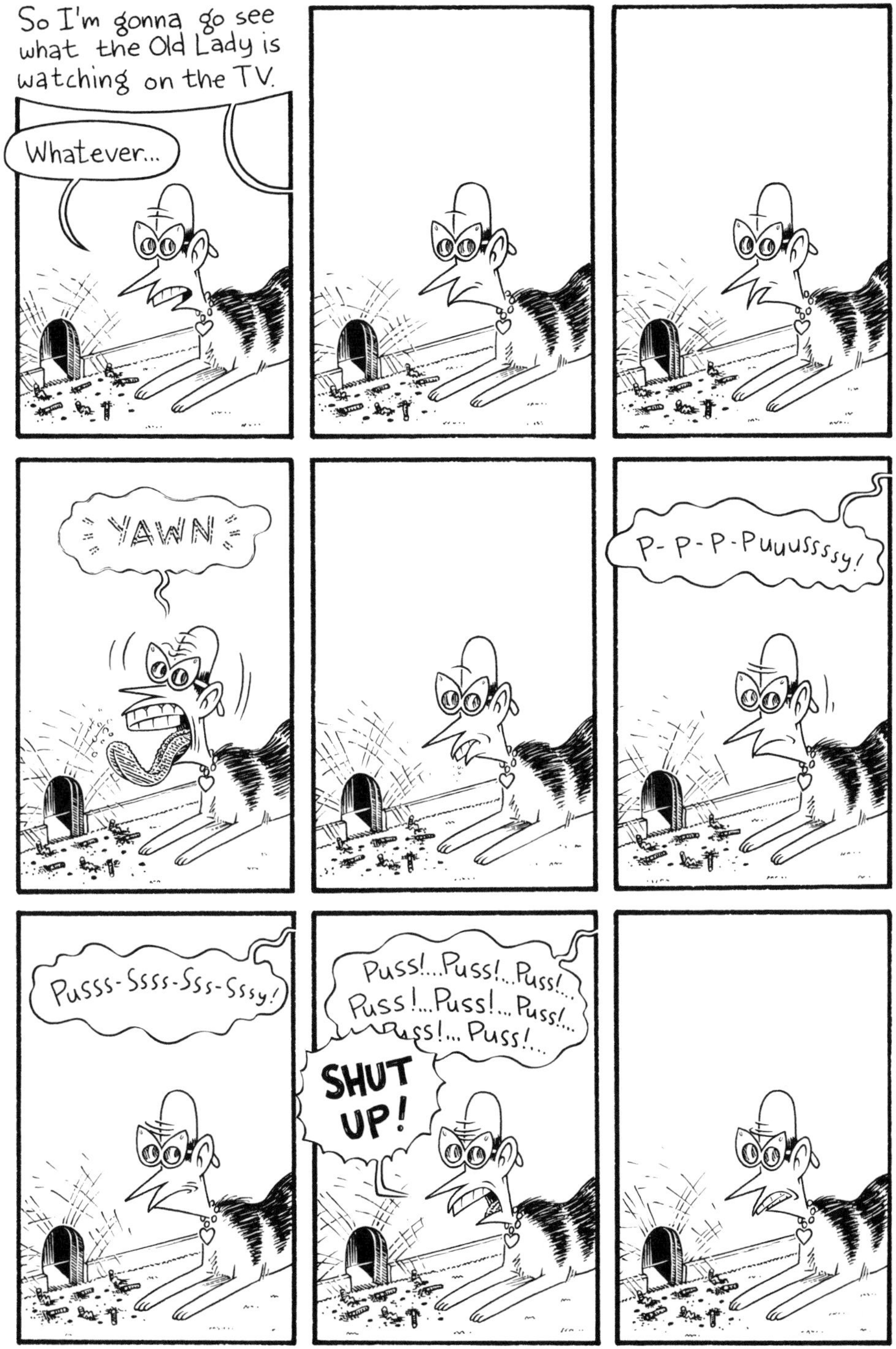
So I'm gonna go see what the Old Lady is watching on the TV.
Whatever...
YAWN
P- P- P- Puuussssy!
Pusss-Ssss-Sss-Sssy!
Puss!...Puss!...Puss!...
Puss!...Puss!...Puss!...
ss!... Puss!...
SHUT UP!

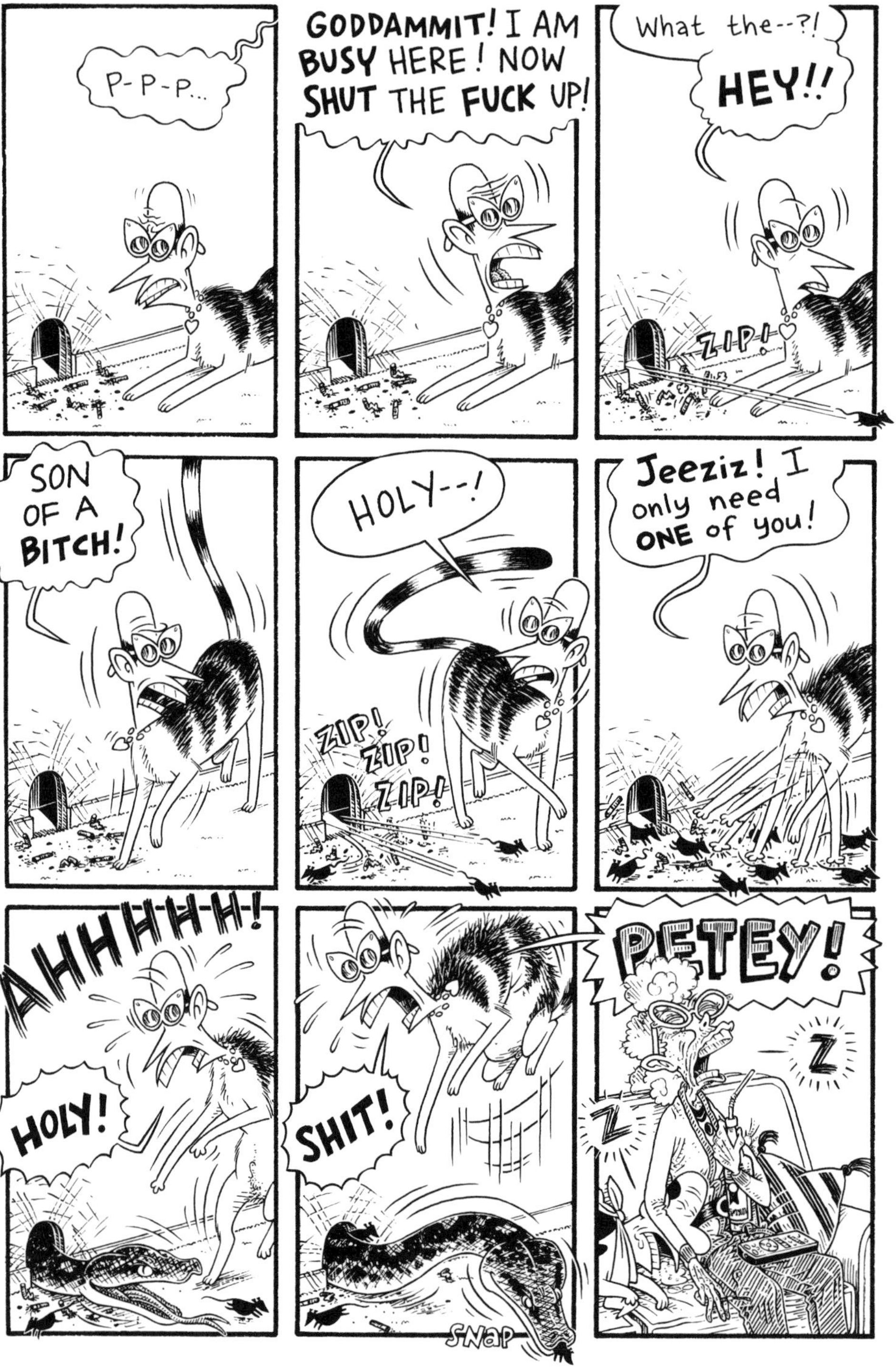
P-P-P...
GODDAMMIT! I AM BUSY HERE! NOW SHUT THE FUCK UP!
What the--?!
HEY!!
ZIP!
SON OF A BITCH!
HOLY--!
ZIP! ZIP! ZIP!
Jeeziz! I only need ONE of you!
AHHHHHH!
HOLY!
SHIT!
SNAP
PETEY!
Z
Z

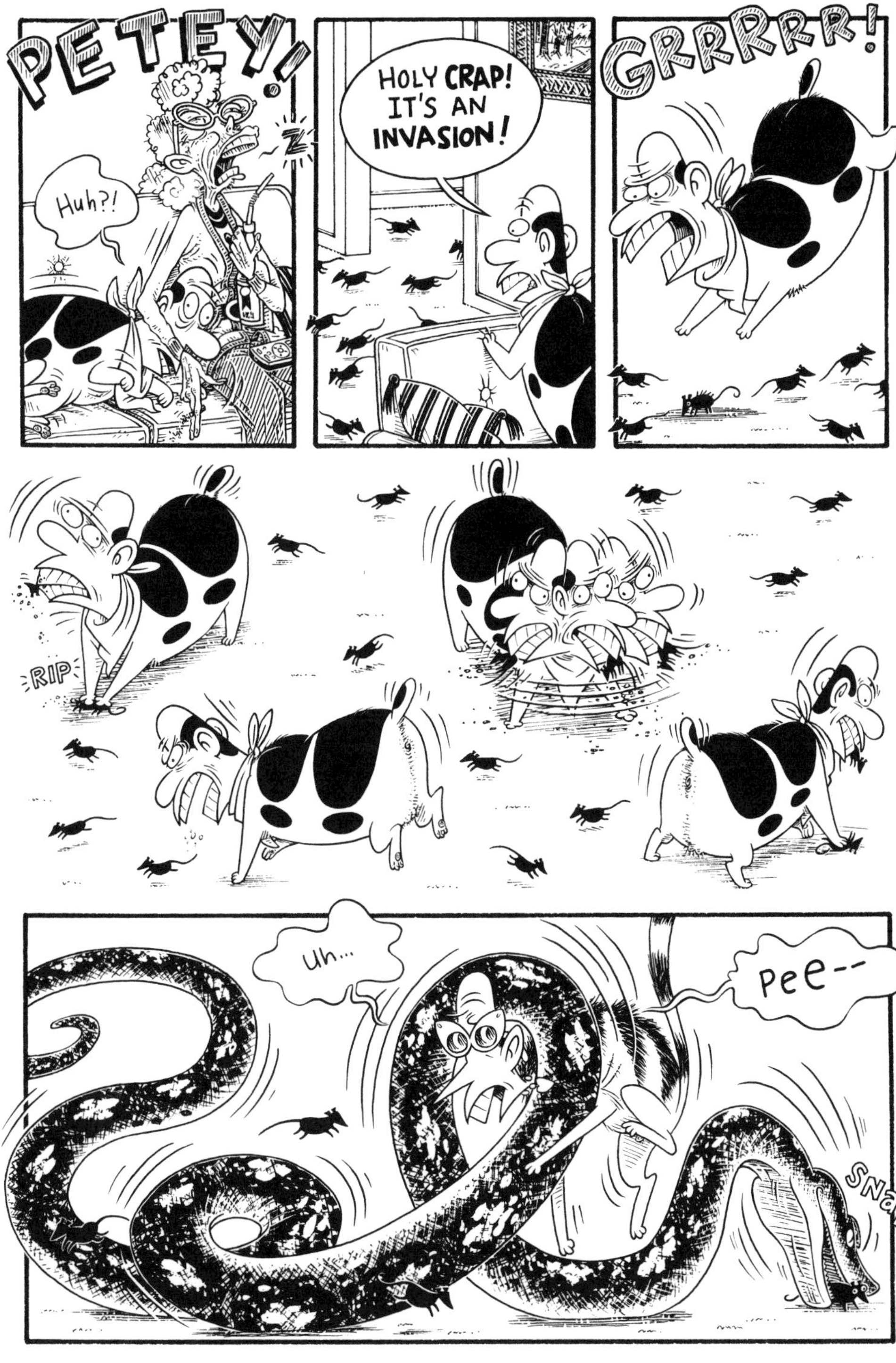
PETEY!
Huh?!
HOLY CRAP! IT'S AN INVASION!
GRRRRRR!
RIP
Uh...
Pee--
SNAP!

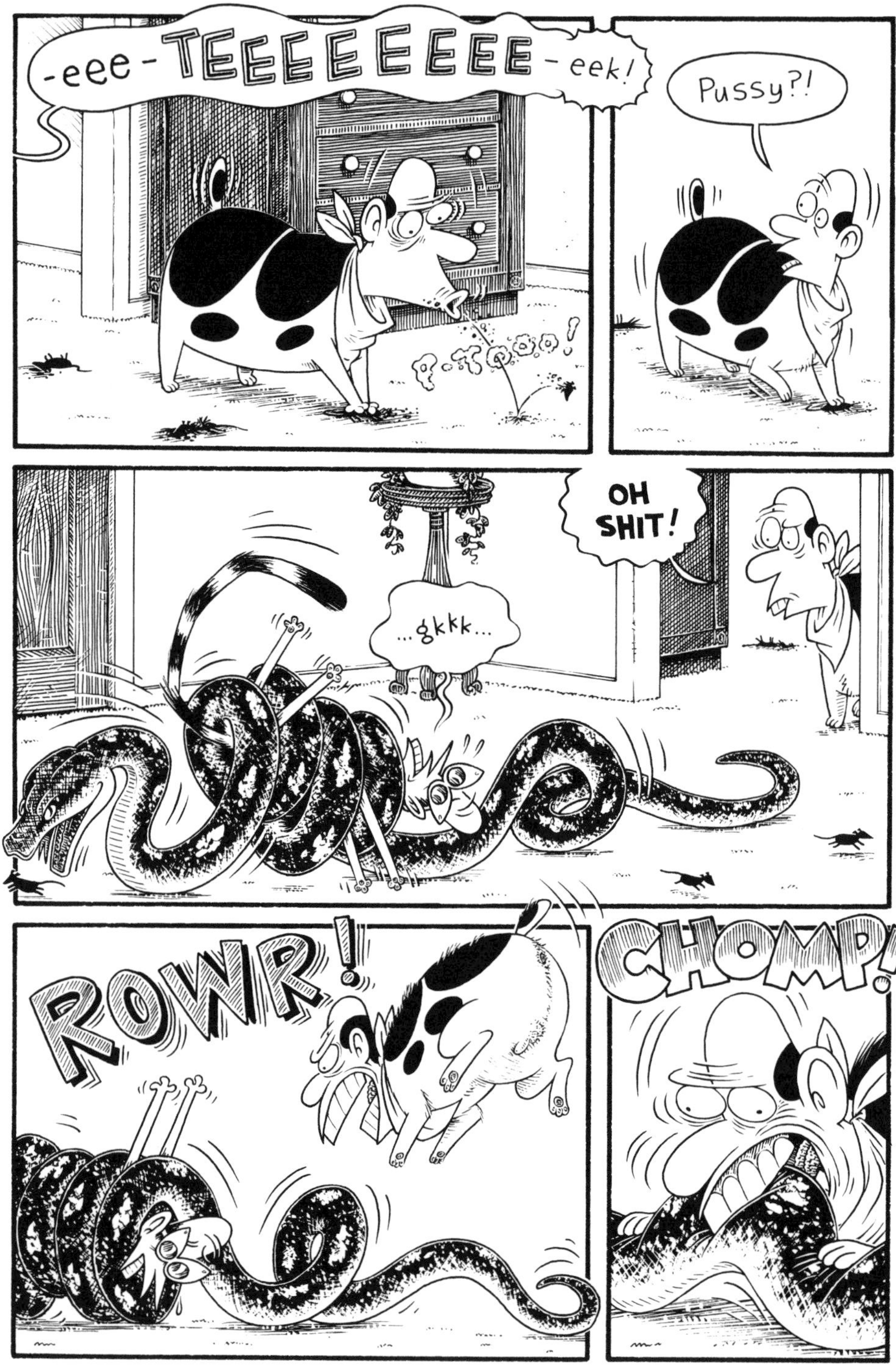

-eee-TEEEEEEEE-eek!
P-TOOO!
Pussy?!
OH SHIT!
...gkkk...
ROWR!
CHOMP!

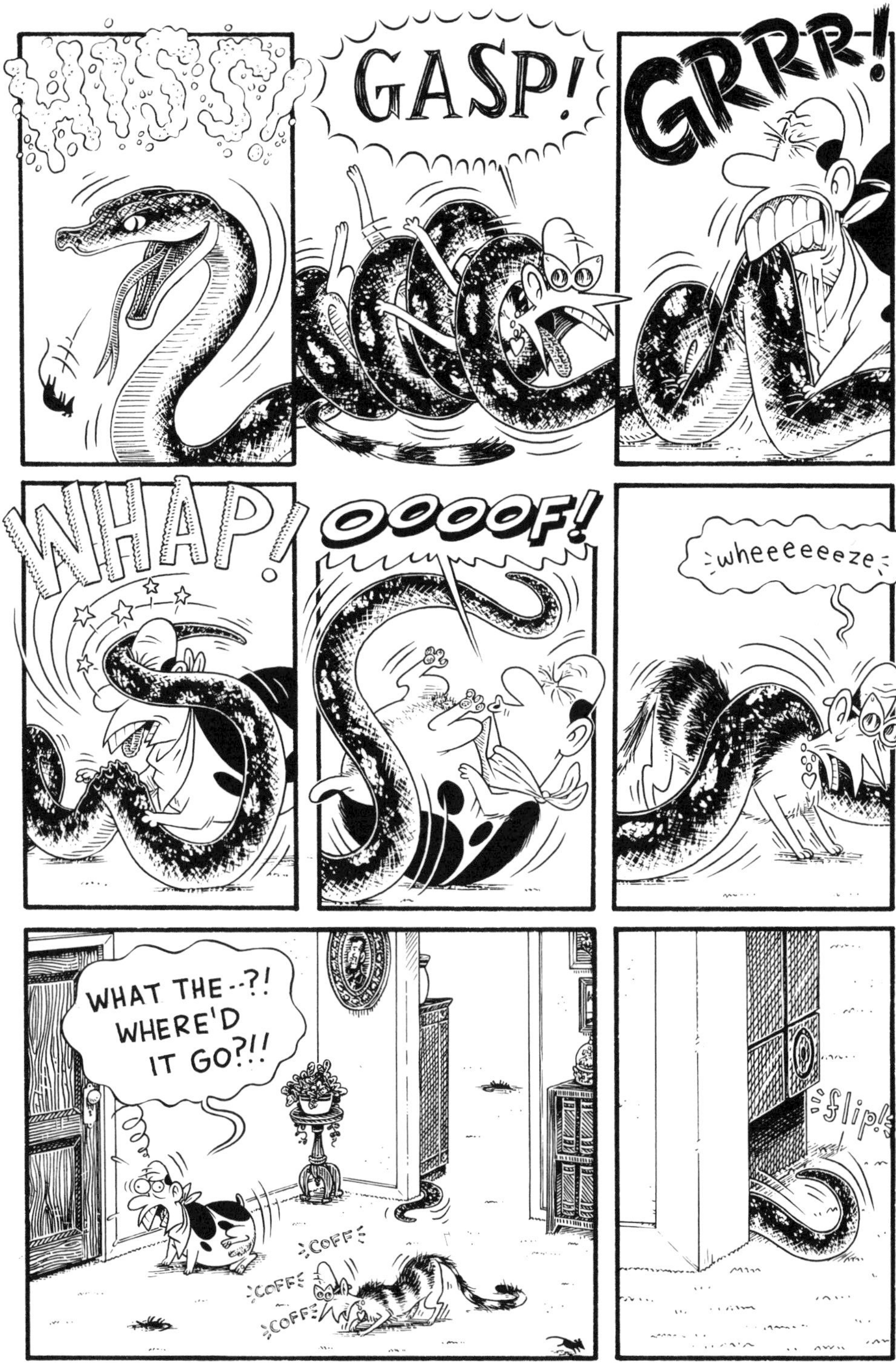
WHSST!
GASP!
GRRR!
WHAP!
OOOOOF!
wheeeeeeze
WHAT THE--?! WHERE'D IT GO?!!
COFF
COFF
COFF
flip!

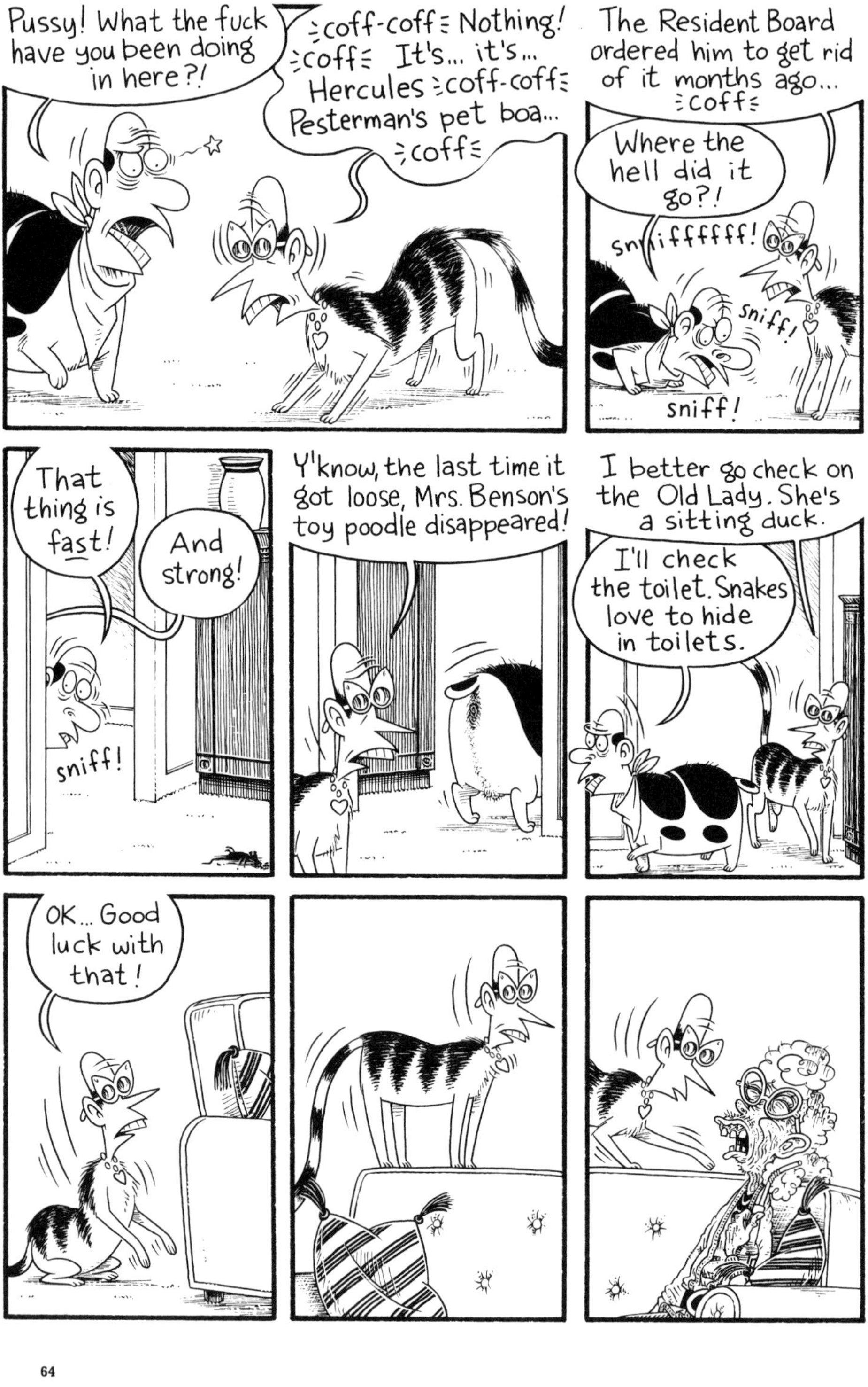
Pussy! What the fuck have you been doing in here?!
coff-coff Nothing! coff It's... it's... Hercules coff-coff Pesterman's pet boa... coff
The Resident Board ordered him to get rid of it months ago... coff
Where the hell did it go?!
sniffffff!
sniff!
sniff!
That thing is fast!
And strong!
sniff!
Y'know, the last time it got loose, Mrs. Benson's toy poodle disappeared!
I better go check on the Old Lady. She's a sitting duck.
I'll check the toilet. Snakes love to hide in toilets.
OK... Good luck with that!

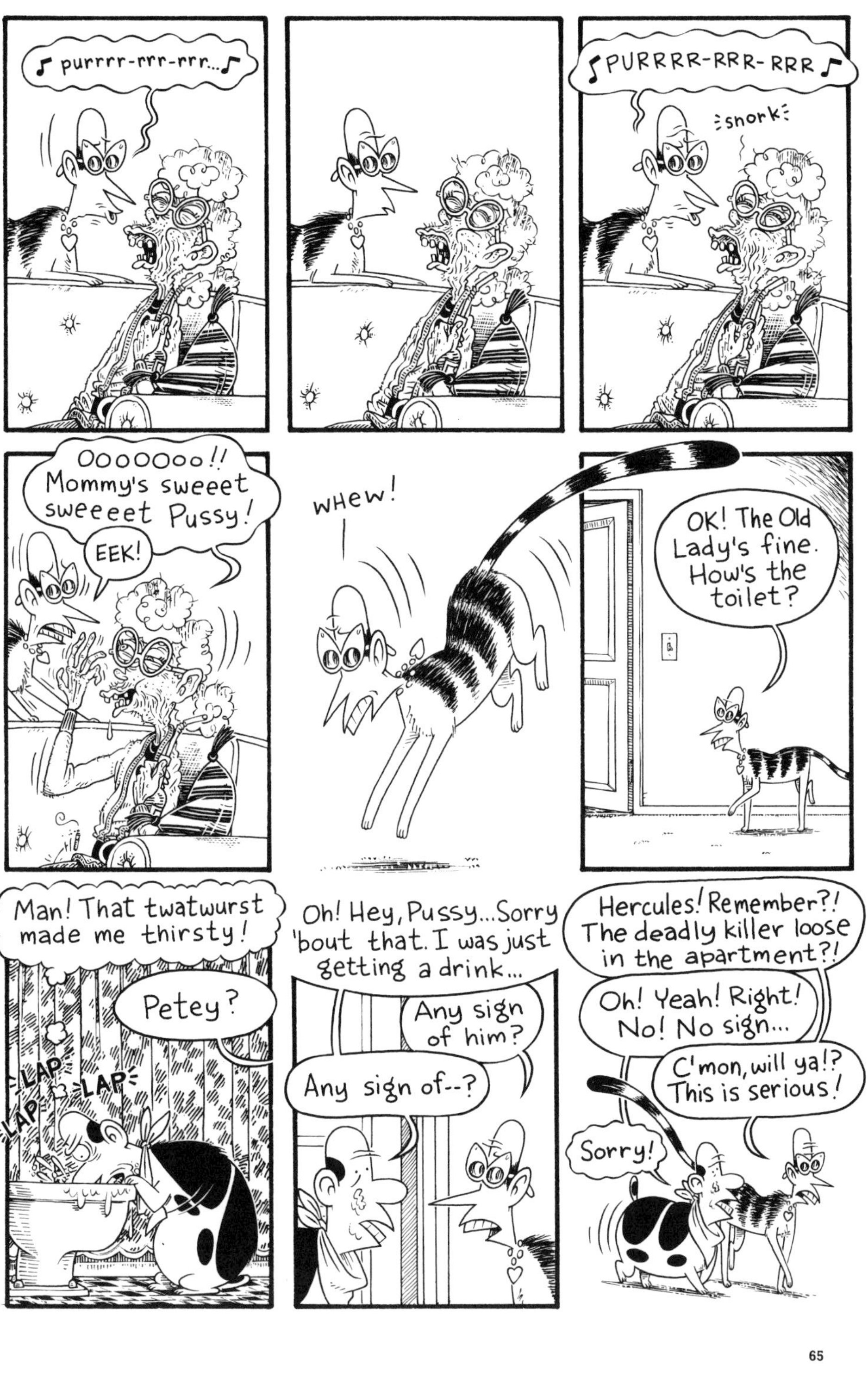
purrrr-rrr-rrr...
PURRRR-RRR-RRR
snork
OOOOOOo!! Mommy's sweeet sweeeet Pussy!
EEK!
WHEW!
OK! The Old Lady's fine. How's the toilet?
Man! That twatwurst made me thirsty!
Petey?
LAP
LAP
LAP
Oh! Hey, Pussy...Sorry 'bout that. I was just getting a drink...
Any sign of him?
Any sign of--?
Hercules! Remember?! The deadly killer loose in the apartment?!
Oh! Yeah! Right! No! No sign...
C'mon, will ya!? This is serious!
Sorry!

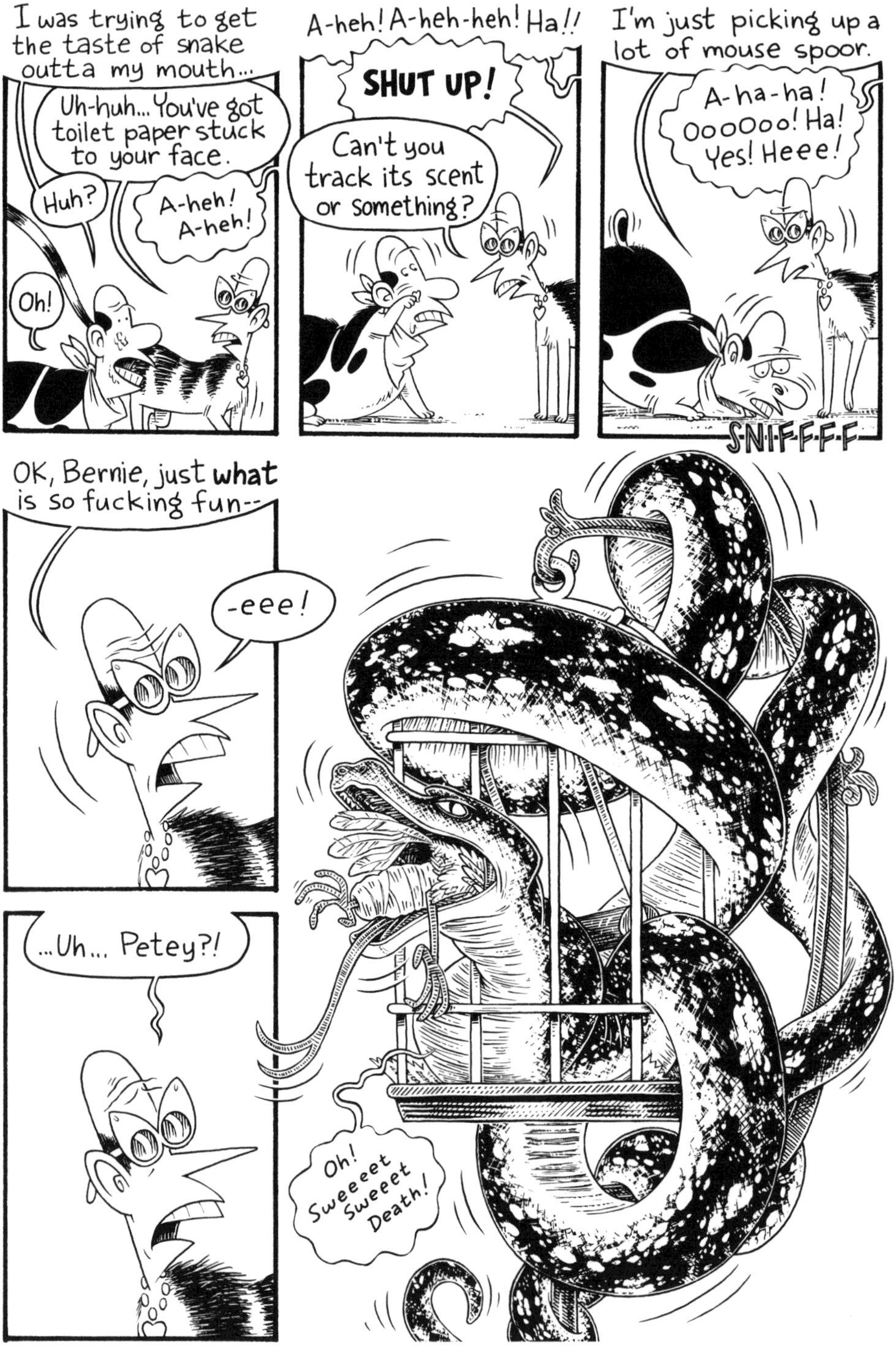
I was trying to get the taste of snake outta my mouth...
Uh-huh... You've got toilet paper stuck to your face.
Huh?
A-heh! A-heh!
Oh!
A-heh! A-heh-heh! Ha!!
SHUT UP!
Can't you track its scent or something?
I'm just picking up a lot of mouse spoor.
A-ha-ha! OooOoo! Ha! Yes! Heee!
SNIFFFF
OK, Bernie, just **what** is so fucking fun--
-eee!
...Uh... Petey?!
Oh! Sweeeet Sweeet Death!

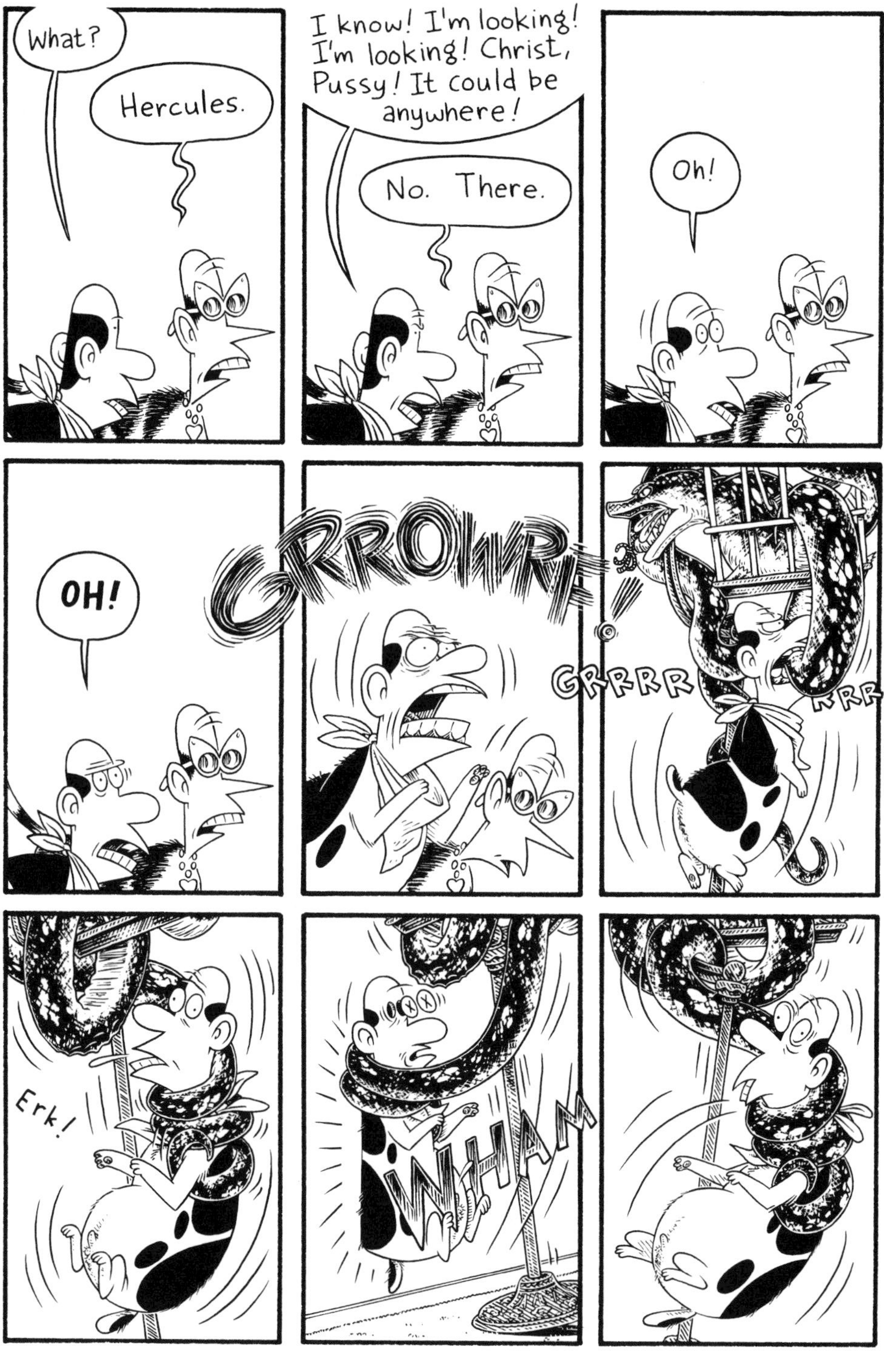
What?
Hercules.
I know! I'm looking! I'm looking! Christ, Pussy! It could be anywhere!
No. There.
Oh!
OH!
GRROWRF!
GRRRR
RRRR
Erk!
WHAM

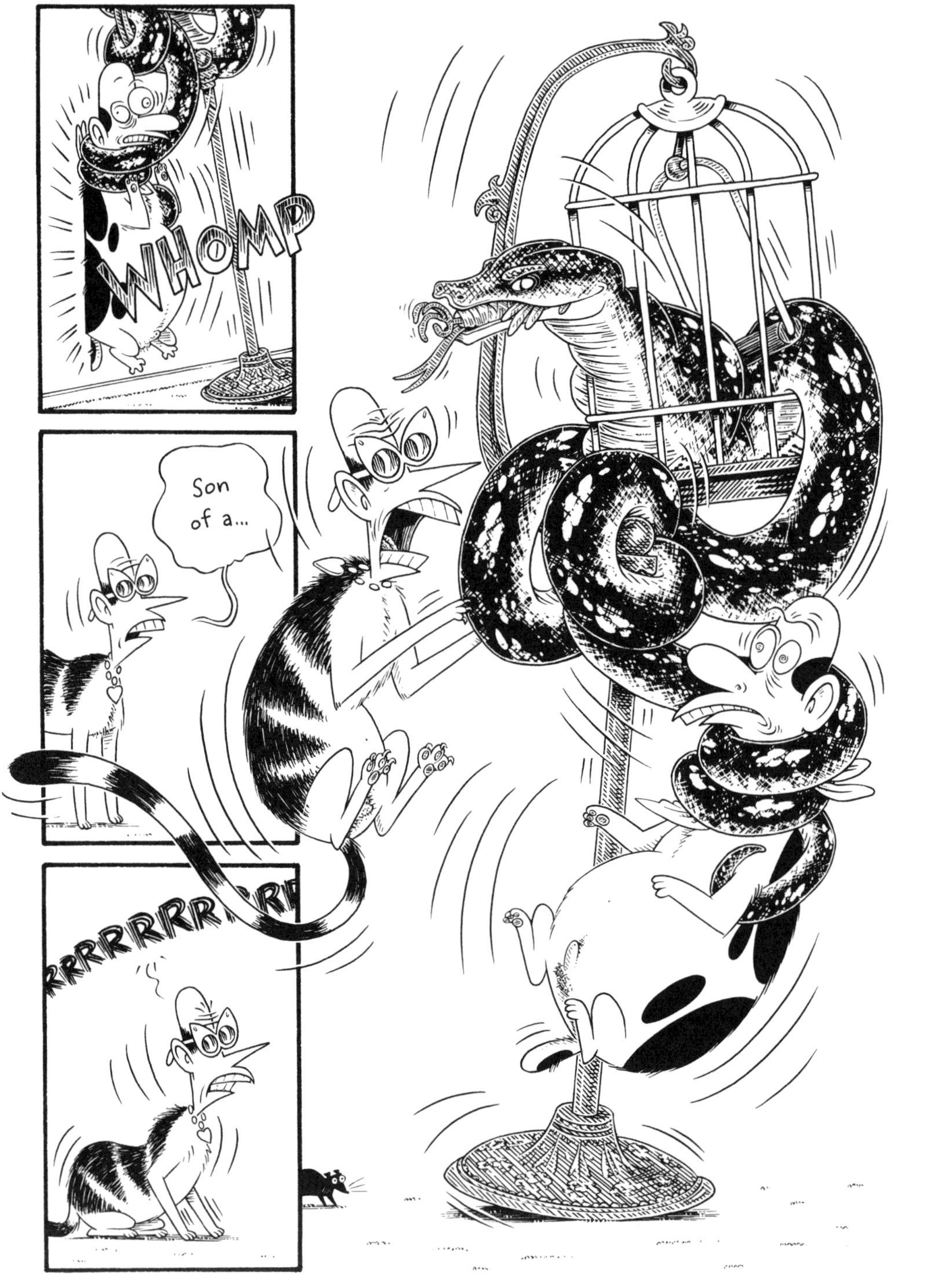
WHOMP
Son of a...
RRRRRRRRRRR

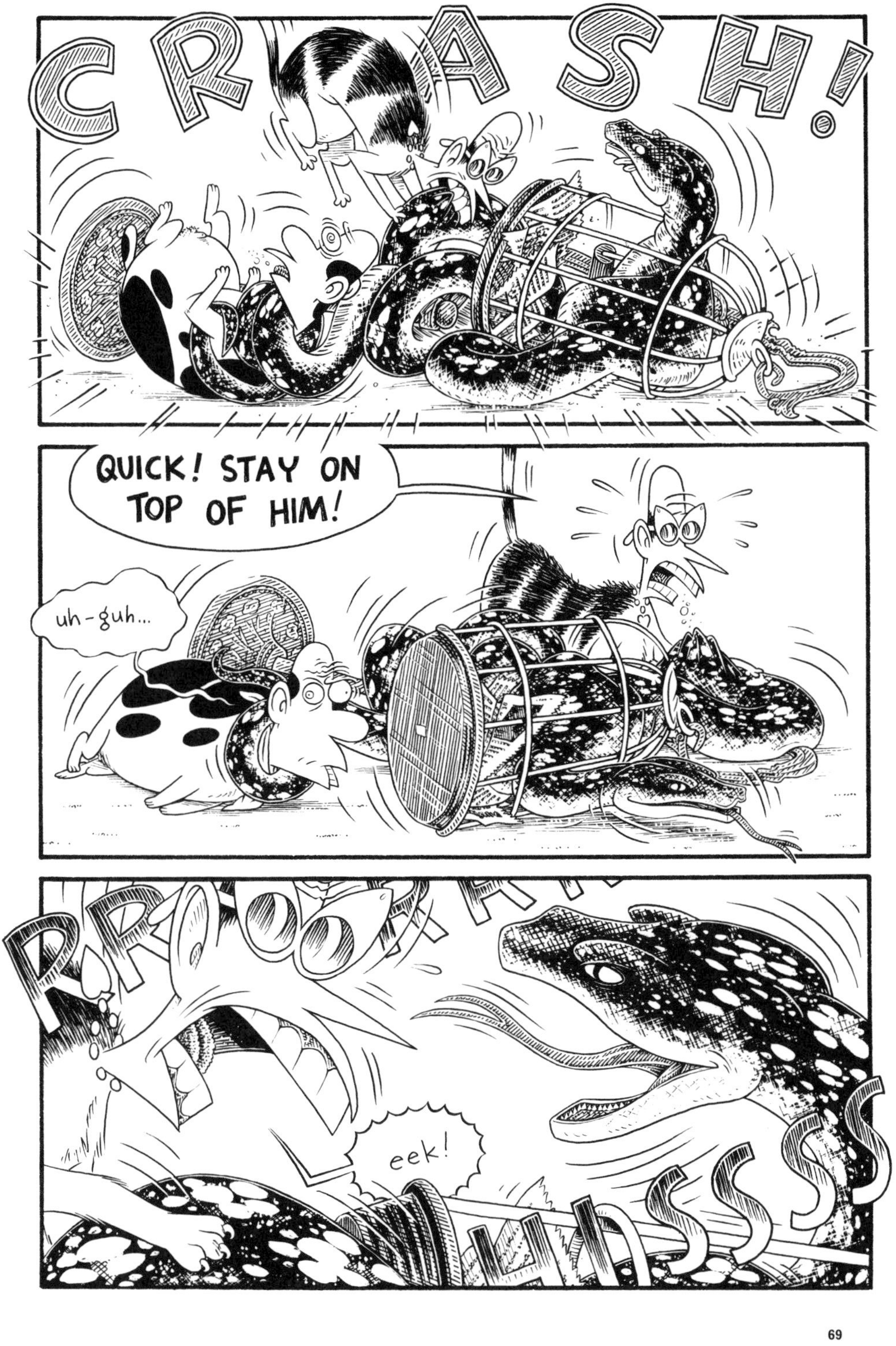
CRASH!
QUICK! STAY ON TOP OF HIM!
uh-guh...
RROOAR
eek!
HISSSS

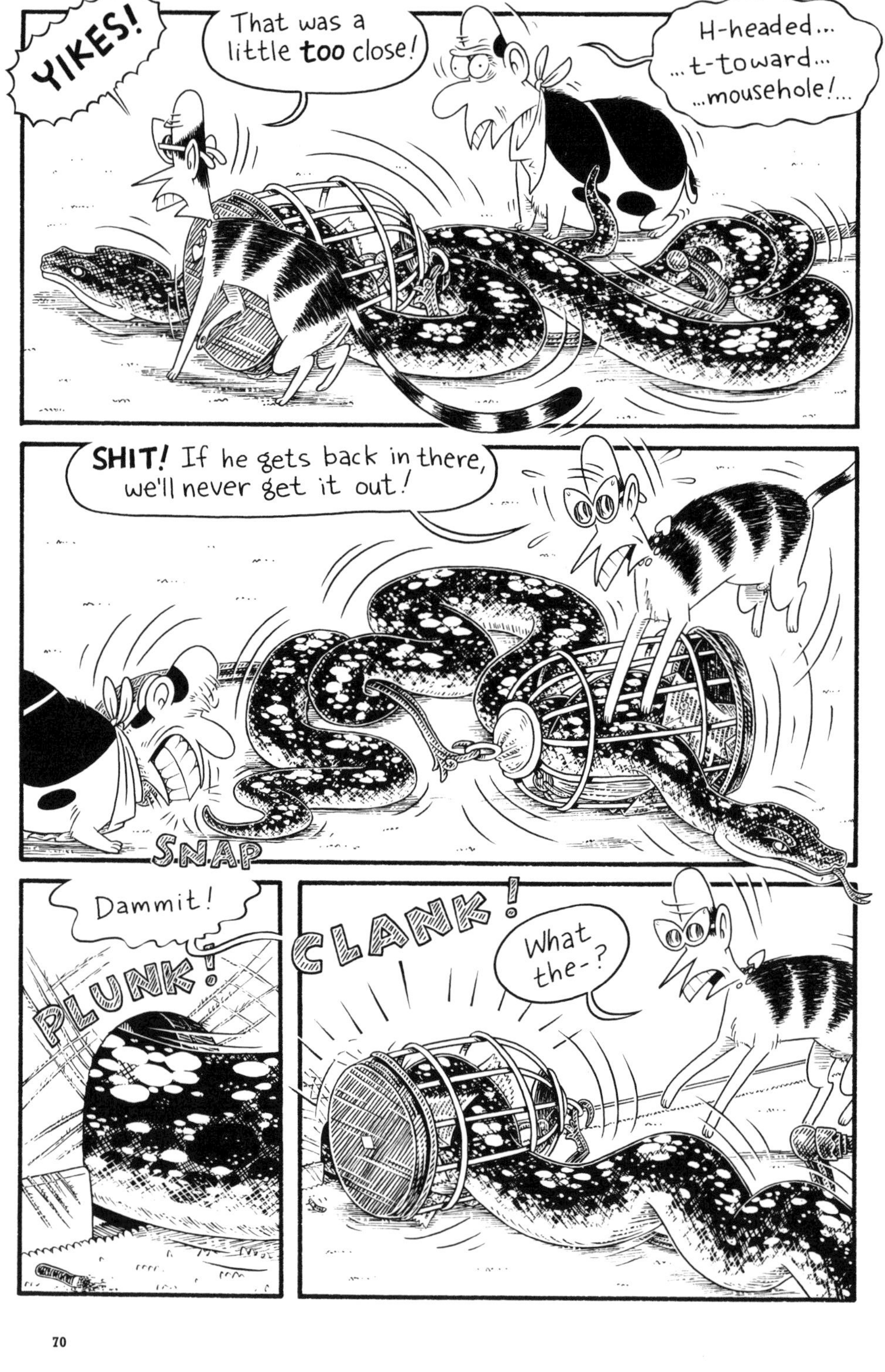
YIKES!
That was a little **too** close!
H-headed... ...t-toward... ...mousehole!...
SHIT! If he gets back in there, we'll never get it out!
SNAP
Dammit!
PLUNK!
CLANK!
What the-?

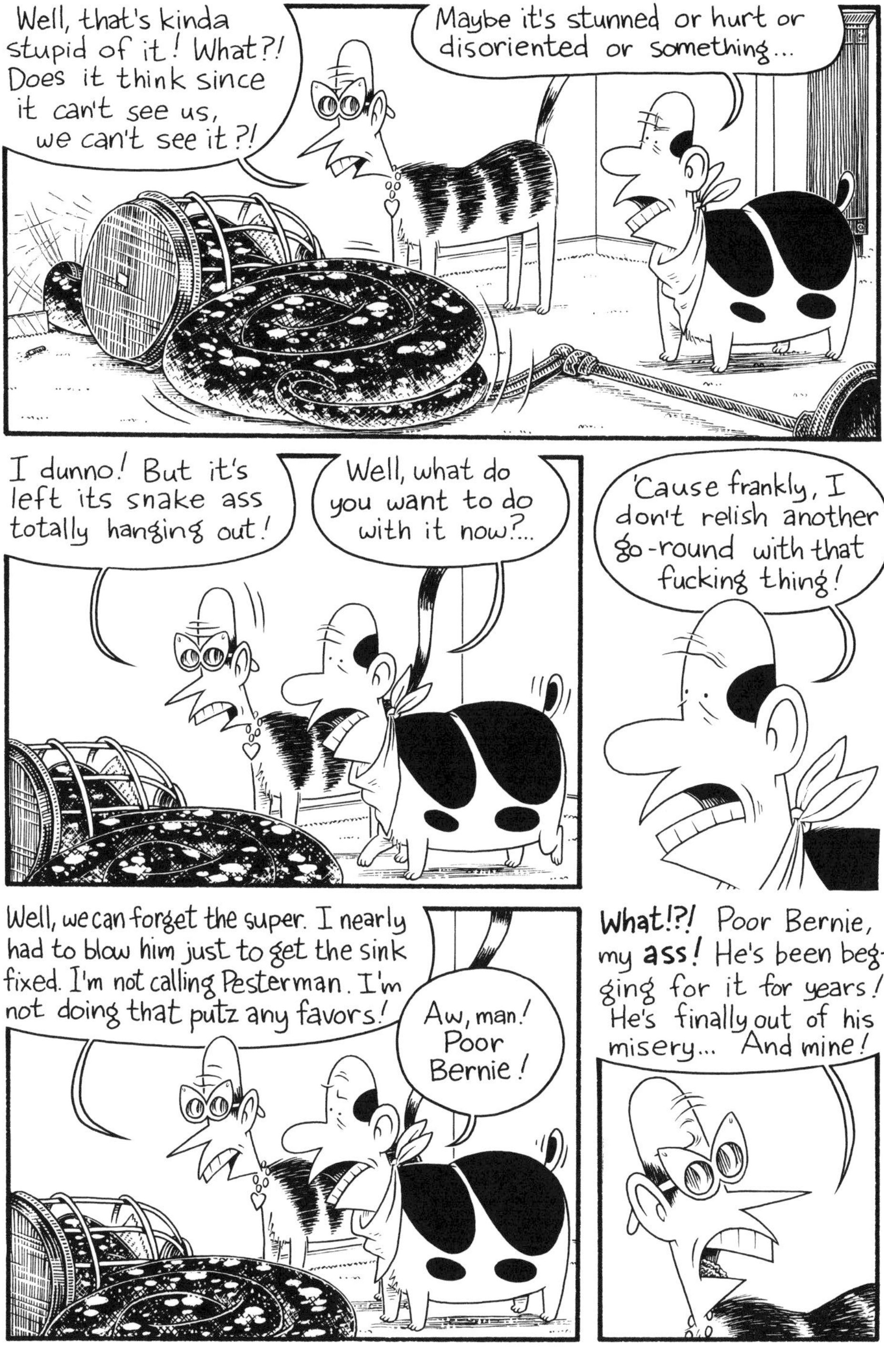
Well, that's kinda stupid of it! What?! Does it think since it can't see us, we can't see it?!
Maybe it's stunned or hurt or disoriented or something...
I dunno! But it's left its snake ass totally hanging out!
Well, what do you want to do with it now?...
'Cause frankly, I don't relish another go-round with that fucking thing!
Well, we can forget the super. I nearly had to blow him just to get the sink fixed. I'm not calling Pesterman. I'm not doing that putz any favors!
Aw, man! Poor Bernie!
What!?! Poor Bernie, my ass! He's been begging for it for years! He's finally out of his misery... And mine!

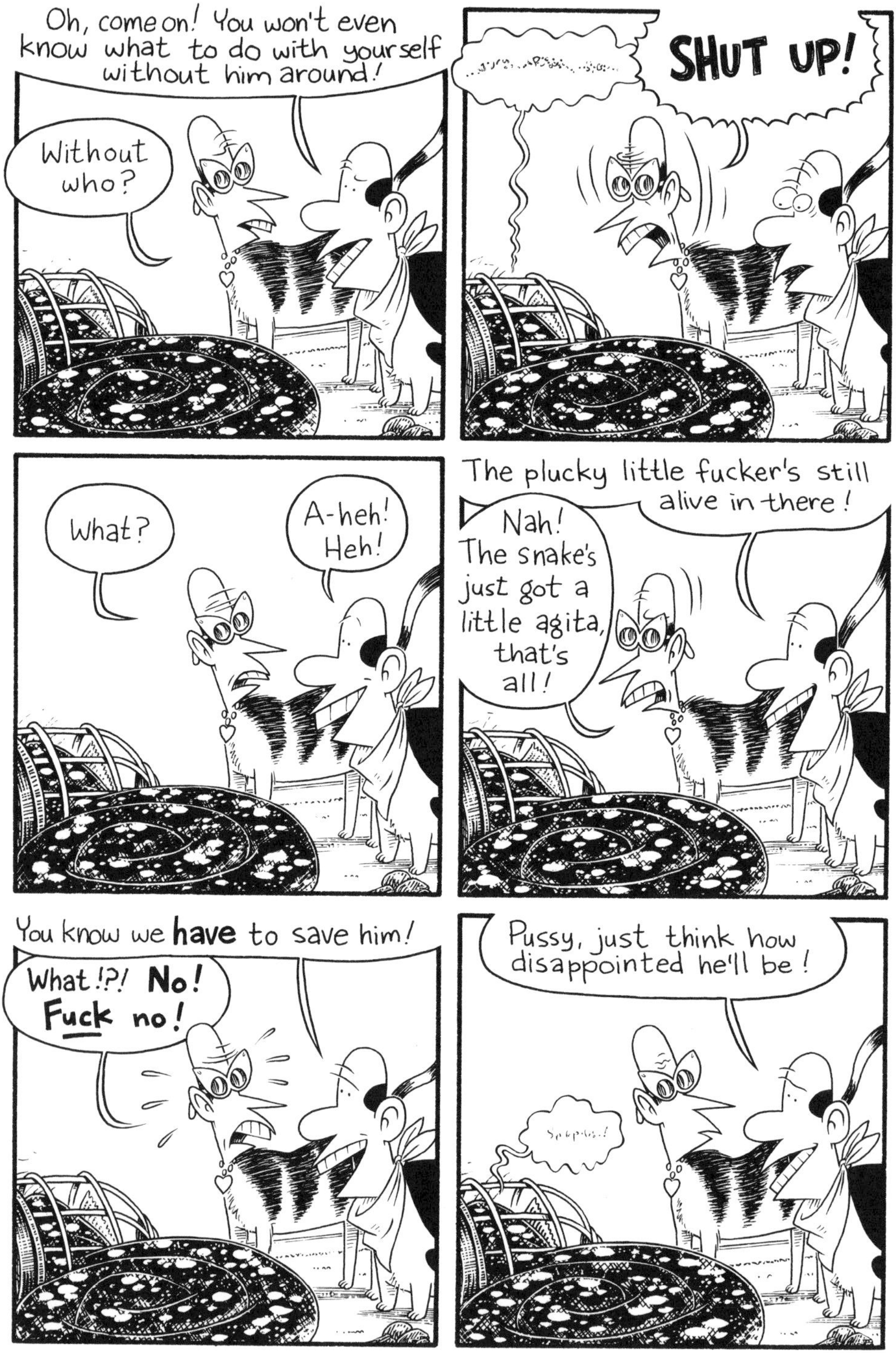
Oh, come on! You won't even know what to do with yourself without him around!
Without who?
SHUT UP!
What?
A-heh! Heh!
The plucky little fucker's still alive in there!
Nah! The snake's just got a little agita, that's all!
You know we **have** to save him!
What!?! **No! Fuck no!**
Pussy, just think how disappointed he'll be!

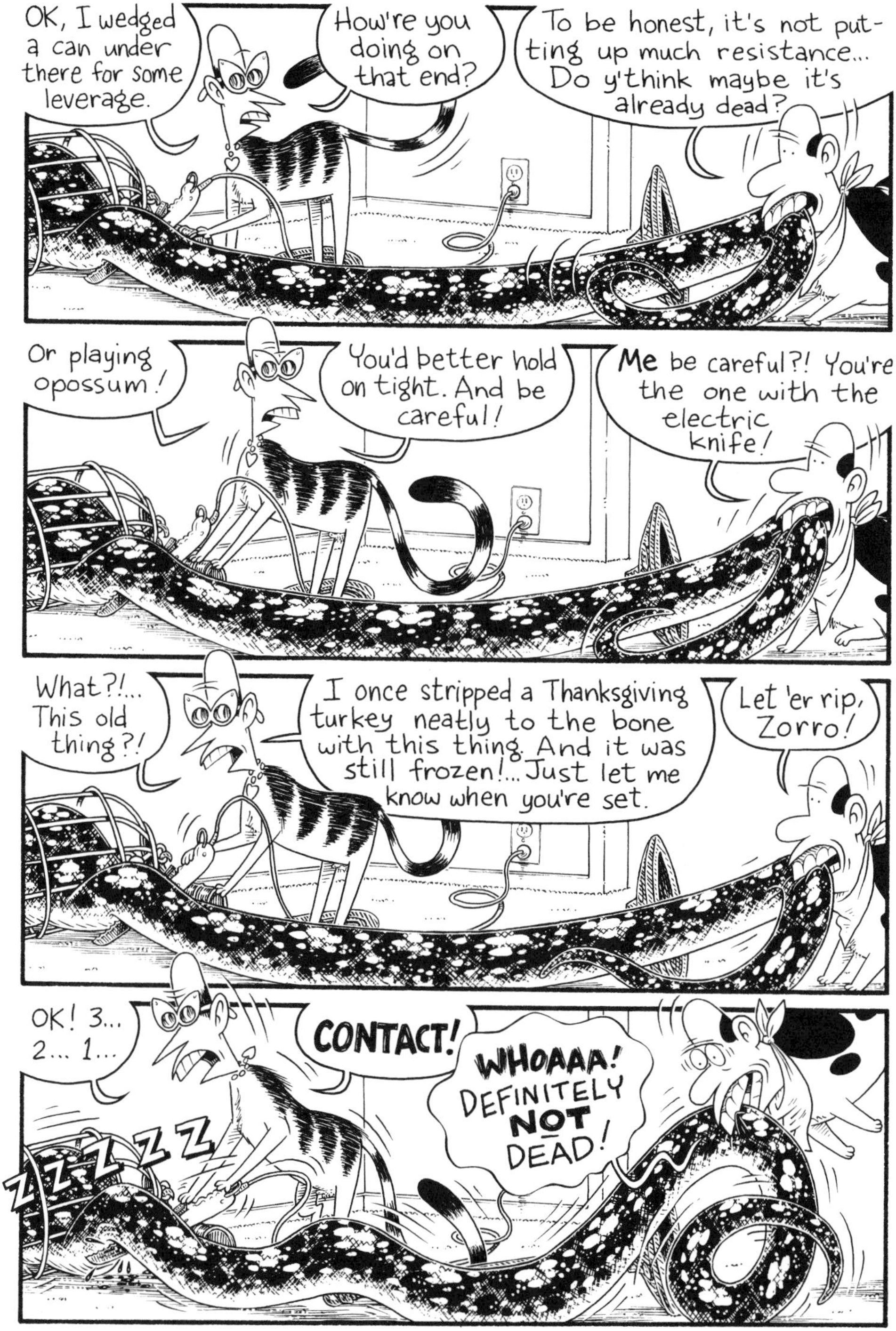
OK, I wedged a can under there for some leverage.
How're you doing on that end?
To be honest, it's not putting up much resistance... Do y'think maybe it's already dead?
Or playing opossum!
You'd better hold on tight. And be careful!
Me be careful?! You're the one with the electric knife!
What?!... This old thing?!
I once stripped a Thanksgiving turkey neatly to the bone with this thing. And it was still frozen!... Just let me know when you're set.
Let 'er rip, Zorro!
OK! 3... 2... 1...
CONTACT!
ZZZZZZ
WHOAAA! DEFINITELY NOT DEAD!

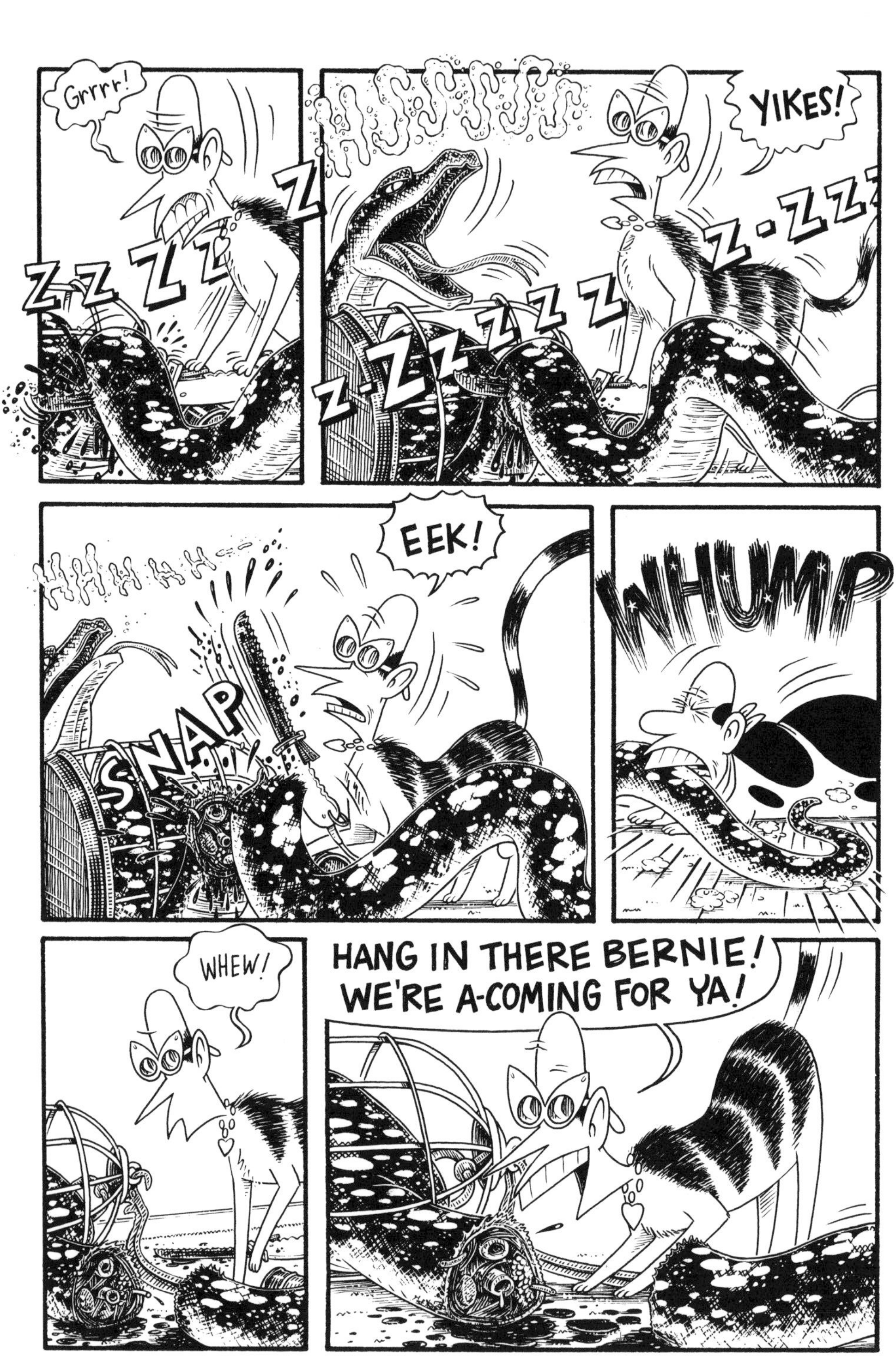
Grrrr!
YIKES!
EEK!
SNAP
WHUMP
WHEW!
HANG IN THERE BERNIE!
WE'RE A-COMING FOR YA!

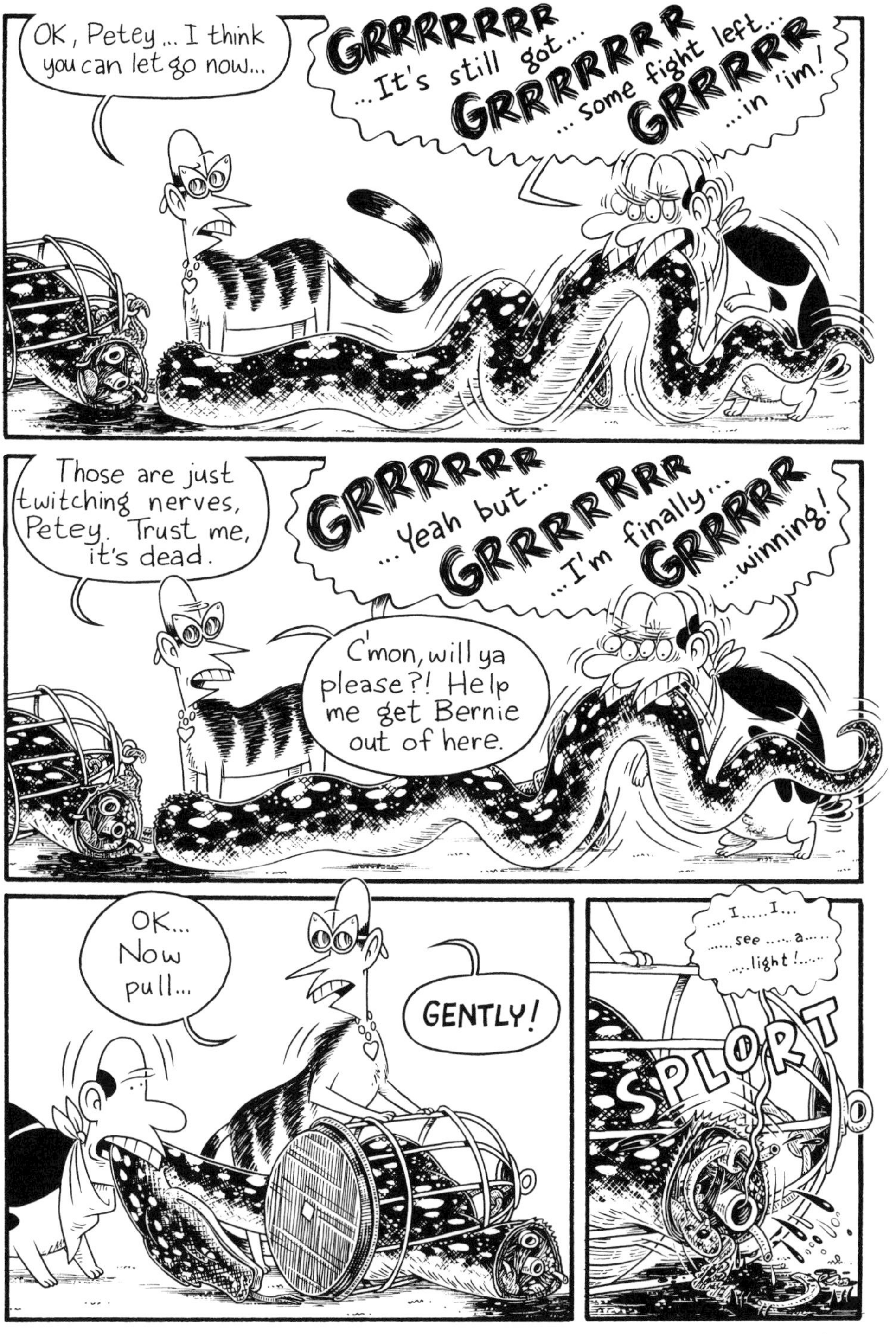
OK, Petey... I think you can let go now...
GRRRRRRR ...It's still got... GRRRRRRR ...some fight left... GRRRRRR ...in 'im!
Those are just twitching nerves, Petey. Trust me, it's dead.
GRRRRRRR ...Yeah but... GRRRRRRR ...I'm finally... GRRRRRR ...winning!
C'mon, will ya please?! Help me get Bernie out of here.
OK... Now pull...
GENTLY!
...I.....I... .....see .....a..... .....light!.....
SPLORT

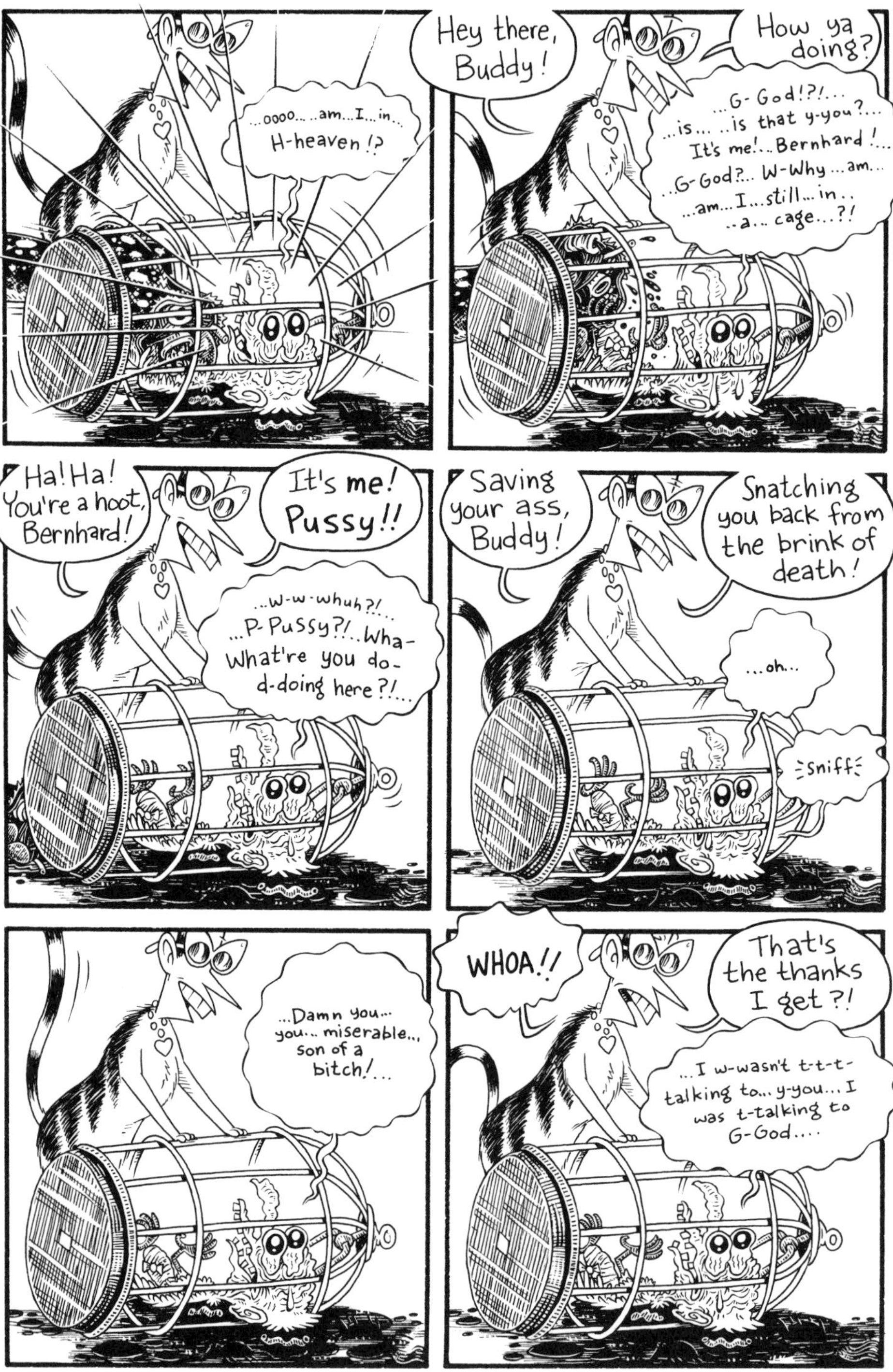
...oooo... ...am...I...in...
H-heaven!?
Hey there, Buddy!
How ya doing?
...G-God!?!...
...is... ...is that y-you?...
It's me!...Bernhard!...
...G-God?... W-Why...am...
...am...I...still...in..
..a...cage...?!
Ha! Ha! You're a hoot, Bernhard!
It's me! Pussy!!
...w-w-whuh?!...
...P-Pussy?!..Wha-
What're you do-
d-doing here?!...
Saving your ass, Buddy!
Snatching you back from the brink of death!
...oh...
sniff
...Damn you...
you... miserable...
son of a
bitch!...
WHOA!!
That's the thanks I get?!
...I w-wasn't t-t-t-
talking to... y-you... I
was t-talking to
G-God....

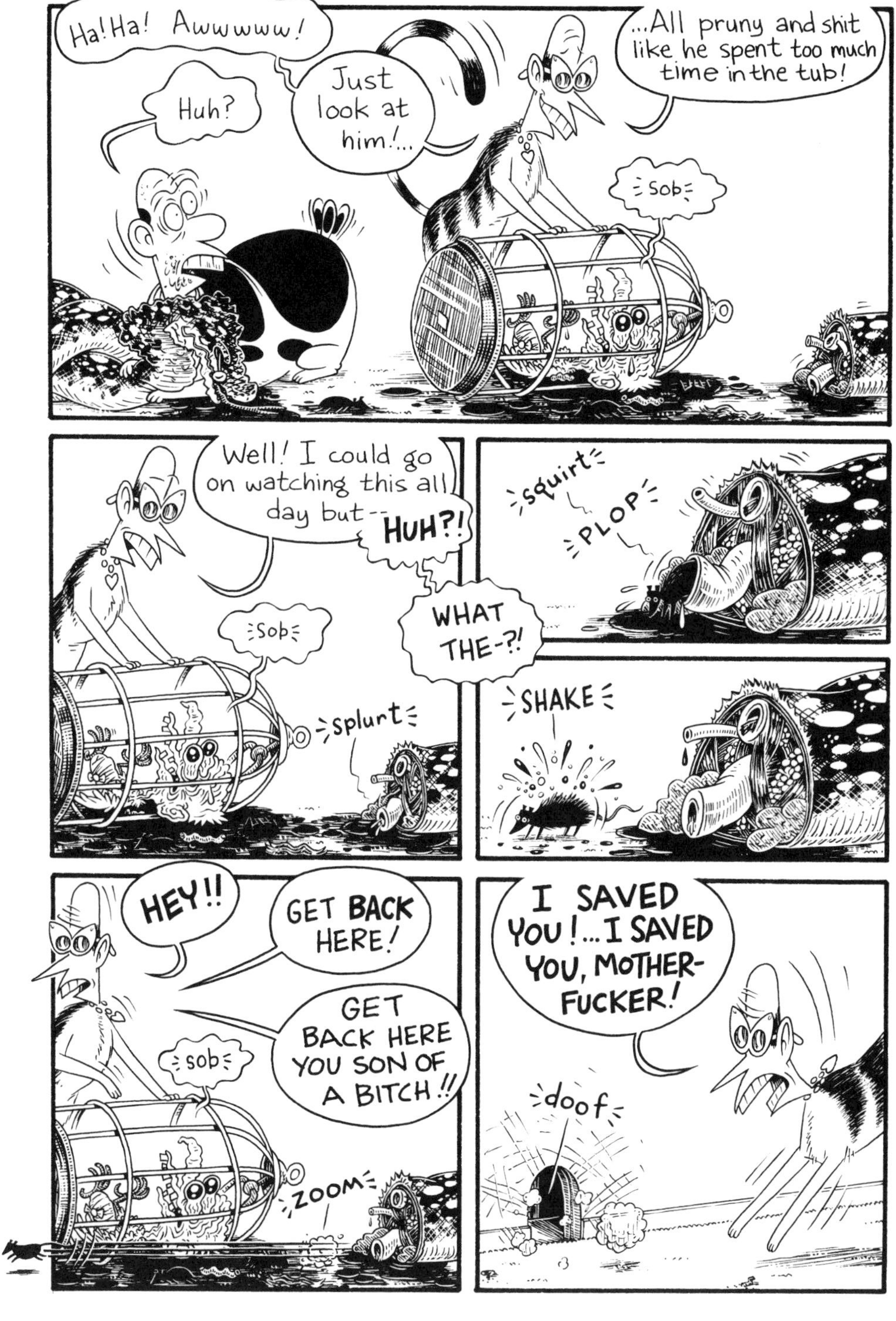
Ha! Ha! Awwwww!
Huh?
Just look at him!...
...All pruny and shit like he spent too much time in the tub!
Sob
Well! I could go on watching this all day but--
HUH?!
WHAT THE-?!
Sob
splurt
squirt
PLOP
SHAKE
HEY!!
GET BACK HERE!
GET BACK HERE YOU SON OF A BITCH!!
sob
ZOOM
I SAVED YOU!...I SAVED YOU, MOTHER-FUCKER!
doof

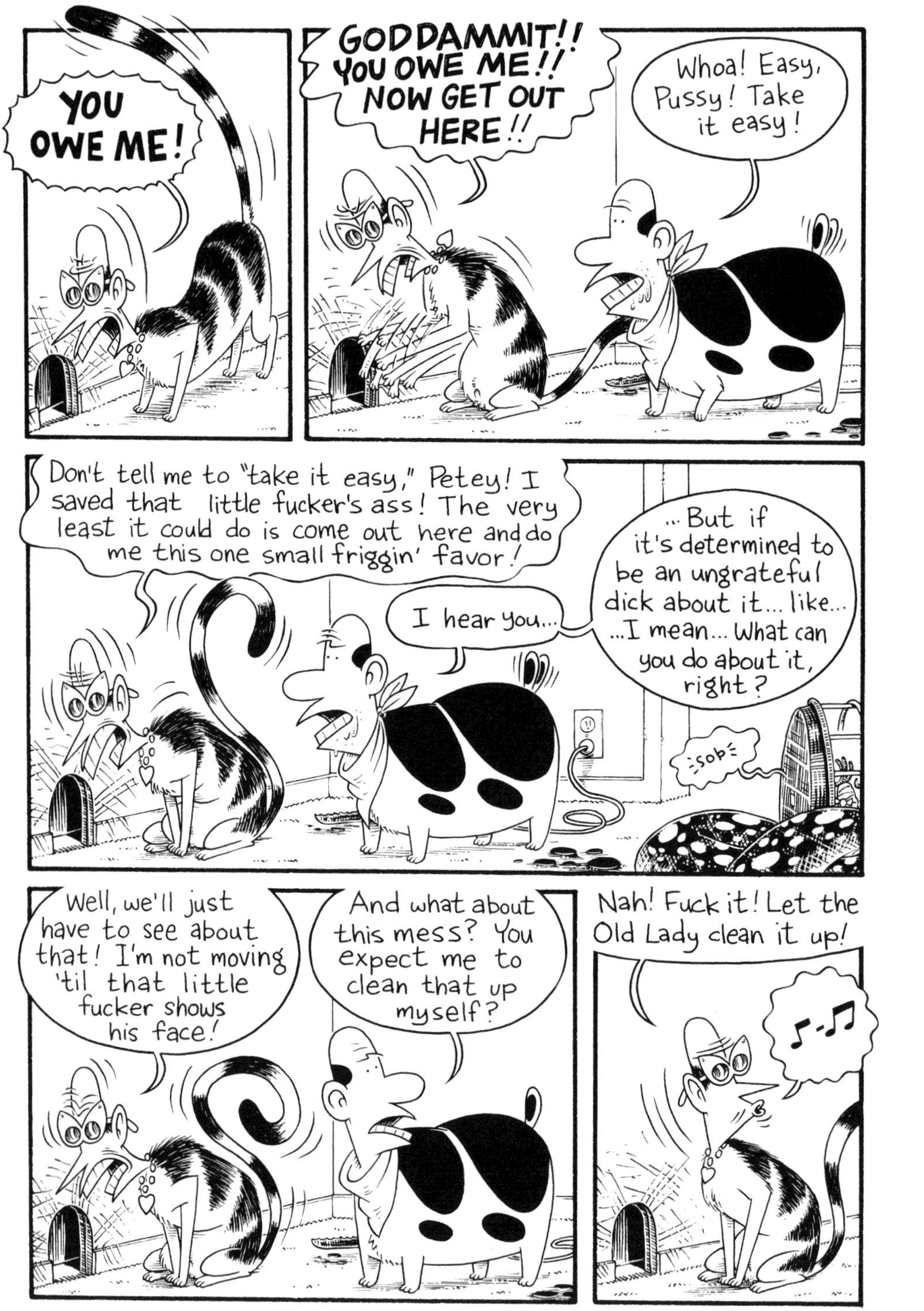
YOU OWE ME!
GODDAMMIT!! YOU OWE ME!! NOW GET OUT HERE!!
Whoa! Easy, Pussy! Take it easy!
Don't tell me to "take it easy," Petey! I saved that little fucker's ass! The very least it could do is come out here and do me this one small friggin' favor!
I hear you...
...But if it's determined to be an ungrateful dick about it... like... ...I mean... What can you do about it, right?
sob
Well, we'll just have to see about that! I'm not moving 'til that little fucker shows his face!
And what about this mess? You expect me to clean that up myself?
Nah! Fuck it! Let the Old Lady clean it up!

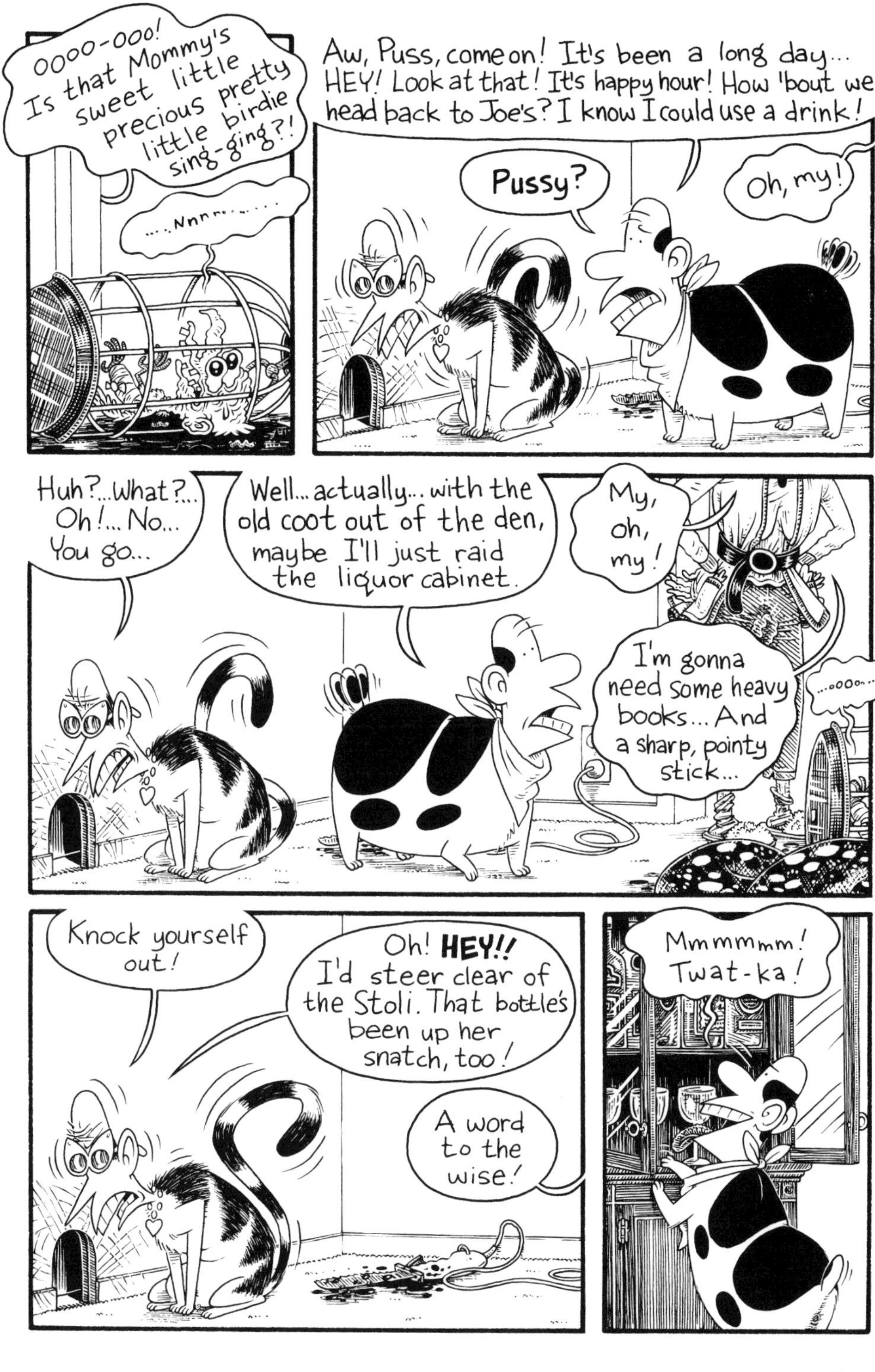
OOOO-OOO! Is that Mommy's sweet little precious pretty little birdie sing-ging?!
....Nnn.......
Aw, Puss, come on! It's been a long day... HEY! Look at that! It's happy hour! How 'bout we head back to Joe's? I know I could use a drink!
Pussy?
Oh, my!
Huh?...What?... Oh!... No... You go...
Well... actually... with the old coot out of the den, maybe I'll just raid the liquor cabinet.
My, oh, my!
I'm gonna need some heavy books... And a sharp, pointy stick...
...ooo...
Knock yourself out!
Oh! HEY!! I'd steer clear of the Stoli. That bottle's been up her snatch, too!
A word to the wise!
Mmmmmm! Twat-ka!

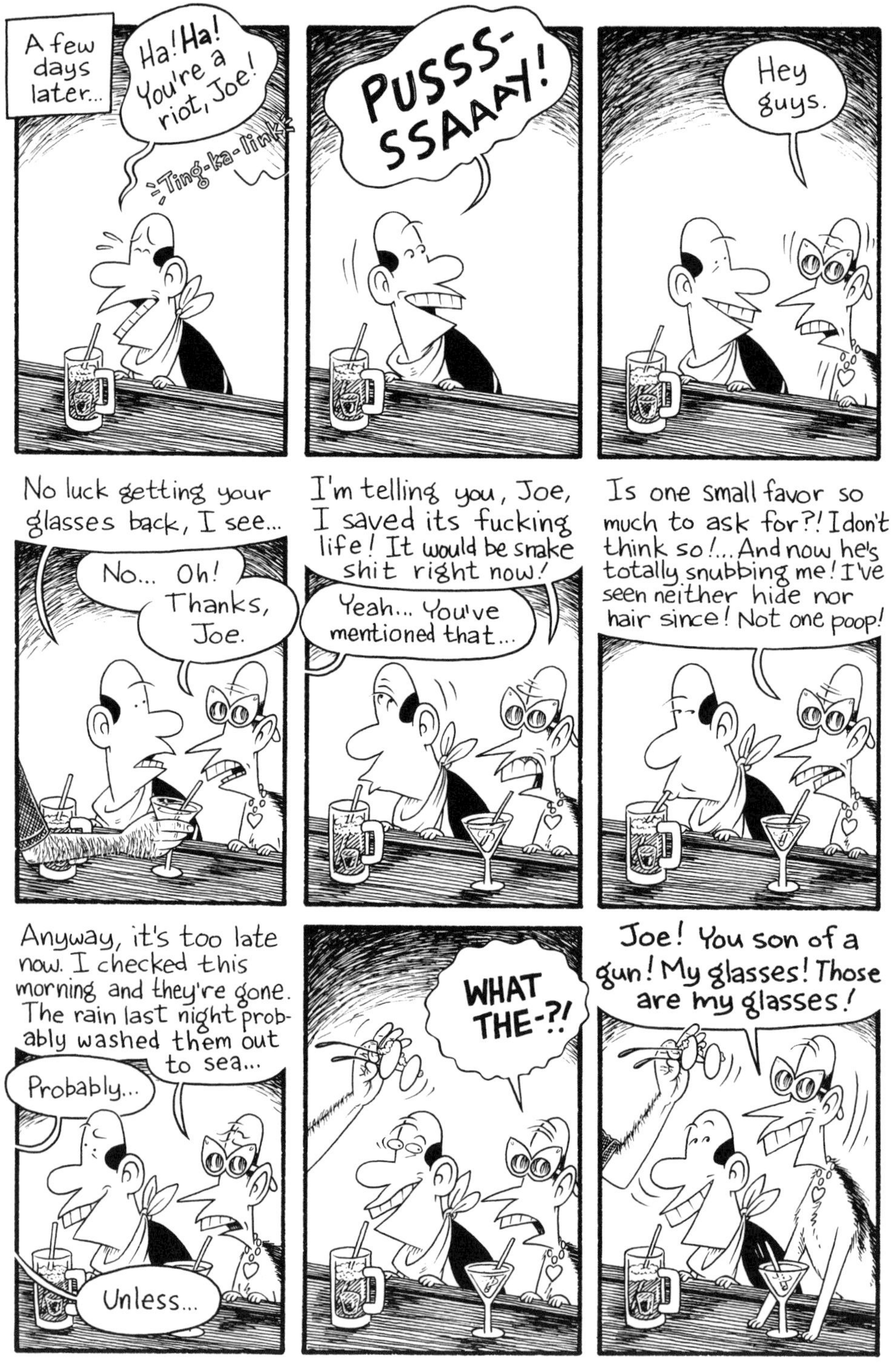

A few days later...
Ha! Ha! You're a riot, Joe!
Ting-ka-link
PUSSS-SSAAAY!
Hey guys.
No luck getting your glasses back, I see...
No... Oh! Thanks, Joe.
I'm telling you, Joe, I saved its fucking life! It would be snake shit right now!
Yeah... You've mentioned that...
Is one small favor so much to ask for?! I don't think so!... And now he's totally snubbing me! I've seen neither hide nor hair since! Not one poop!
Anyway, it's too late now. I checked this morning and they're gone. The rain last night probably washed them out to sea...
Probably...
Unless...
WHAT THE-?!
Joe! You son of a gun! My glasses! Those are my glasses!

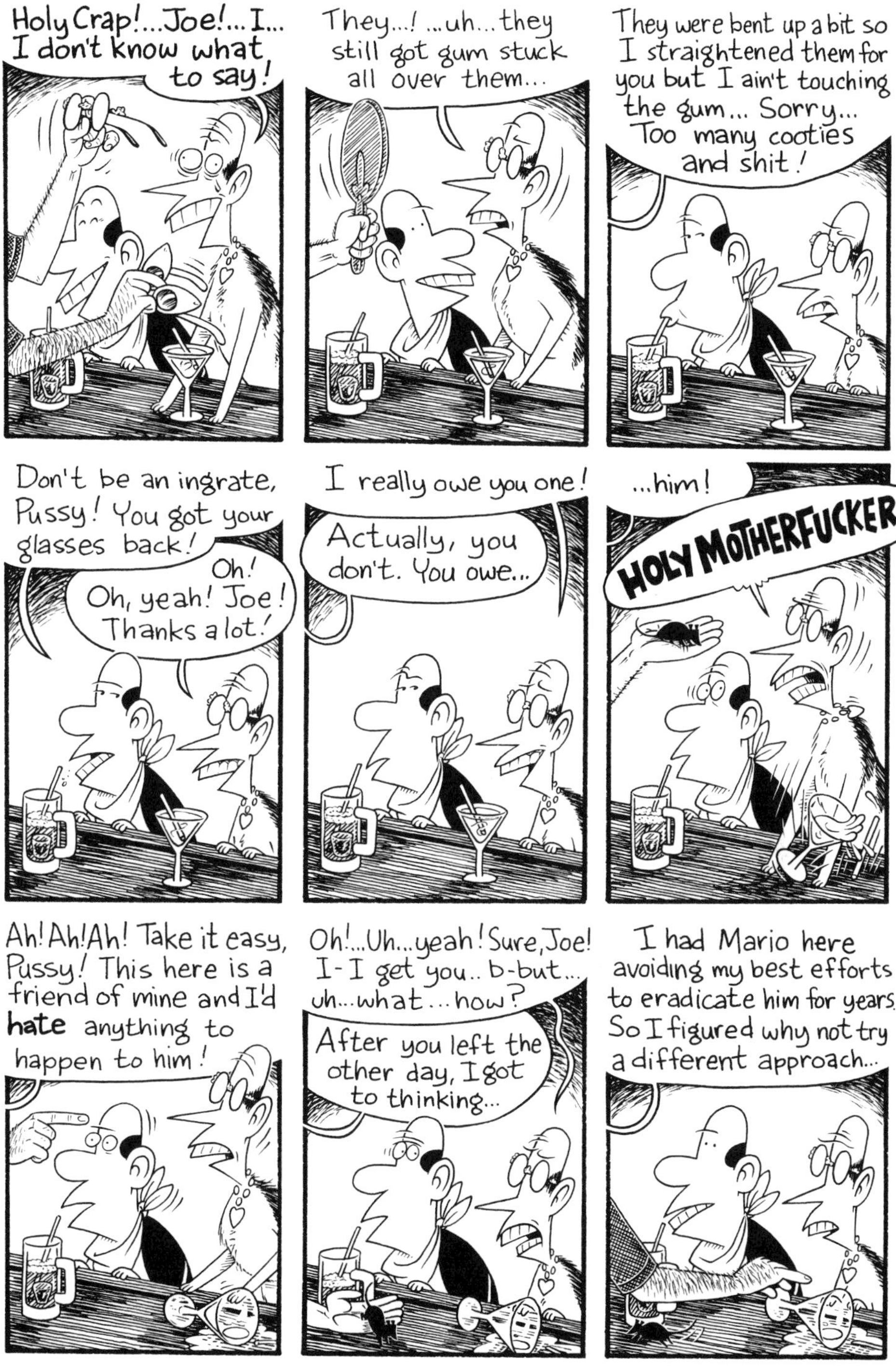
Holy Crap!...Joe!...I... I don't know what to say!
They...! ...uh... they still got gum stuck all over them...
They were bent up a bit so I straightened them for you but I ain't touching the gum... Sorry... Too many cooties and shit!
Don't be an ingrate, Pussy! You got your glasses back!
Oh! Oh, yeah! Joe! Thanks a lot!
I really owe you one!
Actually, you don't. You owe...
...him!
HOLY MOTHERFUCKER!
Ah! Ah! Ah! Take it easy, Pussy! This here is a friend of mine and I'd **hate** anything to happen to him!
Oh!...Uh...yeah! Sure, Joe! I-I get you.. b-but... uh...what...how?
After you left the other day, I got to thinking...
I had Mario here avoiding my best efforts to eradicate him for years. So I figured why not try a different approach...

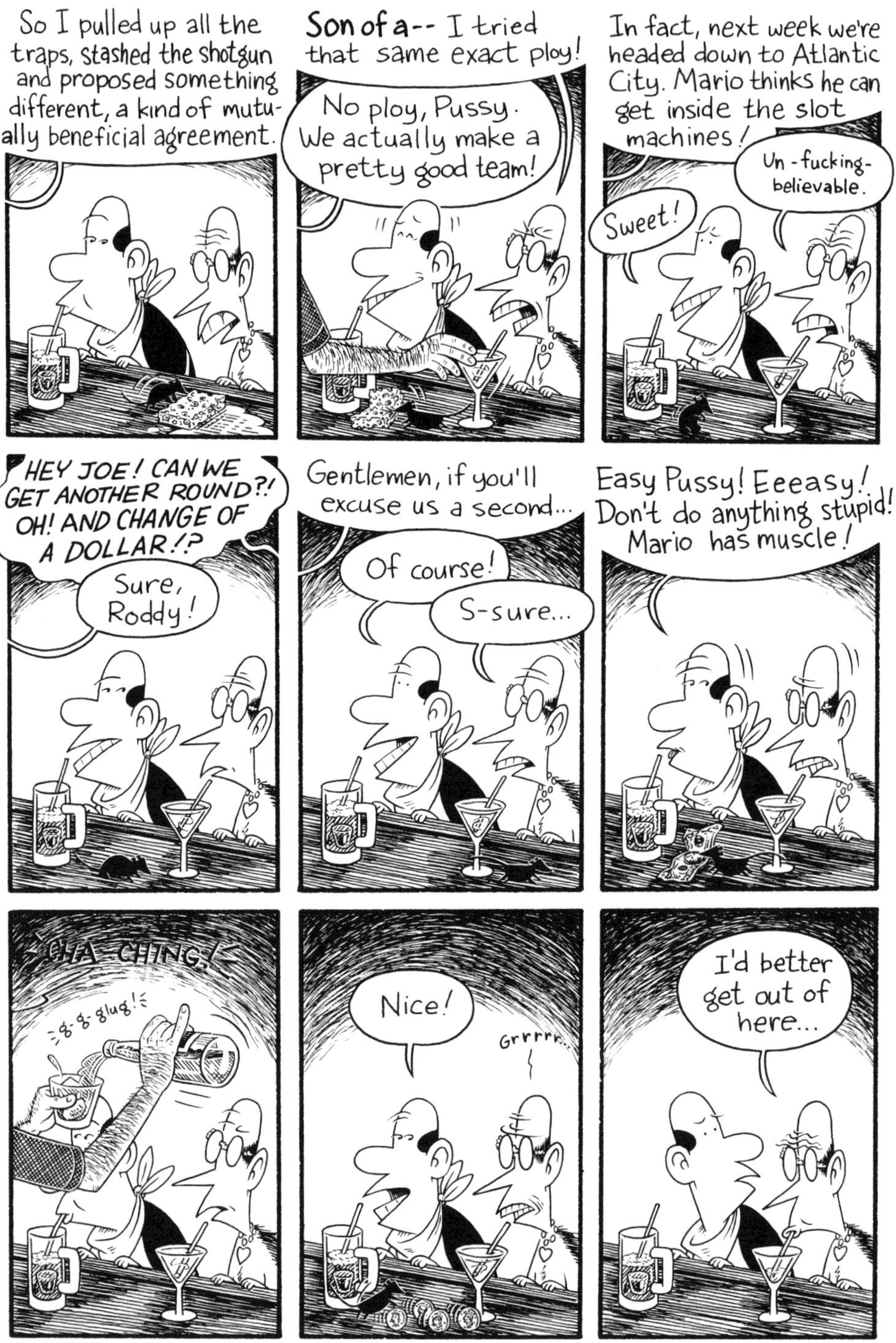

So I pulled up all the traps, stashed the shotgun and proposed something different, a kind of mutually beneficial agreement.
Son of a-- I tried that same exact ploy!
No ploy, Pussy. We actually make a pretty good team!
In fact, next week we're headed down to Atlantic City. Mario thinks he can get inside the slot machines!
Sweet!
Un-fucking-believable.
HEY JOE! CAN WE GET ANOTHER ROUND?! OH! AND CHANGE OF A DOLLAR!?
Sure, Roddy!
Gentlemen, if you'll excuse us a second...
Of course!
S-sure...
Easy Pussy! Eeeasy! Don't do anything stupid! Mario has muscle!
CHA CHING!
g-g-glug!
Nice!
Grrrrr...
I'd better get out of here...

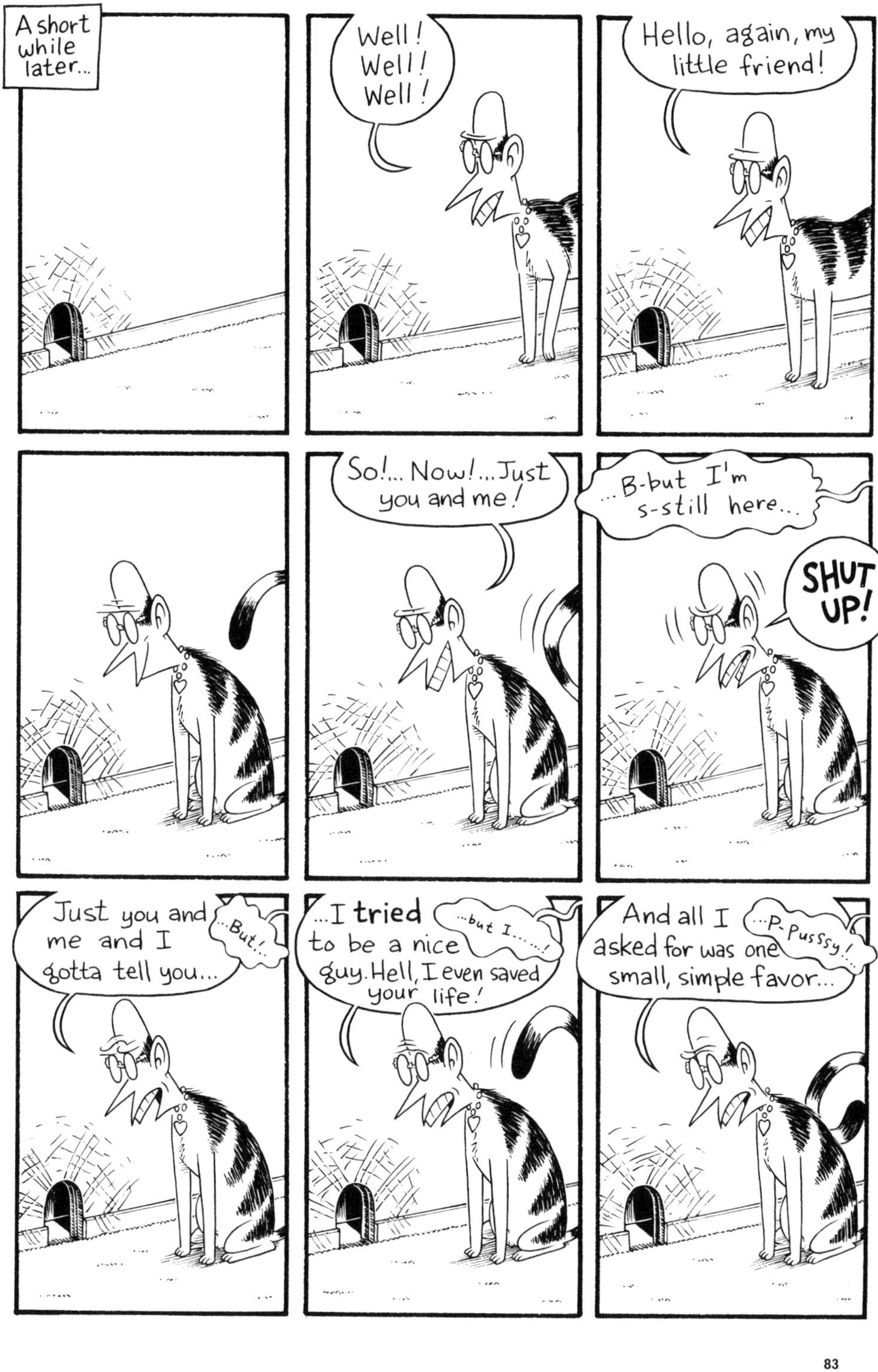
A short while later...
Well! Well! Well!
Hello, again, my little friend!
So!... Now!... Just you and me!
...B-but I'm s-still here...
SHUT UP!
Just you and me and I gotta tell you...
...But!...
...I **tried** to be a nice guy. Hell, I even saved your life!
...but I......!
And all I asked for was one small, simple favor...
...P-Pussssy!...

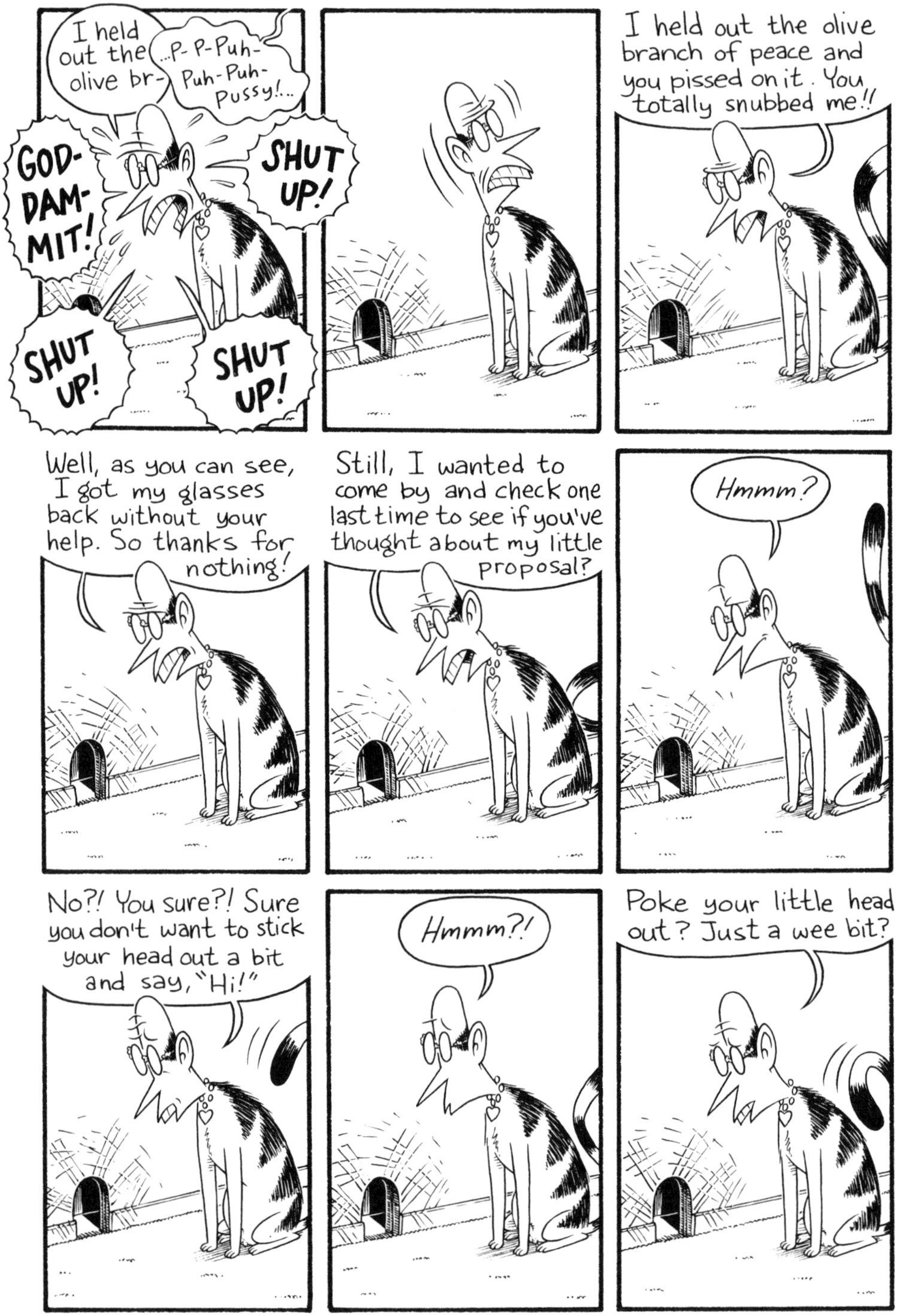

I held out the olive br-
...P-P-Puh-Puh-Puh-Pussy!...
GOD-DAM-MIT!
SHUT UP!
SHUT UP!
SHUT UP!
I held out the olive branch of peace and you pissed on it. You totally snubbed me!!
Well, as you can see, I got my glasses back without your help. So thanks for nothing!
Still, I wanted to come by and check one last time to see if you've thought about my little proposal?
Hmmm?
No?! You sure?! Sure you don't want to stick your head out a bit and say, "Hi!"
Hmmm?!
Poke your little head out? Just a wee bit?

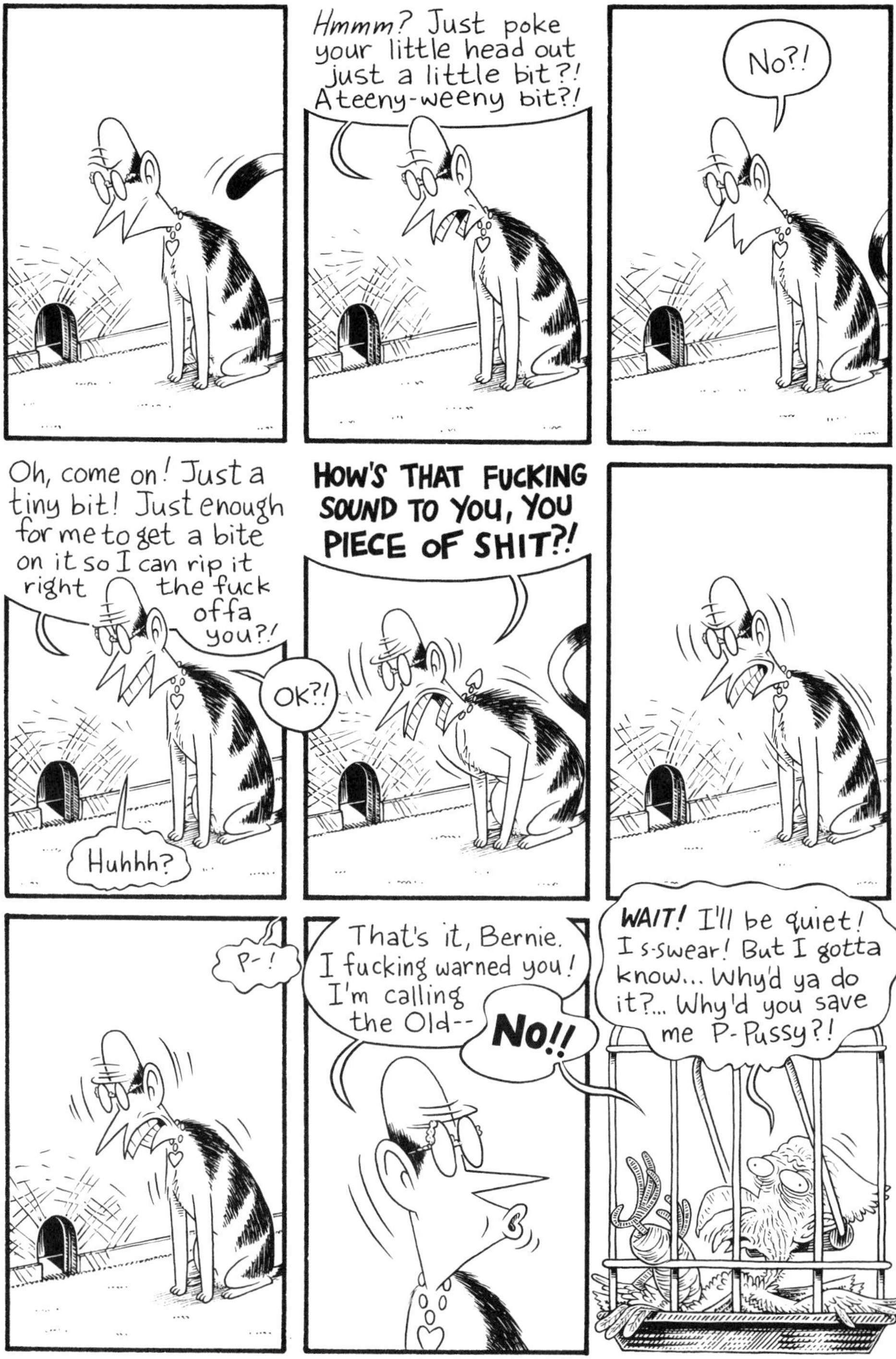

Hmmm? Just poke your little head out just a little bit?! A teeny-weeny bit?!
No?!
Oh, come on! Just a tiny bit! Just enough for me to get a bite on it so I can rip it right the fuck offa you?!
OK?!
Huhhh?
HOW'S THAT FUCKING SOUND TO YOU, YOU PIECE OF SHIT?!
P-!
That's it, Bernie. I fucking warned you! I'm calling the Old--
NO!!
WAIT! I'll be quiet! I s-swear! But I gotta know... Why'd ya do it?... Why'd you save me P-Pussy?!

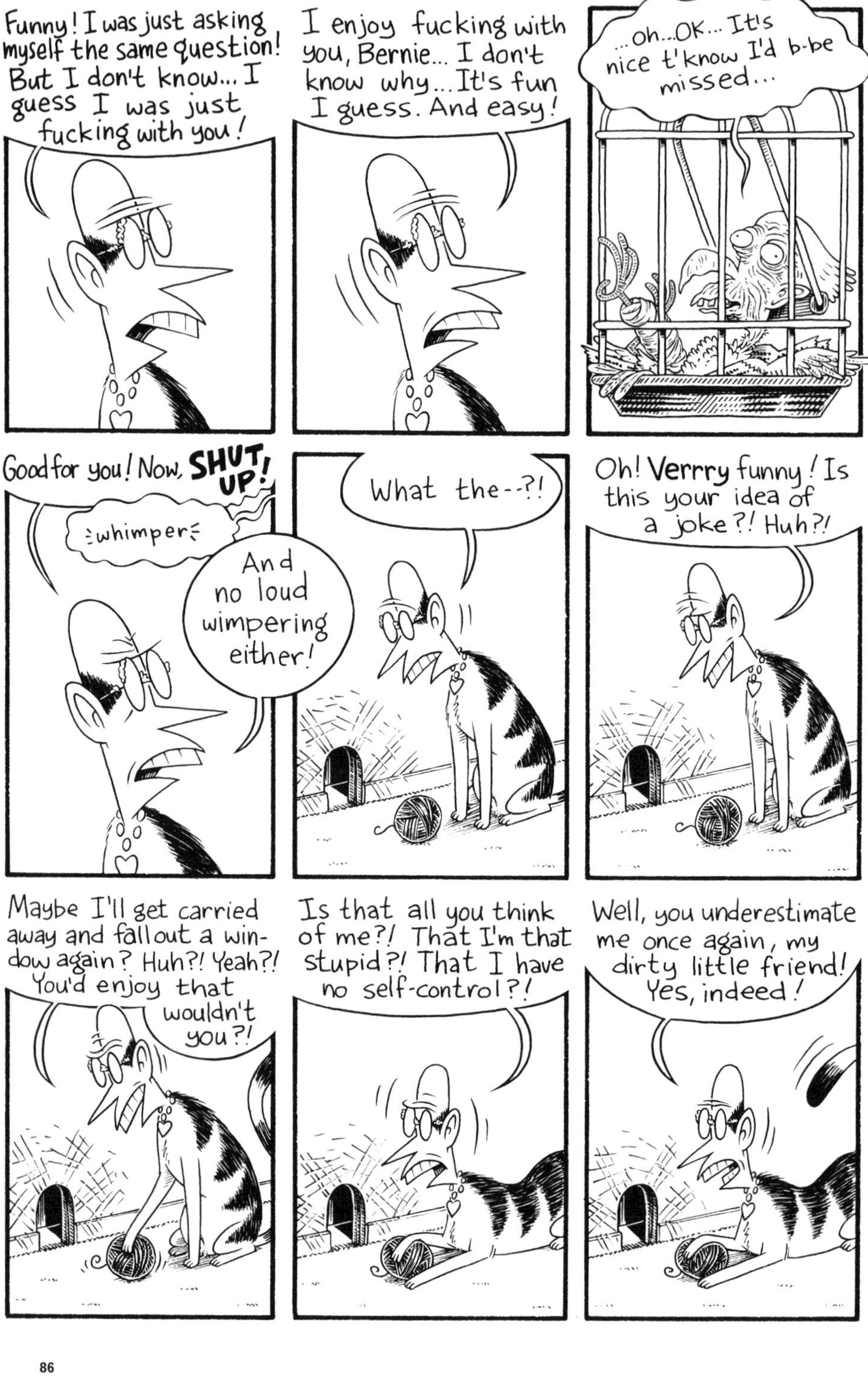
Funny! I was just asking myself the same question! But I don't know... I guess I was just fucking with you!
I enjoy fucking with you, Bernie... I don't know why... It's fun I guess. And easy!
...oh...OK... It's nice t'know I'd b-be missed...
Good for you! Now, SHUT UP!
whimper
And no loud wimpering either!
What the--?!
Oh! Verrry funny! Is this your idea of a joke?! Huh?!
Maybe I'll get carried away and fall out a window again? Huh?! Yeah?! You'd enjoy that wouldn't you?!
Is that all you think of me?! That I'm that stupid?! That I have no self-control?!
Well, you underestimate me once again, my dirty little friend! Yes, indeed!

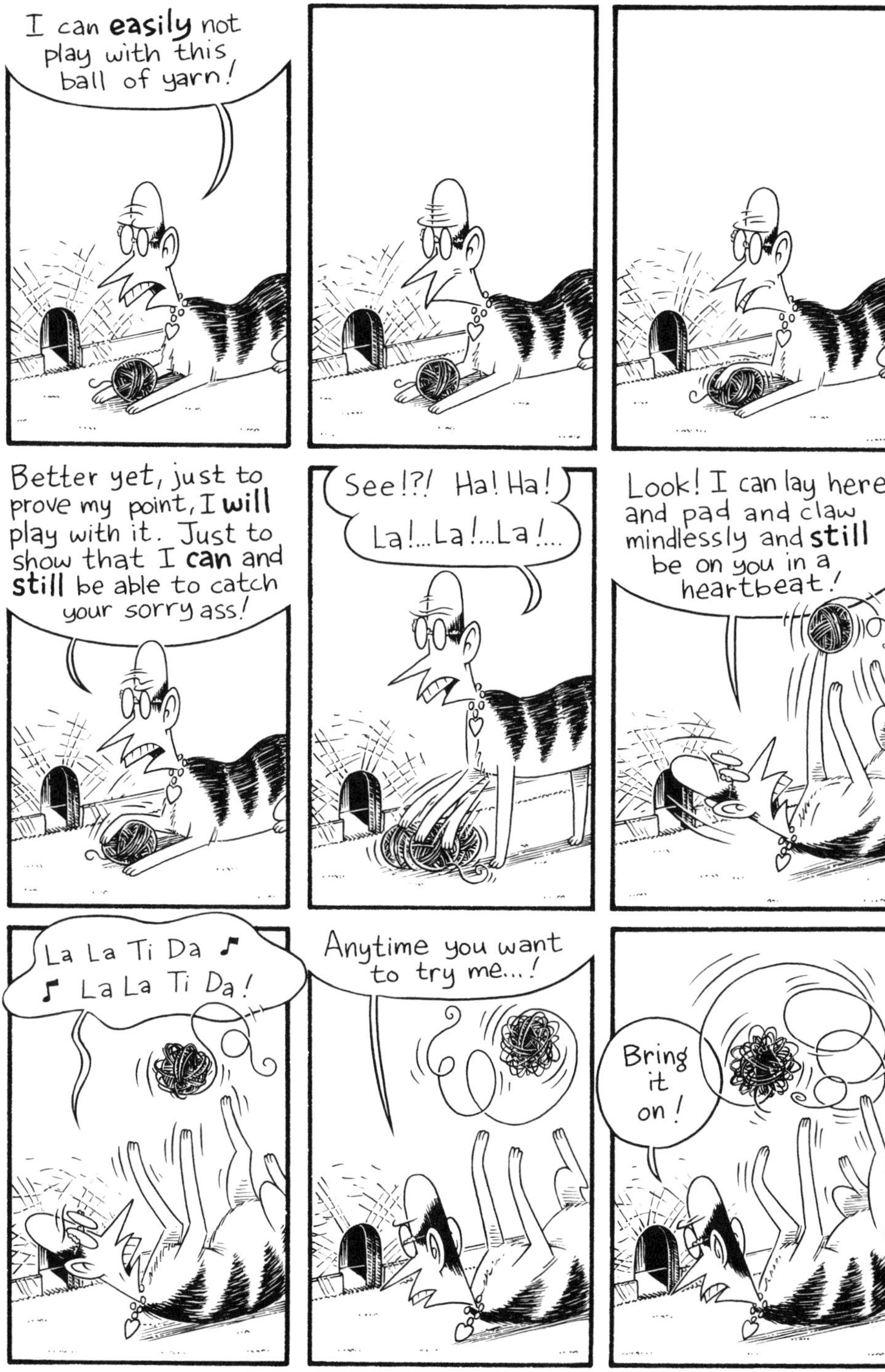
I can **easily** not play with this ball of yarn!
Better yet, just to prove my point, I **will** play with it. Just to show that I **can** and **still** be able to catch your sorry ass!
See!?! Ha! Ha!
La!...La!...La!...
Look! I can lay here and pad and claw mindlessly and **still** be on you in a heartbeat!
La La Ti Da ♪ ♪ La La Ti Da!
Anytime you want to try me...!
Bring it on!

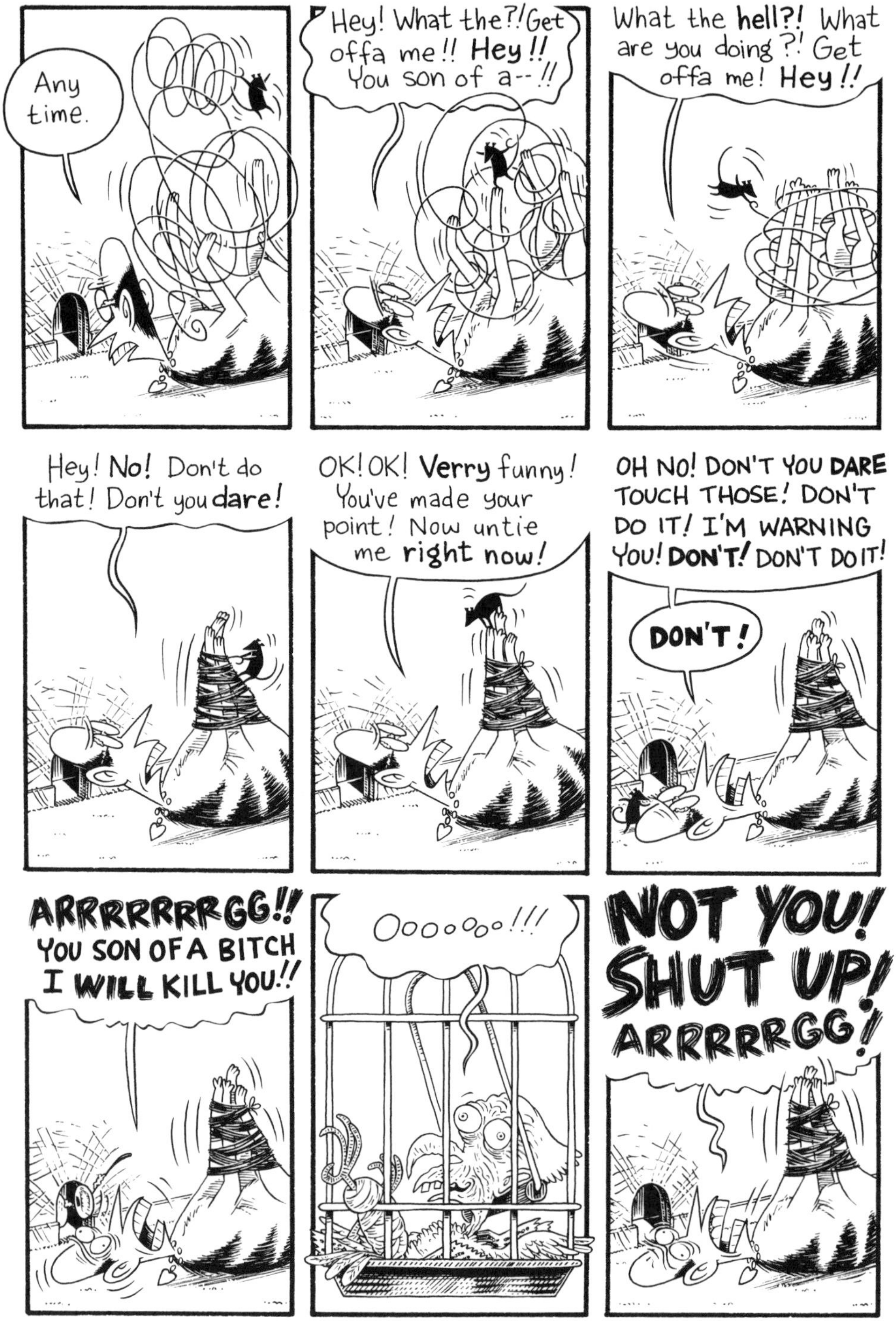
Any time.
Hey! What the?! Get offa me!! Hey!! You son of a--!!
What the hell?! What are you doing?! Get offa me! Hey!!
Hey! No! Don't do that! Don't you dare!
OK! OK! Verry funny! You've made your point! Now untie me right now!
OH NO! DON'T YOU DARE TOUCH THOSE! DON'T DO IT! I'M WARNING YOU! DON'T! DON'T DO IT!
DON'T!
ARRRRRRRGG!! YOU SON OF A BITCH I WILL KILL YOU!!
Oooooo!!!
NOT YOU! SHUT UP! ARRRRRGG!

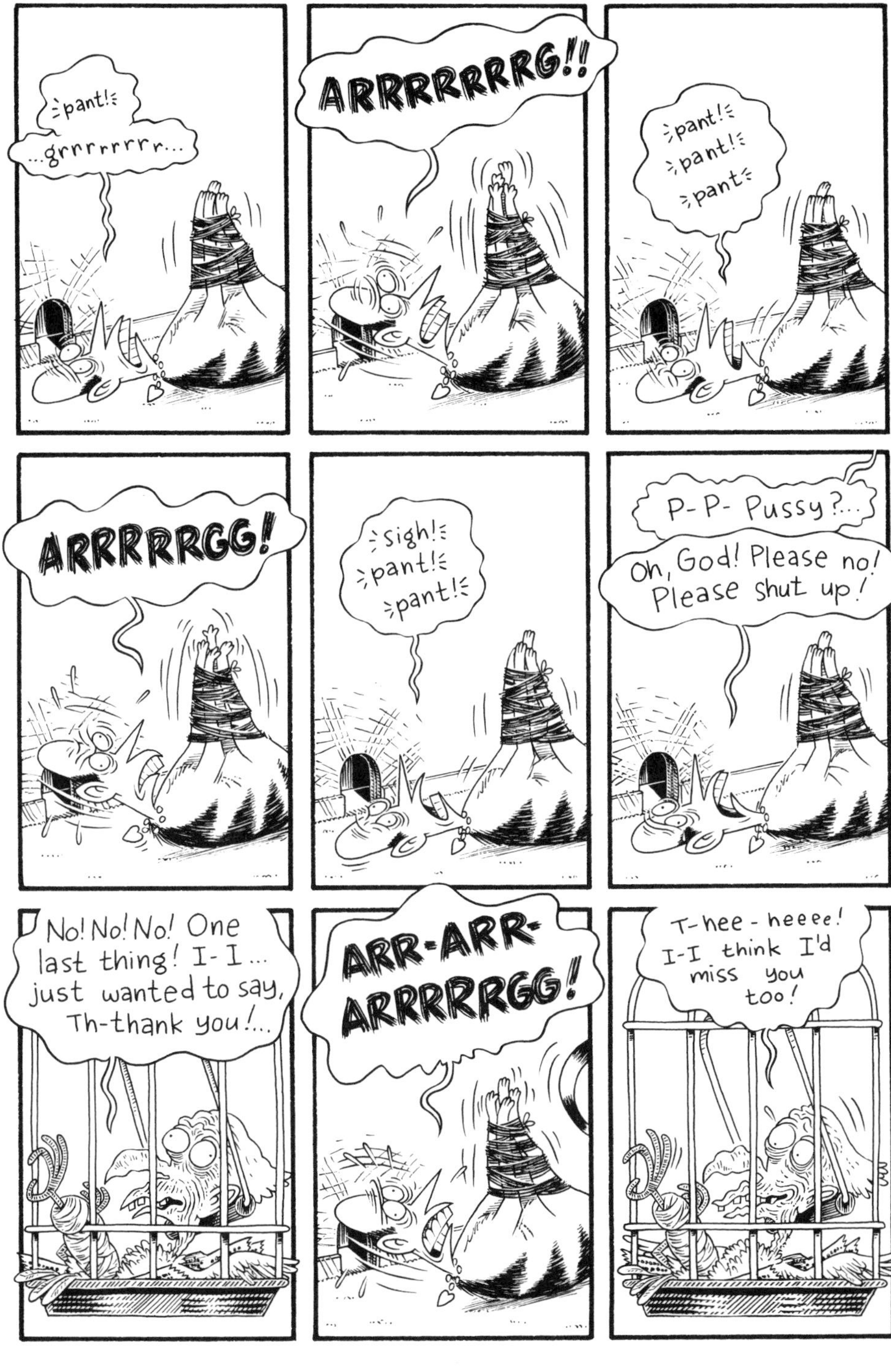
pant!
...grrrrrrr...
ARRRRRRRG!!
pant!
pant!
pant
ARRRRRGG!
sigh!
pant!
pant!
P-P- Pussy?...
Oh, God! Please no! Please shut up!
No! No! No! One last thing! I-I... just wanted to say, Th-thank you!...
ARR-ARR-ARRRRRGG!
T-hee-heeeee! I-I think I'd miss you too!

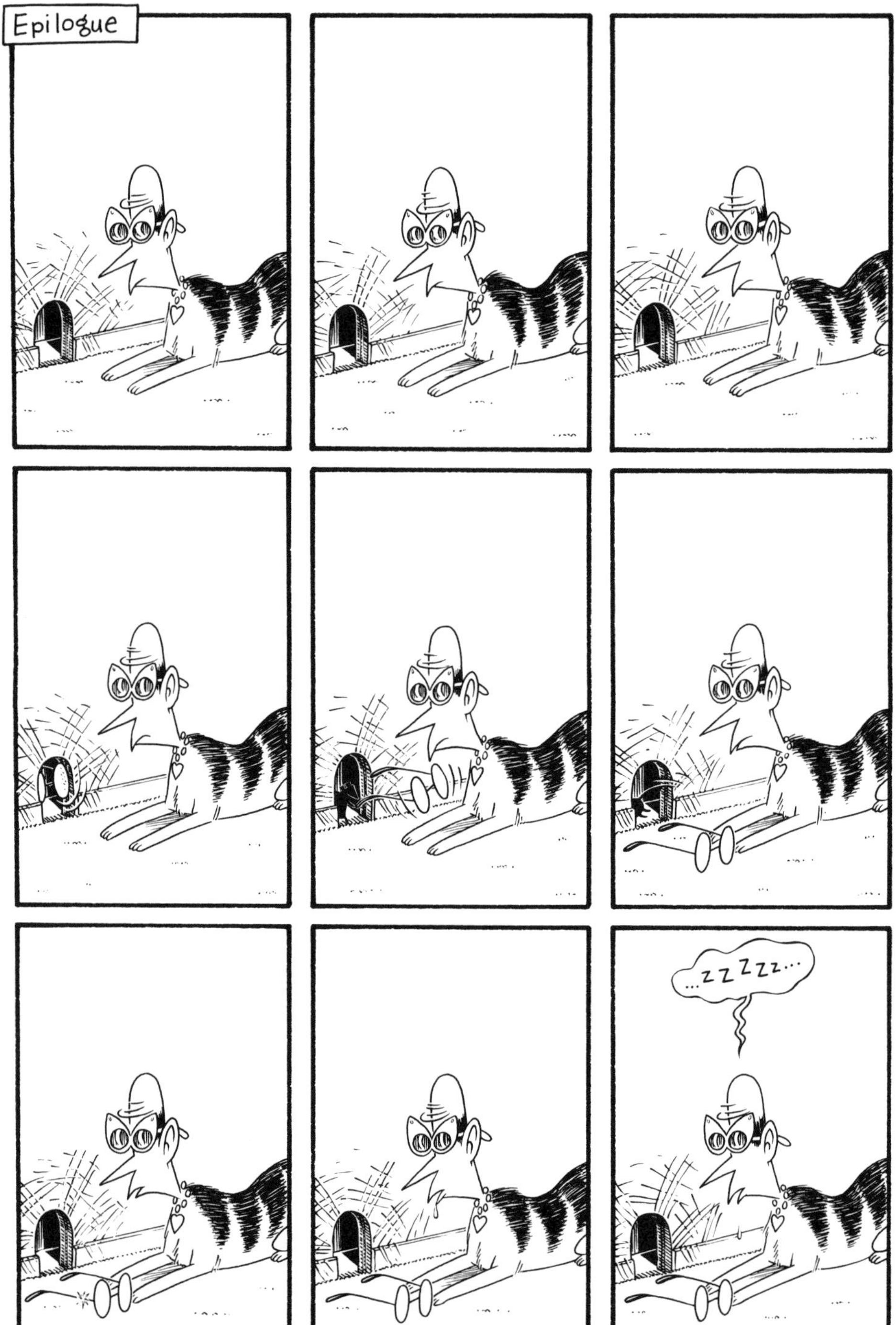
Epilogue
...z z Z z z...
J.K.

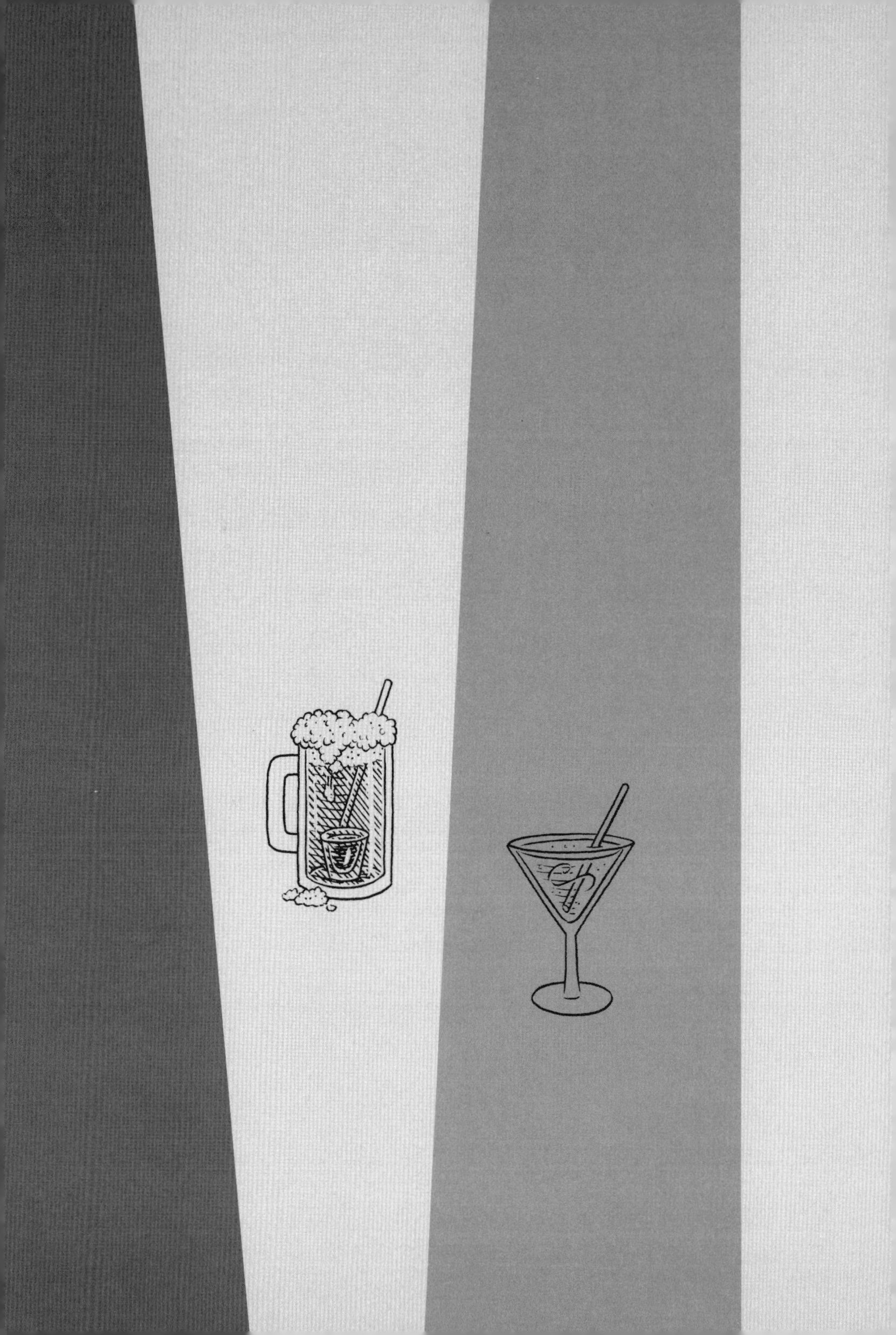

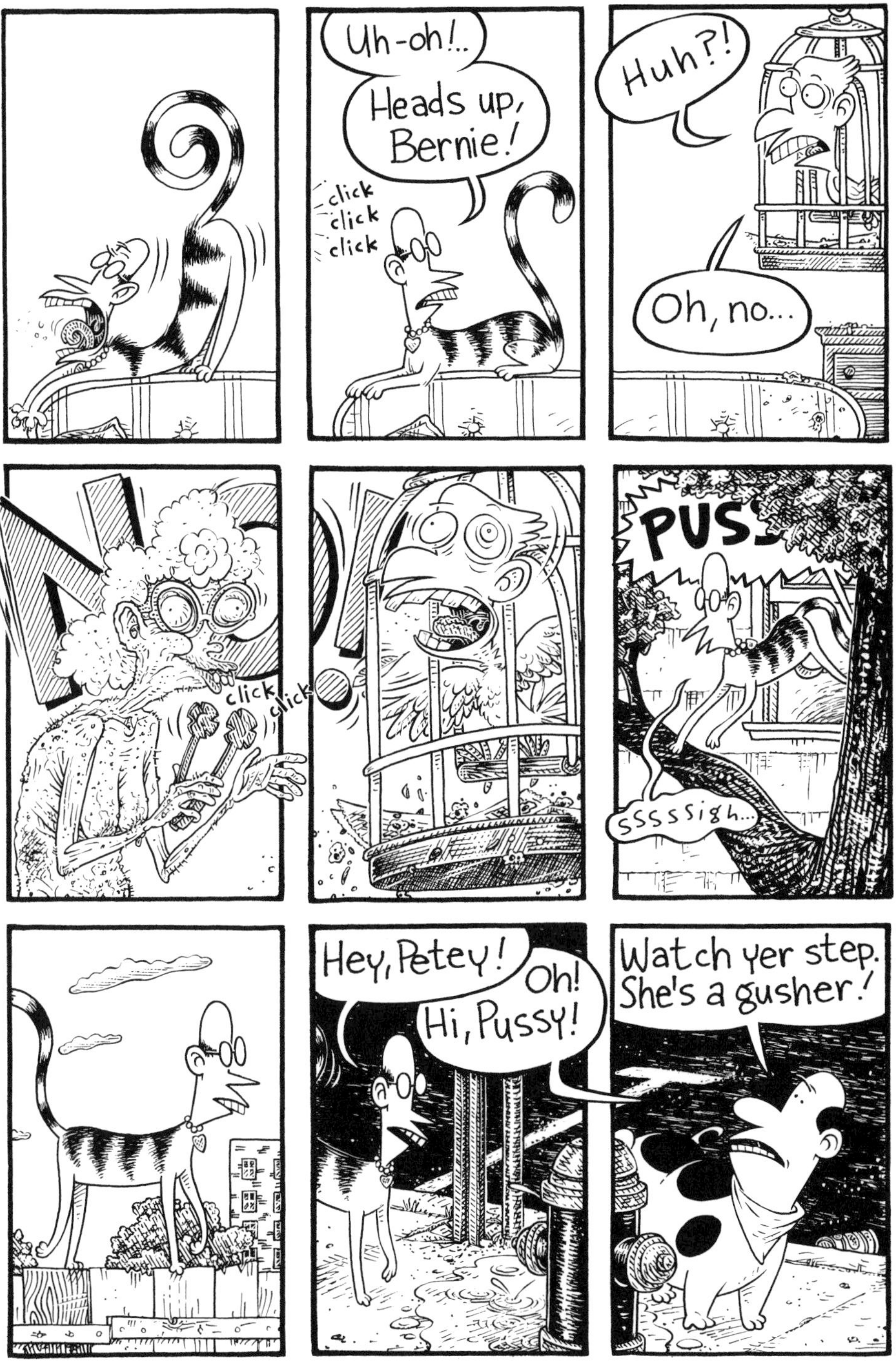
Uh-oh!..
Heads up, Bernie!
click click click
Huh?!
Oh, no...
click click
PUSS
sssssigh...
Hey, Petey!
Oh! Hi, Pussy!
Watch yer step. She's a gusher!

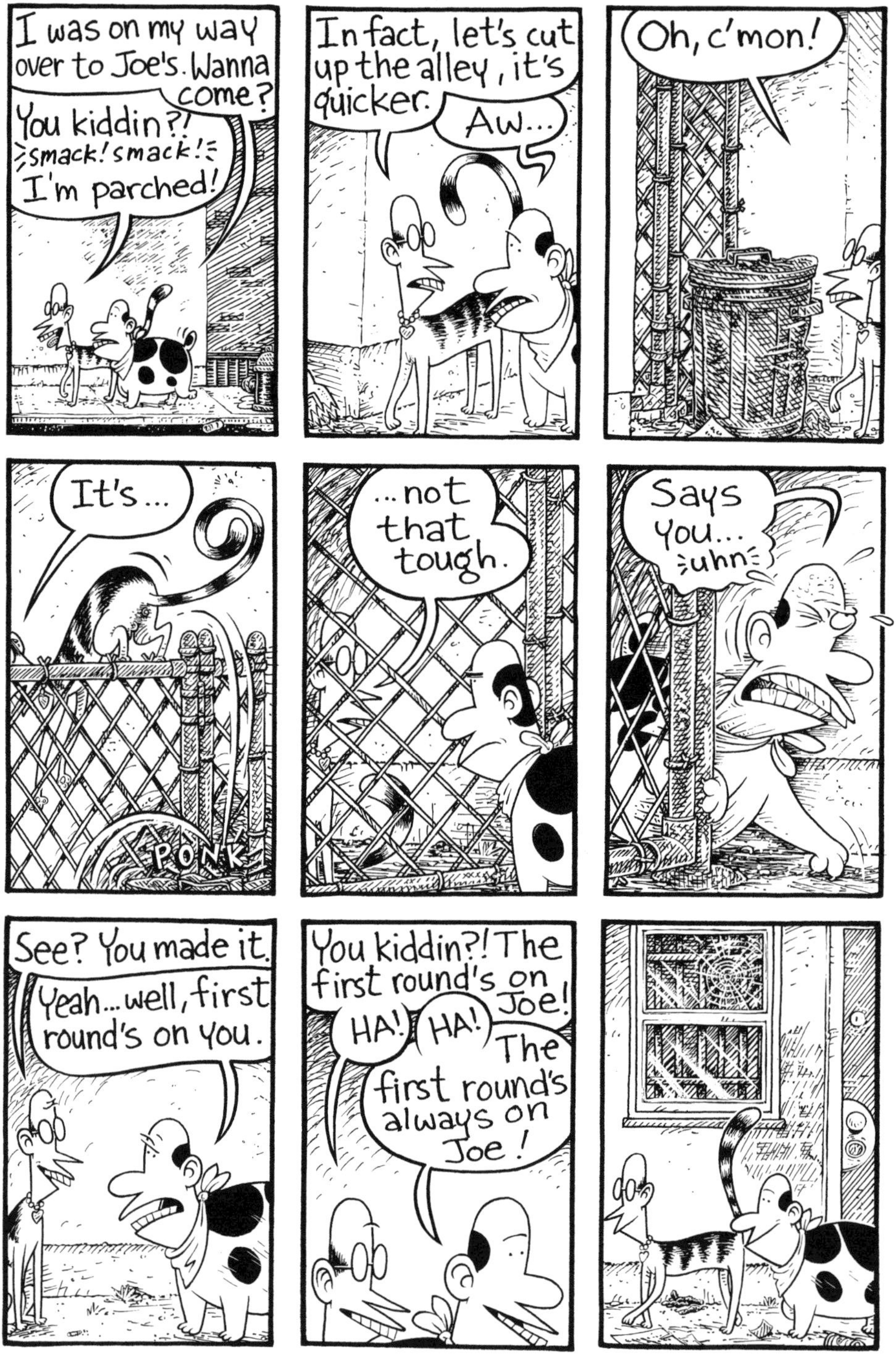
I was on my way over to Joe's. Wanna come?
You kiddin?! smack! smack! I'm parched!
In fact, let's cut up the alley, it's quicker.
Aw...
Oh, c'mon!
It's...
PONK
...not that tough.
Says you... uhn
See? You made it.
Yeah... well, first round's on you.
You kiddin?! The first round's on Joe!
HA!
HA!
The first round's always on Joe!

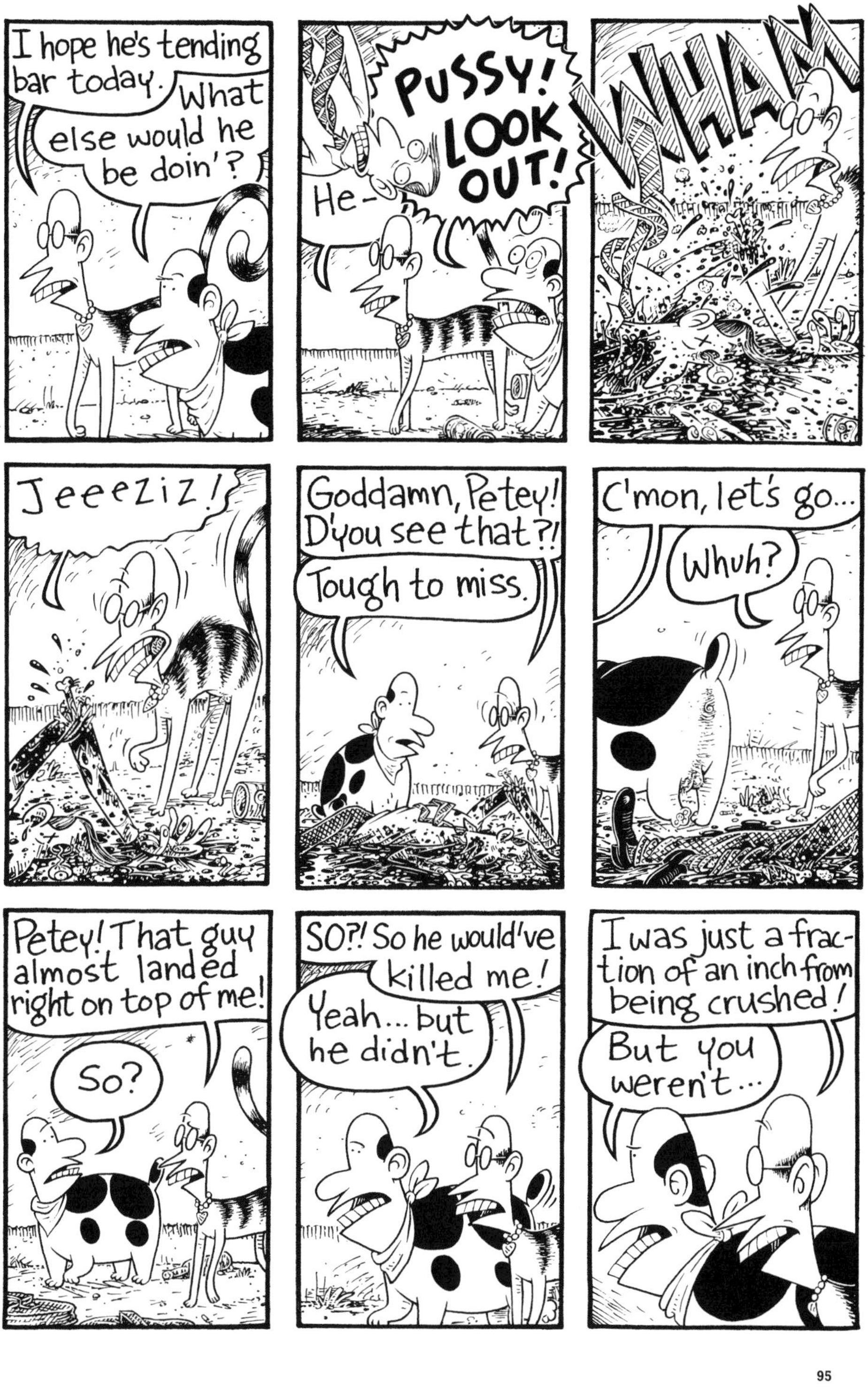
I hope he's tending bar today.
What else would he be doin'?
He-
PUSSY! LOOK OUT!
WHAM
Jeeeziz!
Goddamn, Petey! D'you see that?!
Tough to miss.
C'mon, let's go...
Whuh?
Petey! That guy almost landed right on top of me!
So?
SO?! So he would've killed me!
Yeah... but he didn't.
I was just a fraction of an inch from being crushed!
But you weren't...

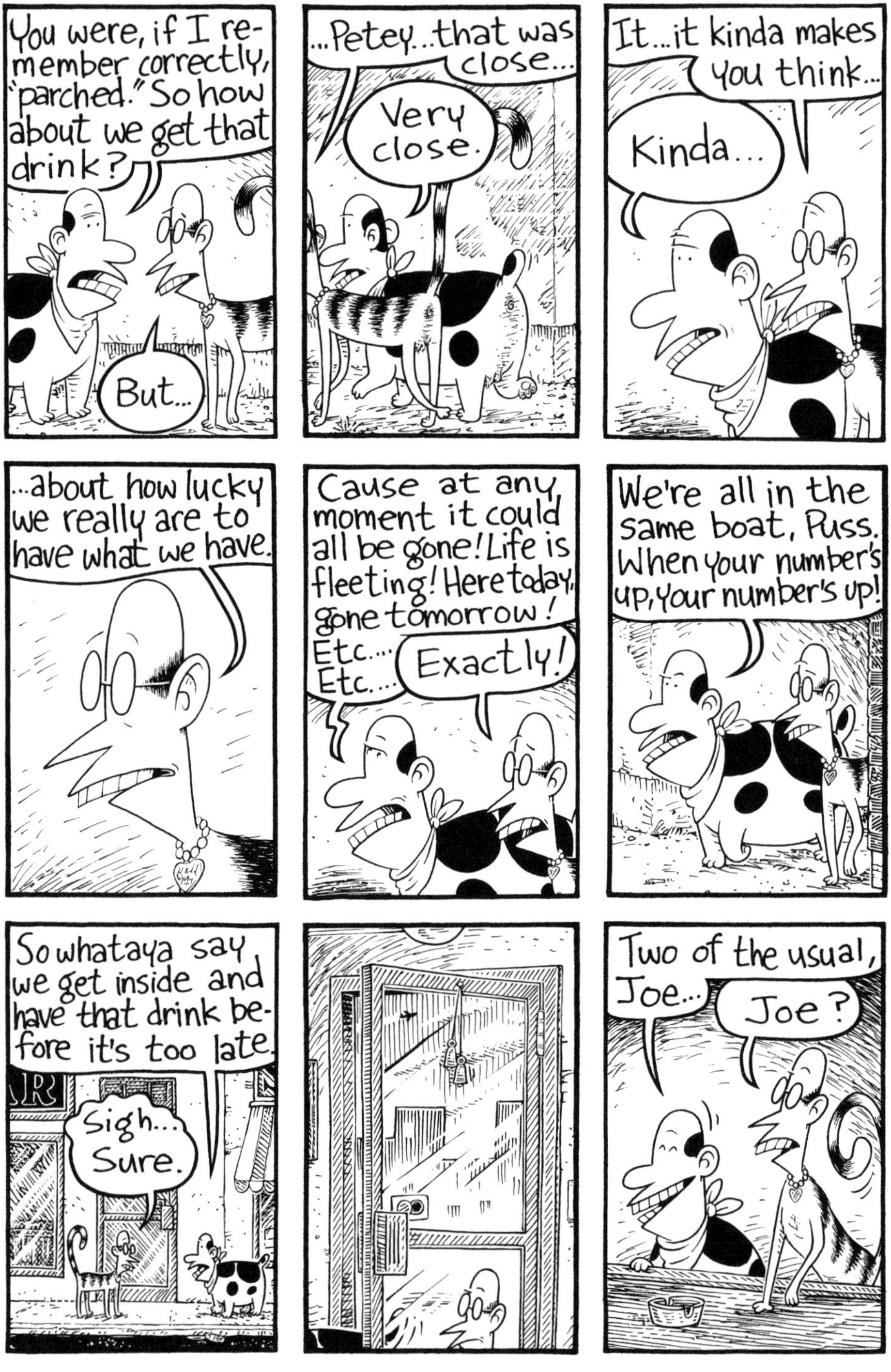

You were, if I remember correctly, "parched." So how about we get that drink?
But...
...Petey...that was close...
Very close.
It...it kinda makes you think...
Kinda...
...about how lucky we really are to have what we have.
Cause at any moment it could all be gone! Life is fleeting! Here today, gone tomorrow! Etc.... Etc....
Exactly!
We're all in the same boat, Puss. When your number's up, your number's up!
So whataya say we get inside and have that drink before it's too late.
Sigh... Sure.
Two of the usual, Joe...
Joe?

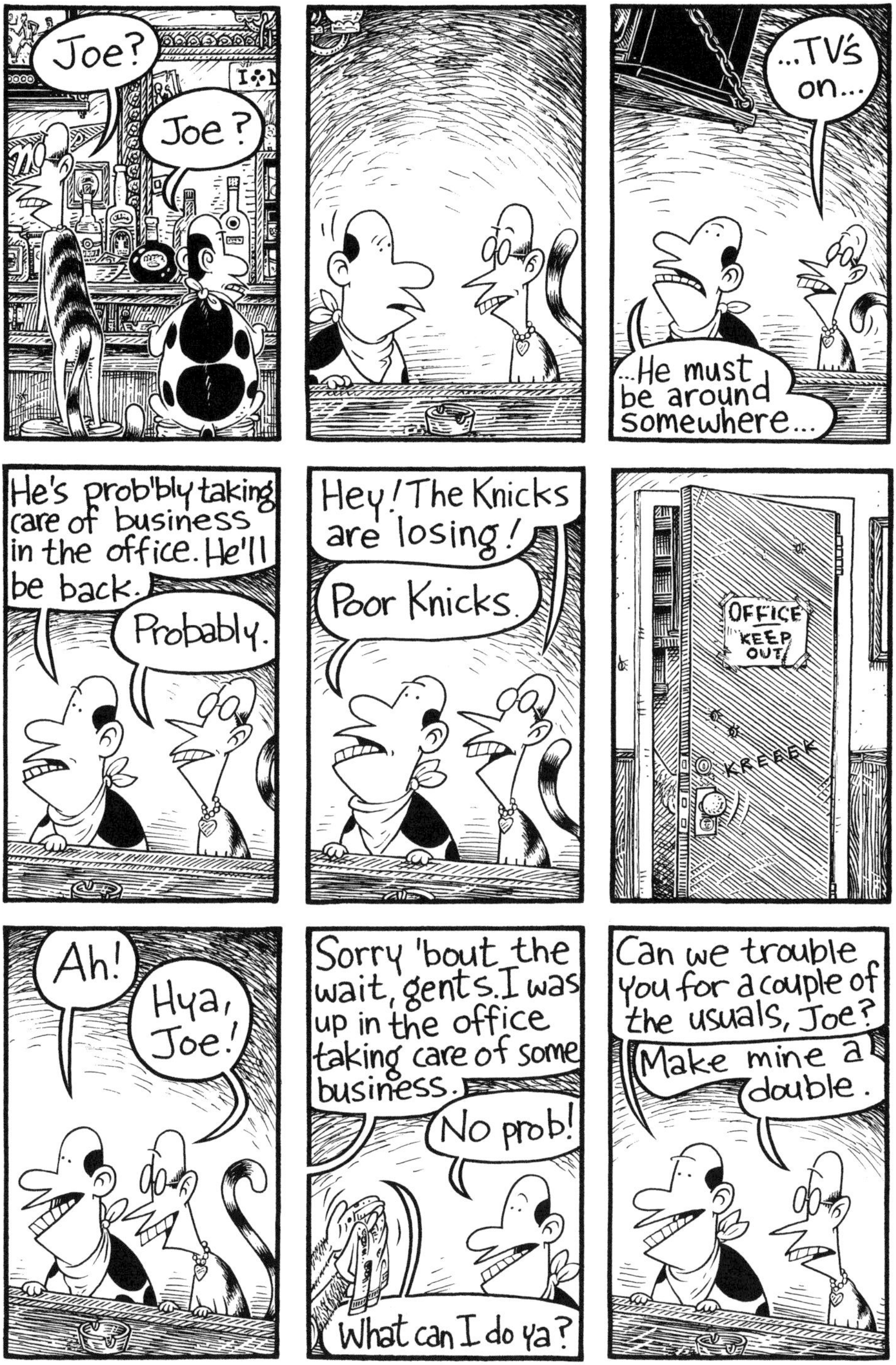
Joe?
Joe?
...TV's on...
...He must be around somewhere...
He's prob'bly taking care of business in the office. He'll be back.
Probably.
Hey! The Knicks are losing!
Poor Knicks.
OFFICE KEEP OUT
KREEEK
Ah!
Hya, Joe!
Sorry 'bout the wait, gents. I was up in the office taking care of some business.
No prob!
What can I do ya?
Can we trouble you for a couple of the usuals, Joe?
Make mine a double.

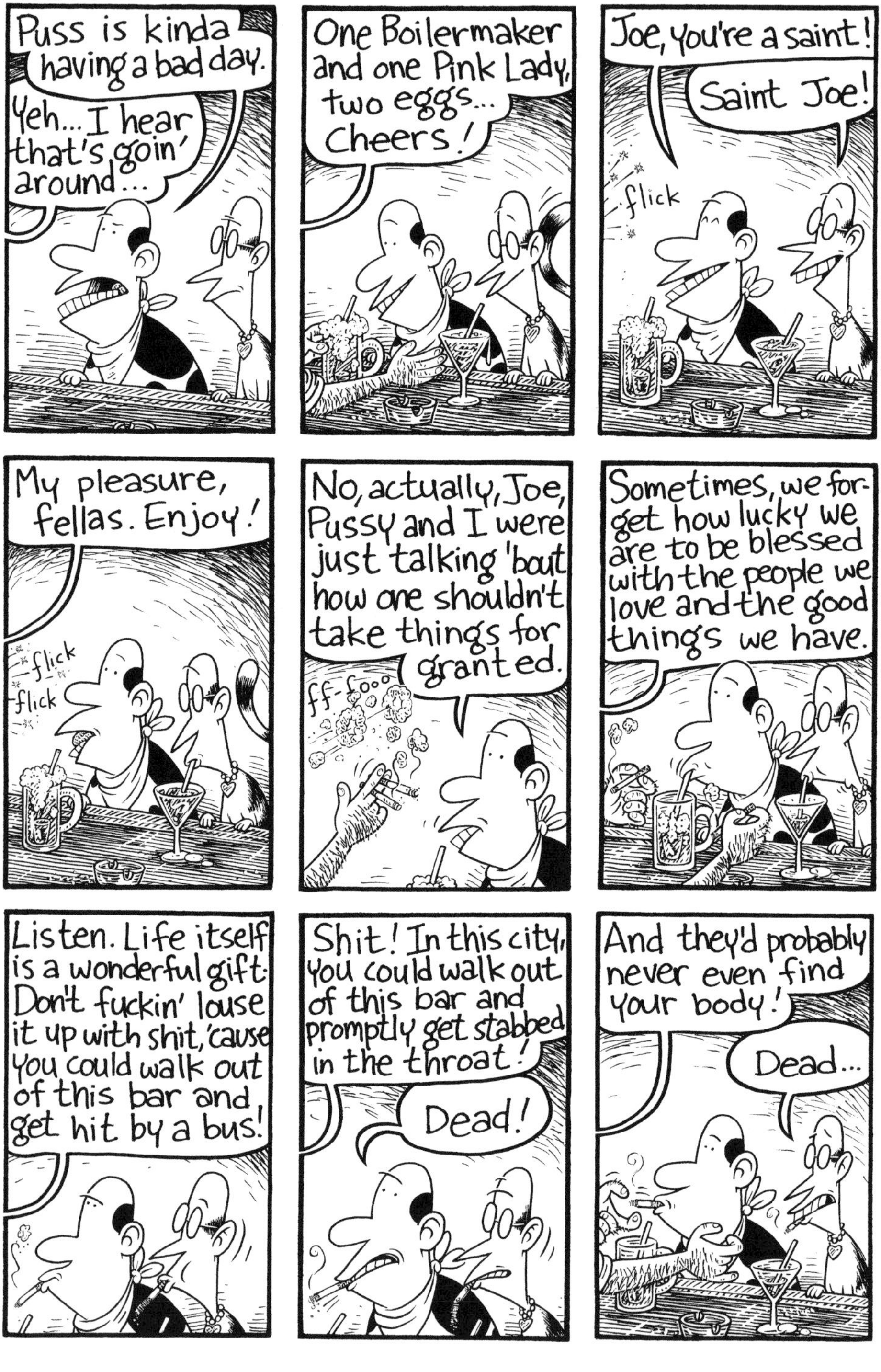
Puss is kinda having a bad day.
Yeh... I hear that's goin' around...
One Boilermaker and one Pink Lady, two eggs... Cheers!
Joe, you're a saint!
Saint Joe!
flick
My pleasure, fellas. Enjoy!
flick
flick
No, actually, Joe, Pussy and I were just talking 'bout how one shouldn't take things for granted.
ff-fooo
Sometimes, we forget how lucky we are to be blessed with the people we love and the good things we have.
Listen. Life itself is a wonderful gift. Don't fuckin' louse it up with shit, 'cause you could walk out of this bar and get hit by a bus!
Shit! In this city, you could walk out of this bar and promptly get stabbed in the throat!
Dead!
And they'd probably never even find your body!
Dead...

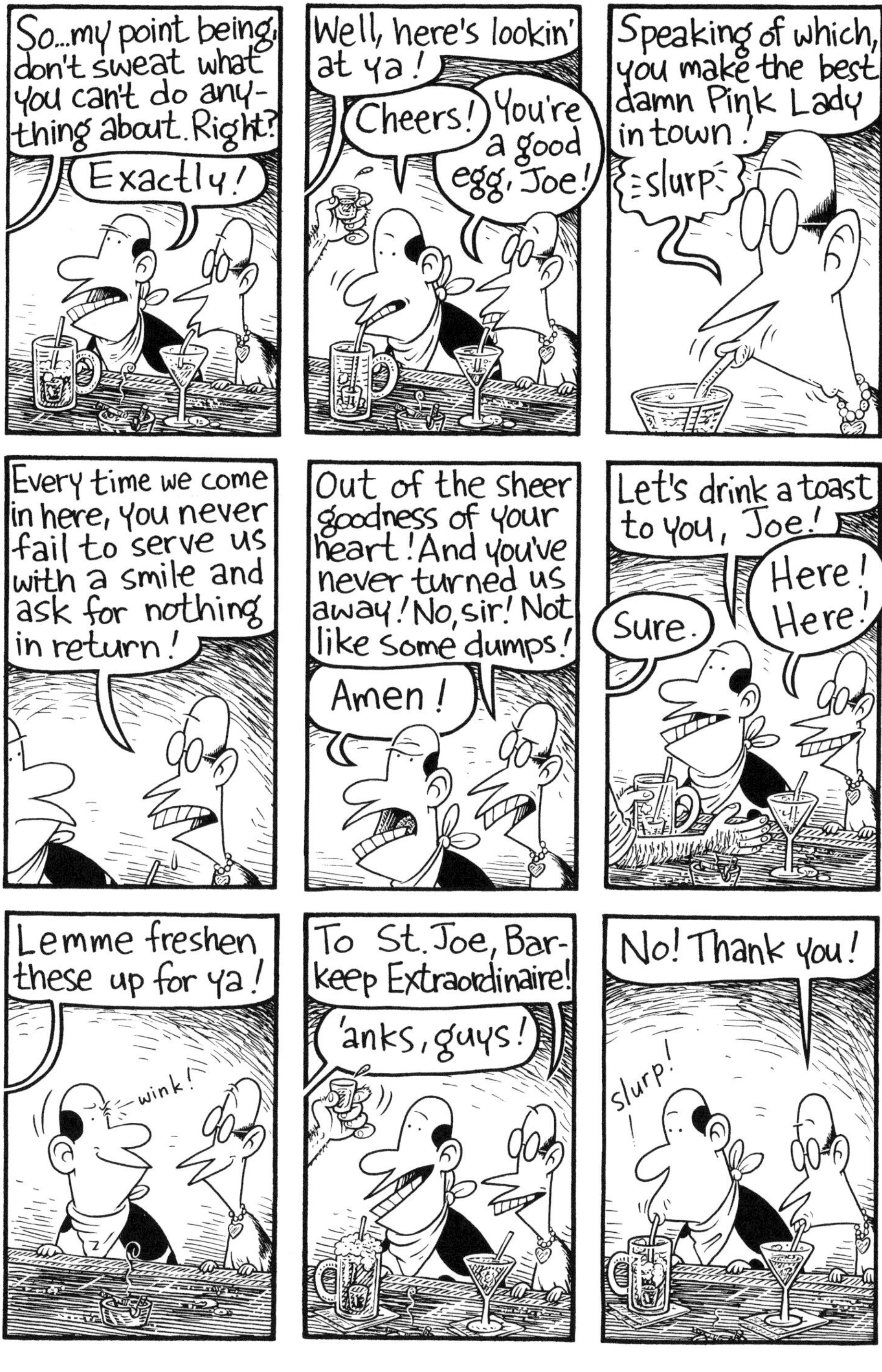
So...my point being, don't sweat what you can't do anything about. Right?
Exactly!
Well, here's lookin' at ya!
Cheers!
You're a good egg, Joe!
Speaking of which, you make the best damn Pink Lady in town!
slurp
Every time we come in here, you never fail to serve us with a smile and ask for nothing in return!
Out of the sheer goodness of your heart! And you've never turned us away! No, sir! Not like some dumps!
Amen!
Let's drink a toast to you, Joe!
Sure.
Here! Here!
Lemme freshen these up for ya!
wink!
To St. Joe, Barkeep Extraordinaire!
'anks, guys!
No! Thank you!
slurp!

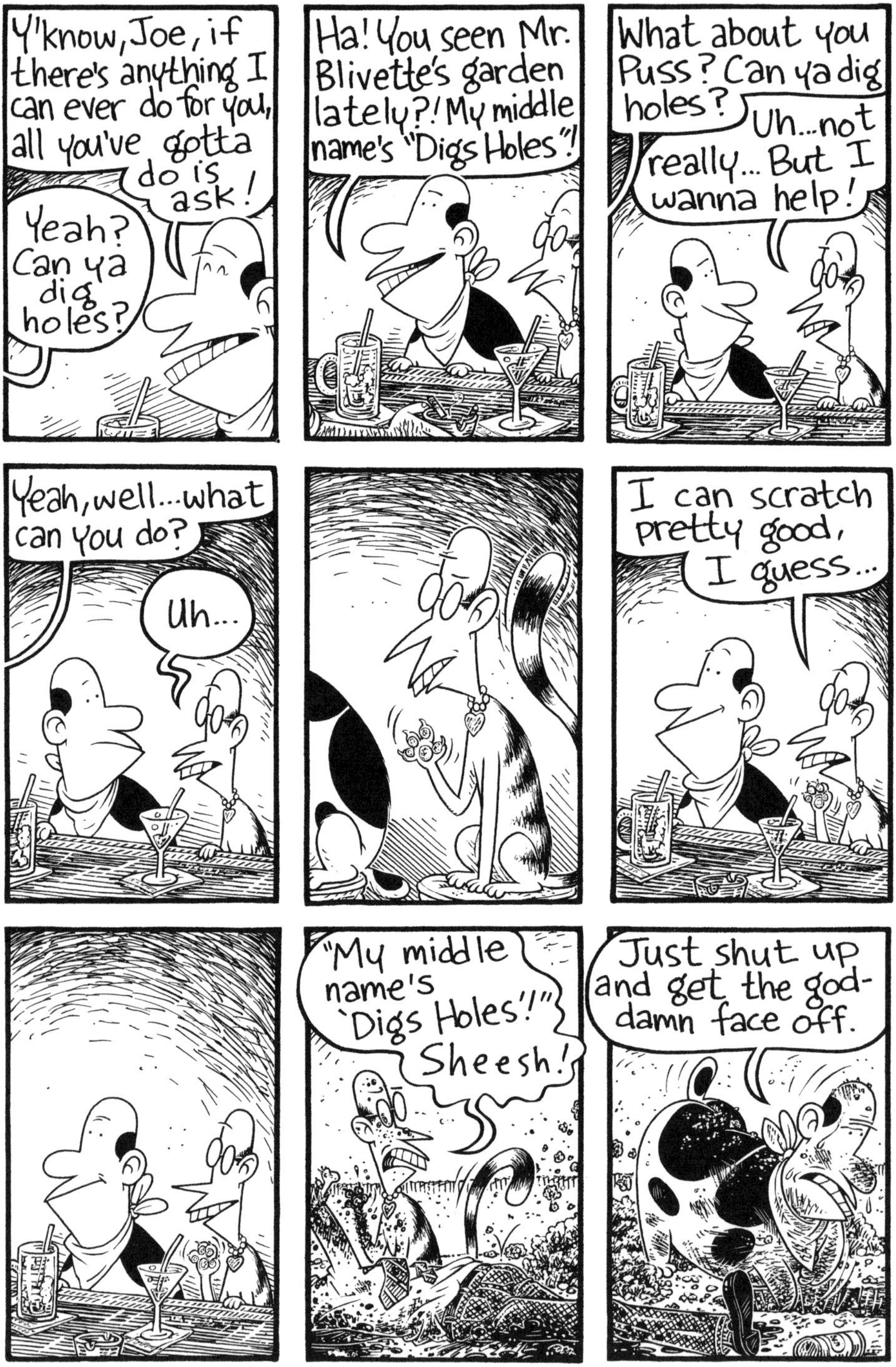
Y'know, Joe, if there's anything I can ever do for you, all you've gotta do is ask!
Yeah? Can ya dig holes?
Ha! You seen Mr. Blivette's garden lately?! My middle name's "Digs Holes"!
What about you Puss? Can ya dig holes?
Uh...not really... But I wanna help!
Yeah, well...what can you do?
Uh...
I can scratch pretty good, I guess...
"My middle name's 'Digs Holes'!" Sheesh!
Just shut up and get the god-damn face off.

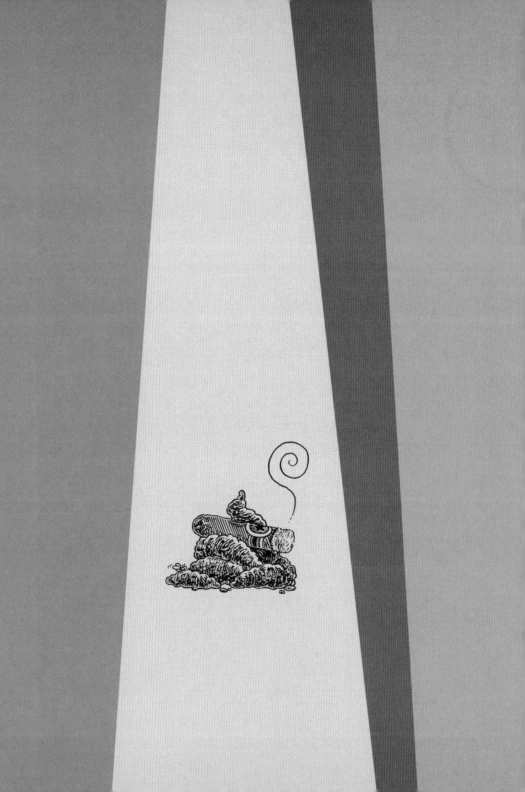

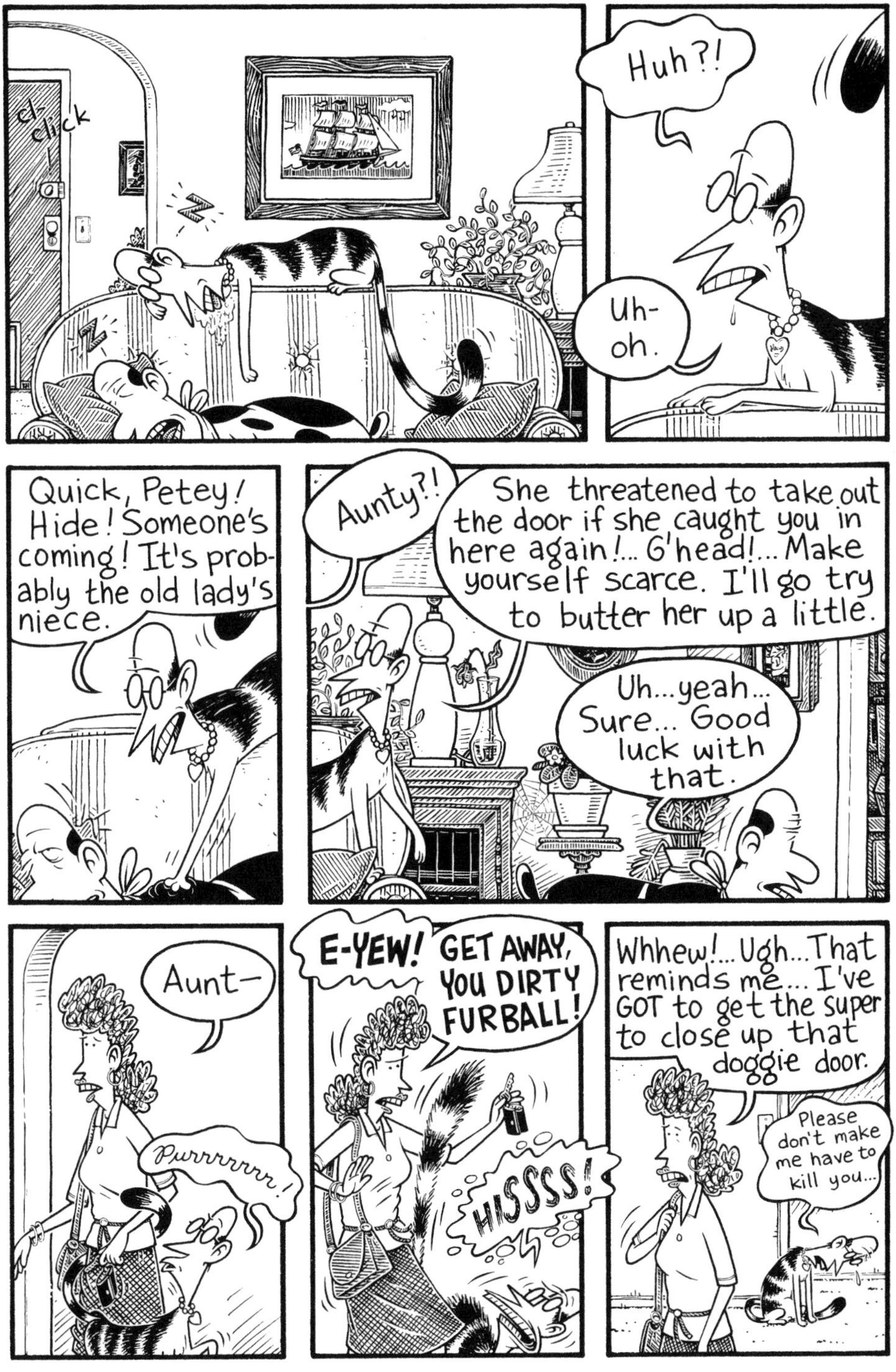
cl-click
Huh?!
Uh-oh.
Quick, Petey! Hide! Someone's coming! It's probably the old lady's niece.
Aunty?!
She threatened to take out the door if she caught you in here again!... G'head!... Make yourself scarce. I'll go try to butter her up a little.
Uh...yeah... Sure... Good luck with that.
Aunt—
Purrrrrrr!
E-YEW!
GET AWAY, YOU DIRTY FURBALL!
HISSSS!
Whhew!... Ugh... That reminds me... I've GOT to get the super to close up that doggie door.
Please don't make me have to kill you...

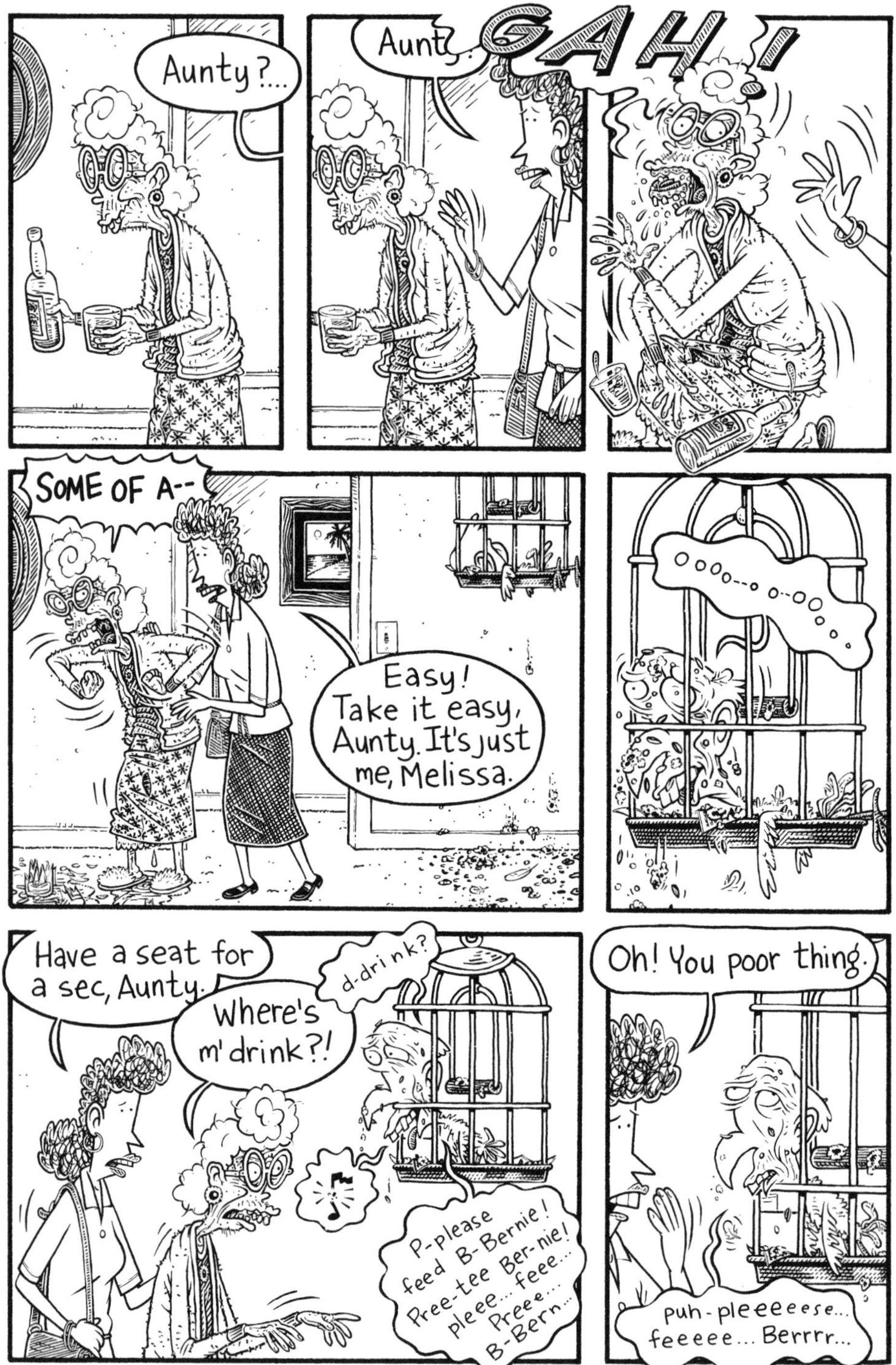
Aunty?...
Aunty...
GAH!
SOME OF A--
Easy! Take it easy, Aunty. It's just me, Melissa.
O O O o--o o--O O o o . .
Have a seat for a sec, Aunty.
Where's m'drink?!
d-drink?
P-please feed B-Bernie! Pree-tee Ber-nie! pleee... feee... Preee... B-Bern...
Oh! You poor thing.
puh-pleeeeese... feeeee... Berrrr...

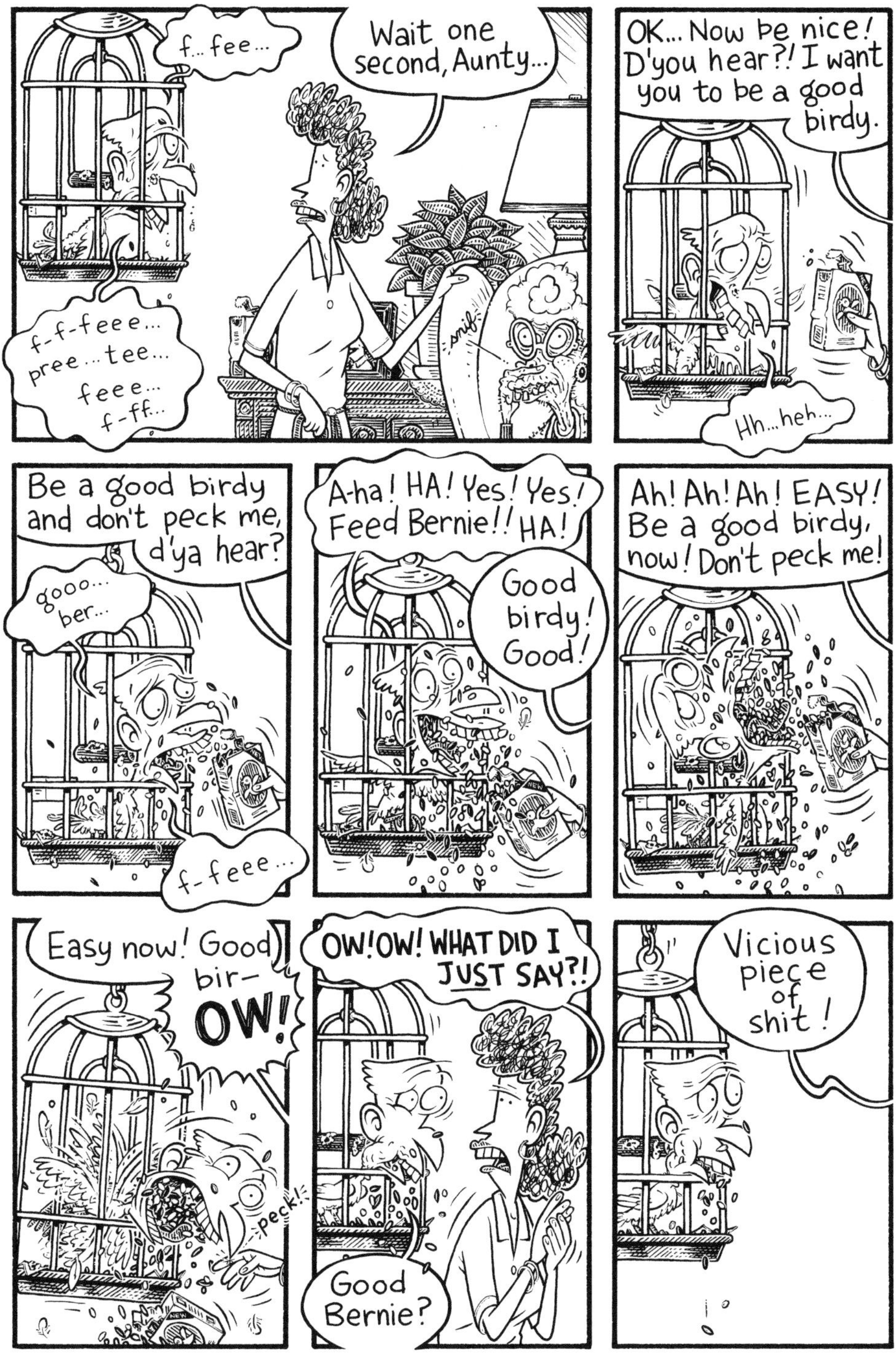

f... fee...
Wait one second, Aunty...
f-f-feee... pree...tee... feee... f-ff...
smif
OK... Now be nice! D'you hear?! I want you to be a good birdy.
Hh...heh...
Be a good birdy and don't peck me, d'ya hear?
gooo... ber...
f-feee...
A-ha! HA! Yes! Yes! Feed Bernie!! HA!
Good birdy! Good!
Ah! Ah! Ah! EASY! Be a good birdy, now! Don't peck me!
Easy now! Good bir-
OW!
peck!
OW! OW! WHAT DID I JUST SAY?!
Good Bernie?
Vicious piece of shit!

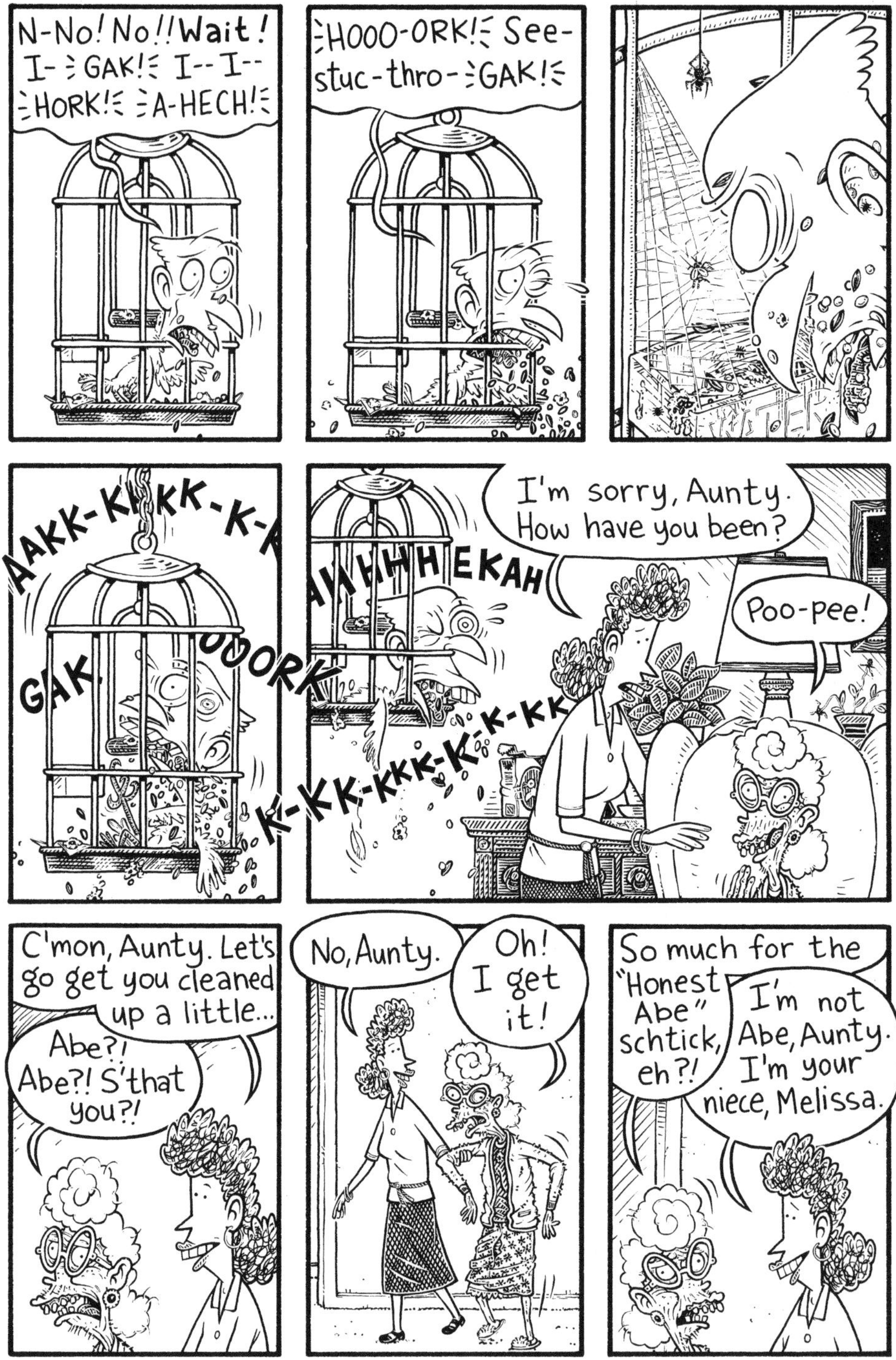

N-No! No!! Wait! I- GAK! I-- I-- HORK! A-HECH!
HOOO-ORK! See- stuc-thro- GAK!
AAKK-KKKK-K-K
GAK
OOORK
AHHHH EKAH
K-KK-KKK-K-K-KK
I'm sorry, Aunty. How have you been?
Poo-pee!
C'mon, Aunty. Let's go get you cleaned up a little...
Abe?! Abe?! S'that you?!
No, Aunty.
Oh! I get it!
So much for the "Honest Abe" schtick, eh?!
I'm not Abe, Aunty. I'm your niece, Melissa.

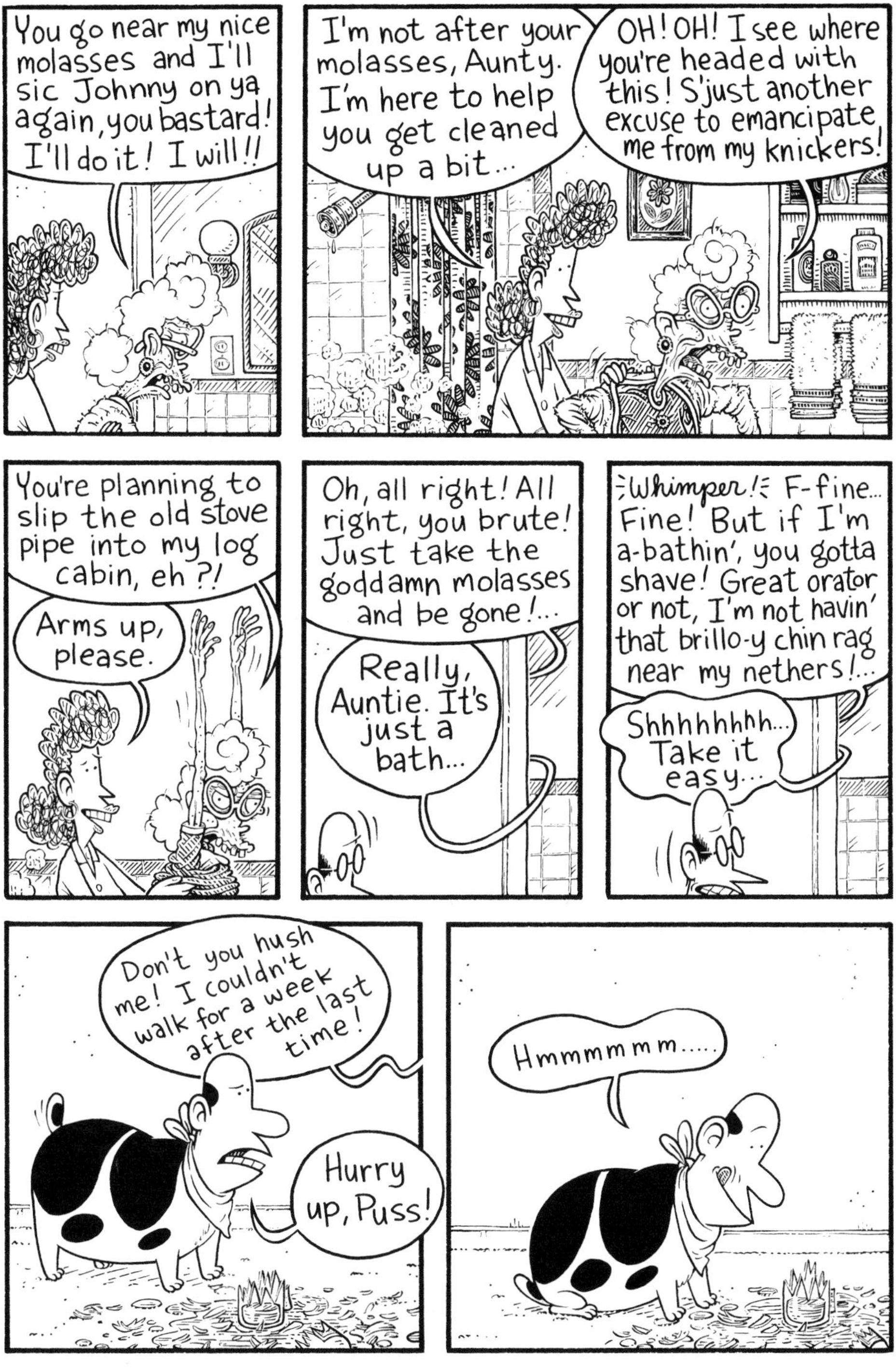
You go near my nice molasses and I'll sic Johnny on ya again, you bastard! I'll do it! I will!!
I'm not after your molasses, Aunty. I'm here to help you get cleaned up a bit...
OH! OH! I see where you're headed with this! S'just another excuse to emancipate me from my knickers!
You're planning to slip the old stove pipe into my log cabin, eh?!
Arms up, please.
Oh, all right! All right, you brute! Just take the goddamn molasses and be gone!...
Really, Auntie. It's just a bath...
Whimper! F-fine... Fine! But if I'm a-bathin', you gotta shave! Great orator or not, I'm not havin' that brillo-y chin rag near my nethers!...
Shhhhhhhh... Take it easy...
Don't you hush me! I couldn't walk for a week after the last time!
Hurry up, Puss!
Hmmmmmm.....

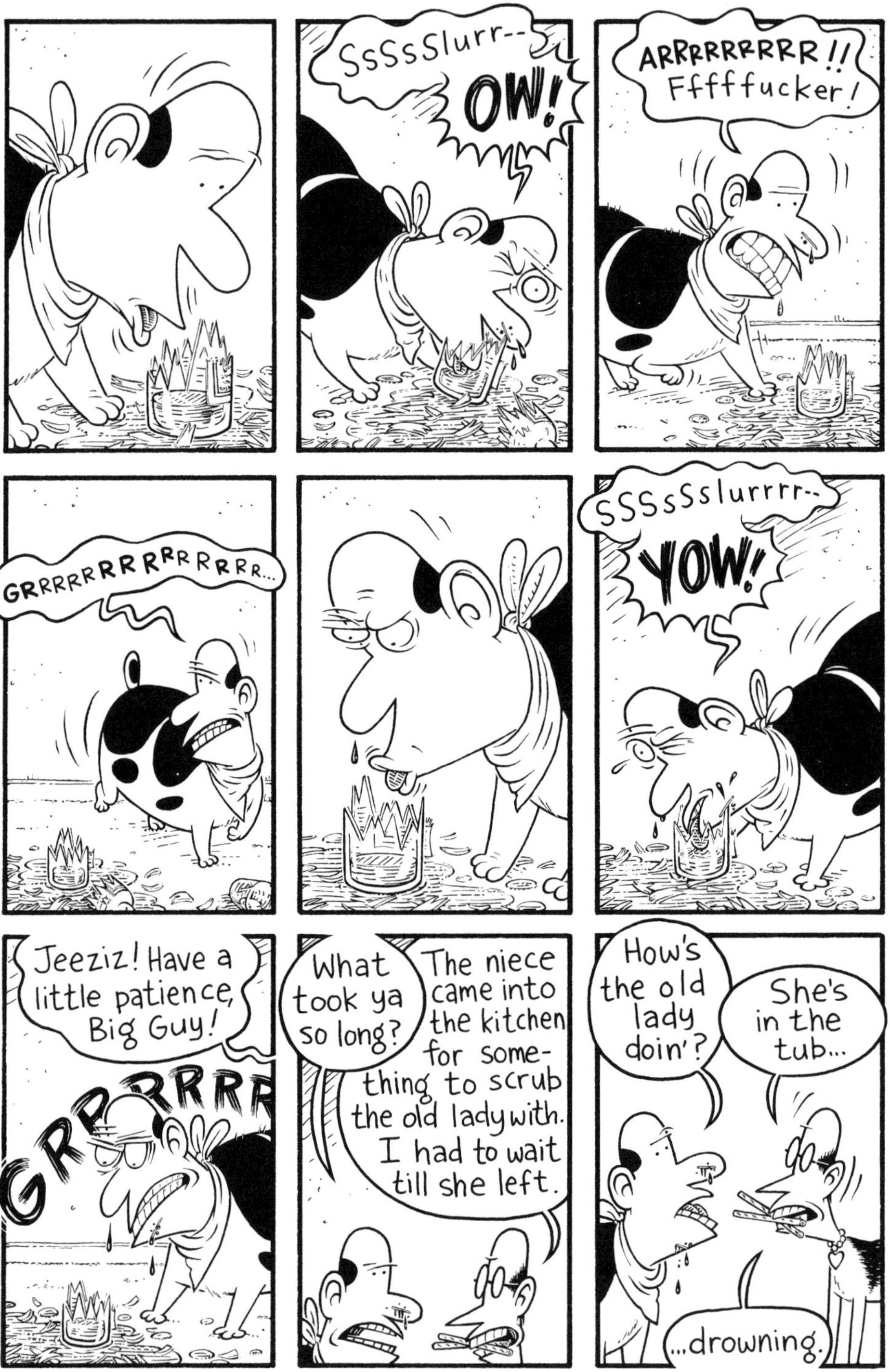

SsSsSlurr--
OW!
ARRRRRRRR!! Fffffucker!
GRRRRRRRRRRRR...
SSSsSslurrrr--
YOW!
Jeeziz! Have a little patience, Big Guy!
GRRRRRR
What took ya so long?
The niece came into the kitchen for something to scrub the old lady with. I had to wait till she left.
How's the old lady doin'?
She's in the tub...
...drowning.

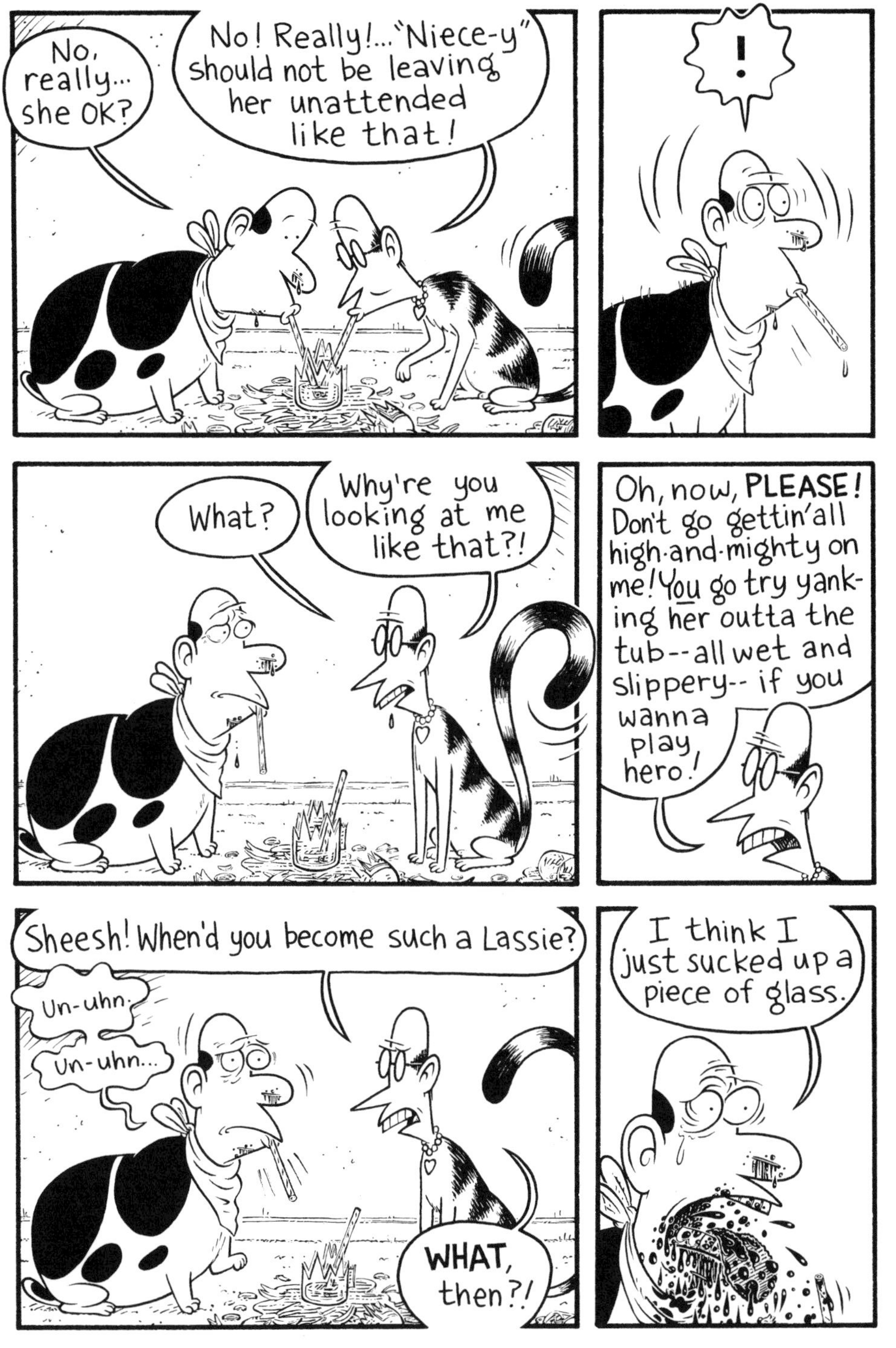
No, really... she OK?
No! Really!..."Niece-y" should not be leaving her unattended like that!
!
What?
Why're you looking at me like that?!
Oh, now, **PLEASE!** Don't go gettin' all high-and-mighty on me! You go try yank-ing her outta the tub--all wet and slippery-- if you wanna play hero!
Sheesh! When'd you become such a Lassie?
Un-uhn.
Un-uhn...
WHAT, then?!
I think I just sucked up a piece of glass.

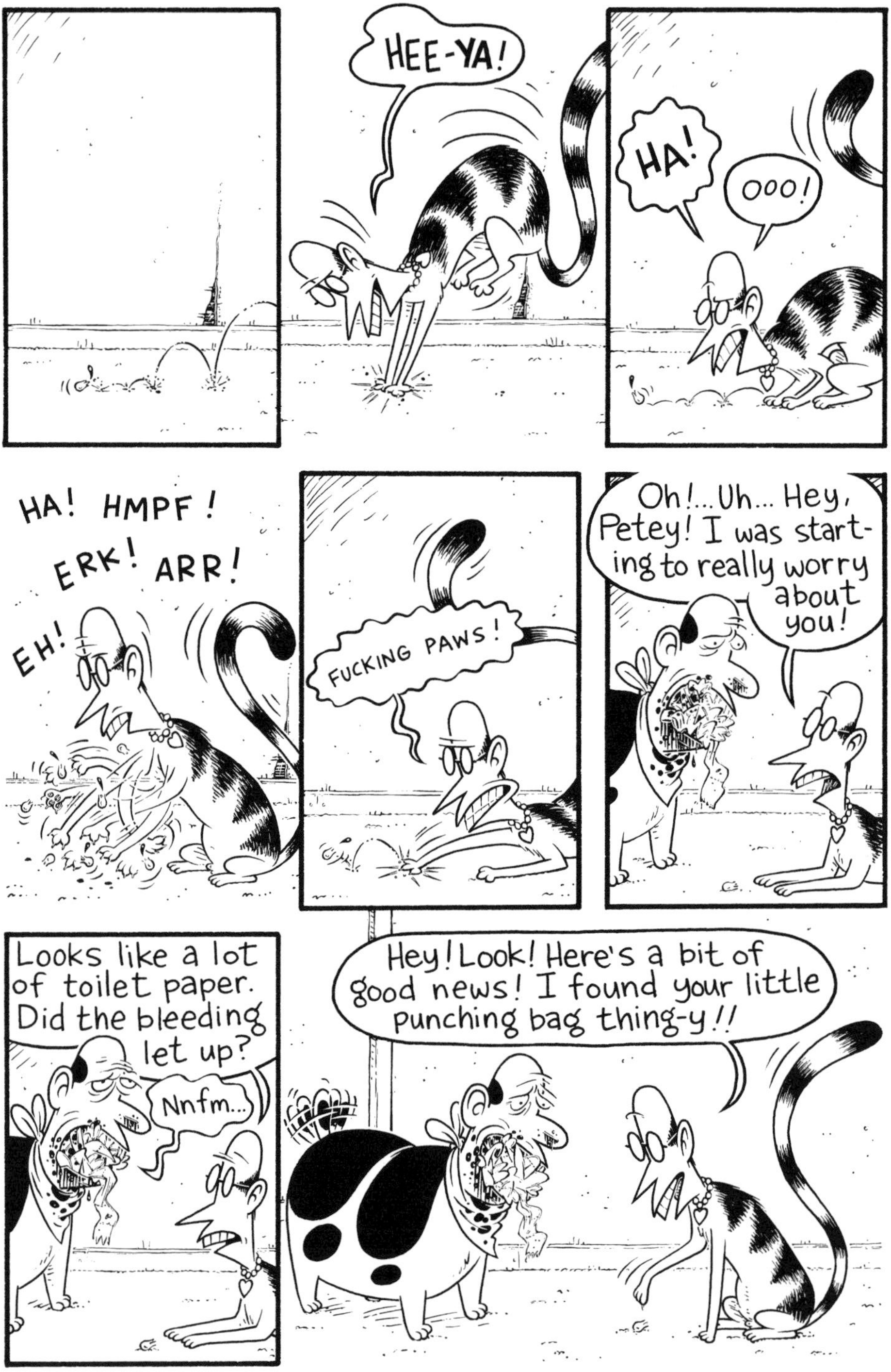
HEE-YA!
HA!
OOO!
HA! HMPF!
ERK! ARR!
EH!
FUCKING PAWS!
Oh!... Uh... Hey, Petey! I was starting to really worry about you!
Looks like a lot of toilet paper. Did the bleeding let up?
Nnfm...
Hey! Look! Here's a bit of good news! I found your little punching bag thing-y!!

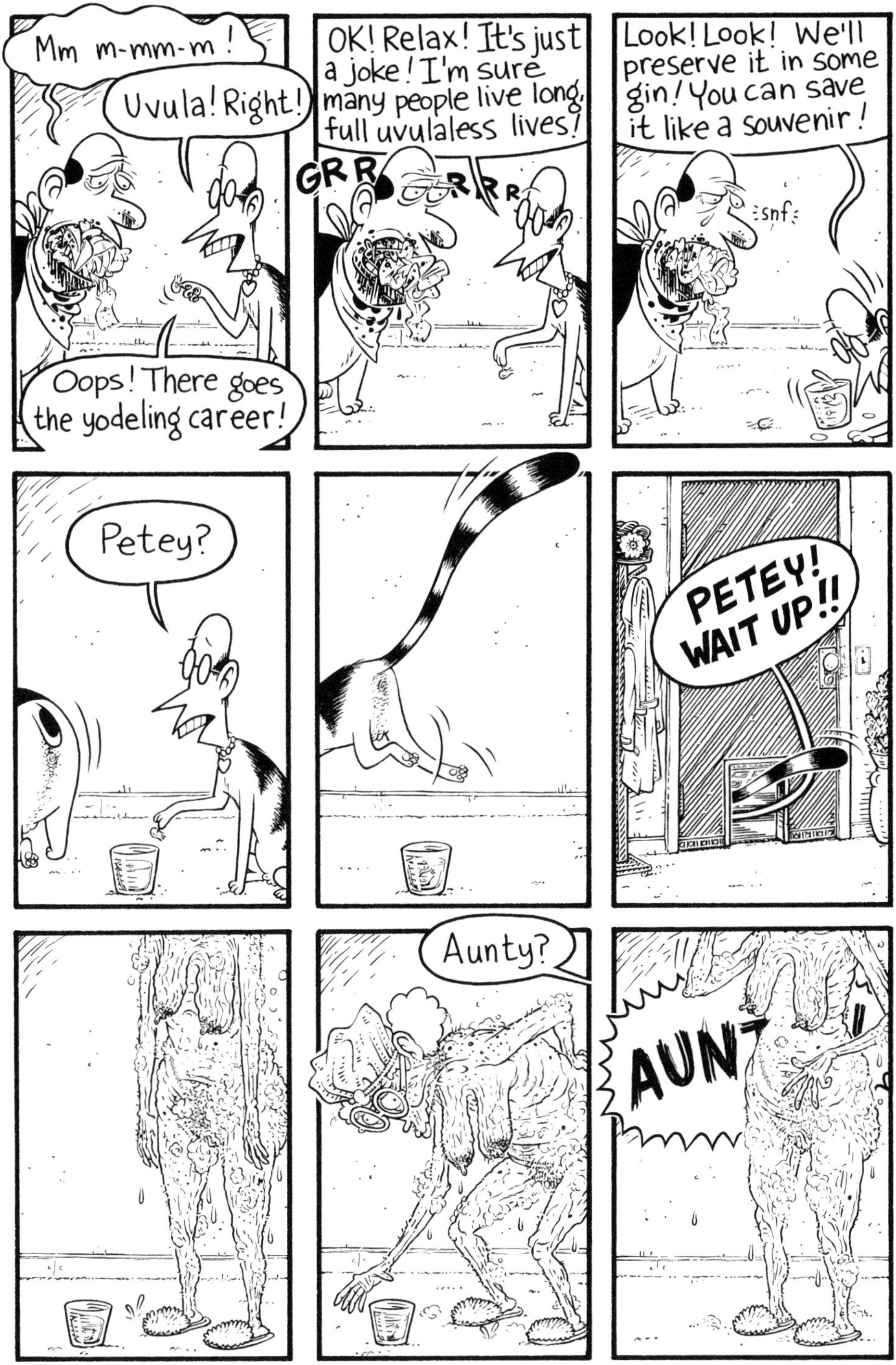
Mm m-mm-m!
Uvula! Right!
Oops! There goes the yodeling career!
OK! Relax! It's just a joke! I'm sure many people live long, full uvulaless lives!
GRRRRRR
Look! Look! We'll preserve it in some gin! You can save it like a souvenir!
snf
Petey?
PETEY! WAIT UP!!
Aunty?
AUNT

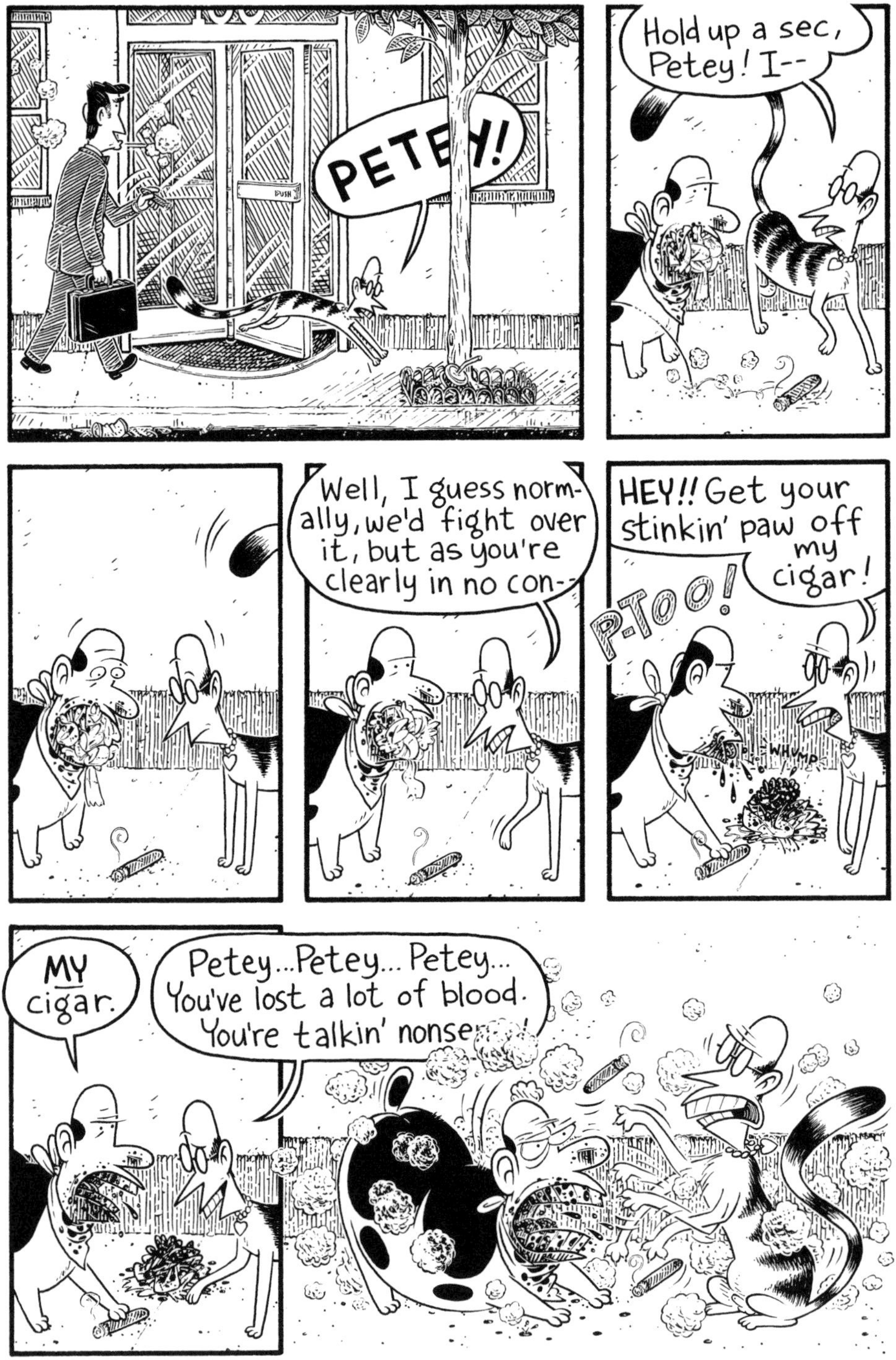
PUSH
PETEY!
Hold up a sec, Petey! I--
Well, I guess normally, we'd fight over it, but as you're clearly in no con--
HEY!! Get your stinkin' paw off my cigar!
P-TOO!
WHUMP
MY cigar.
Petey...Petey... Petey...
You've lost a lot of blood.
You're talkin' nonse

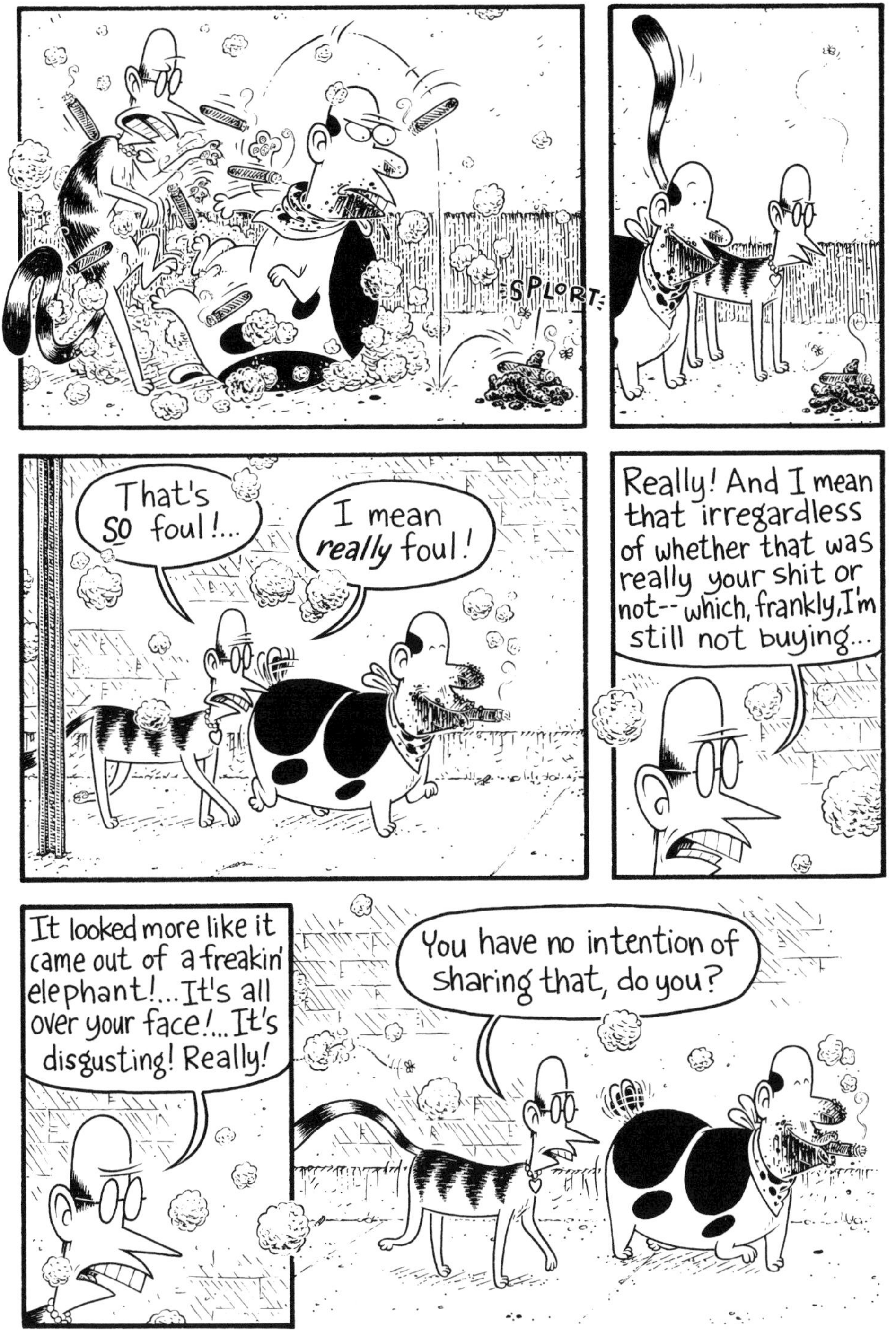
SPLORT
That's SO foul!...
I mean really foul!
Really! And I mean that irregardless of whether that was really your shit or not-- which, frankly, I'm still not buying...
It looked more like it came out of a freakin' elephant!... It's all over your face!... It's disgusting! Really!
You have no intention of sharing that, do you?

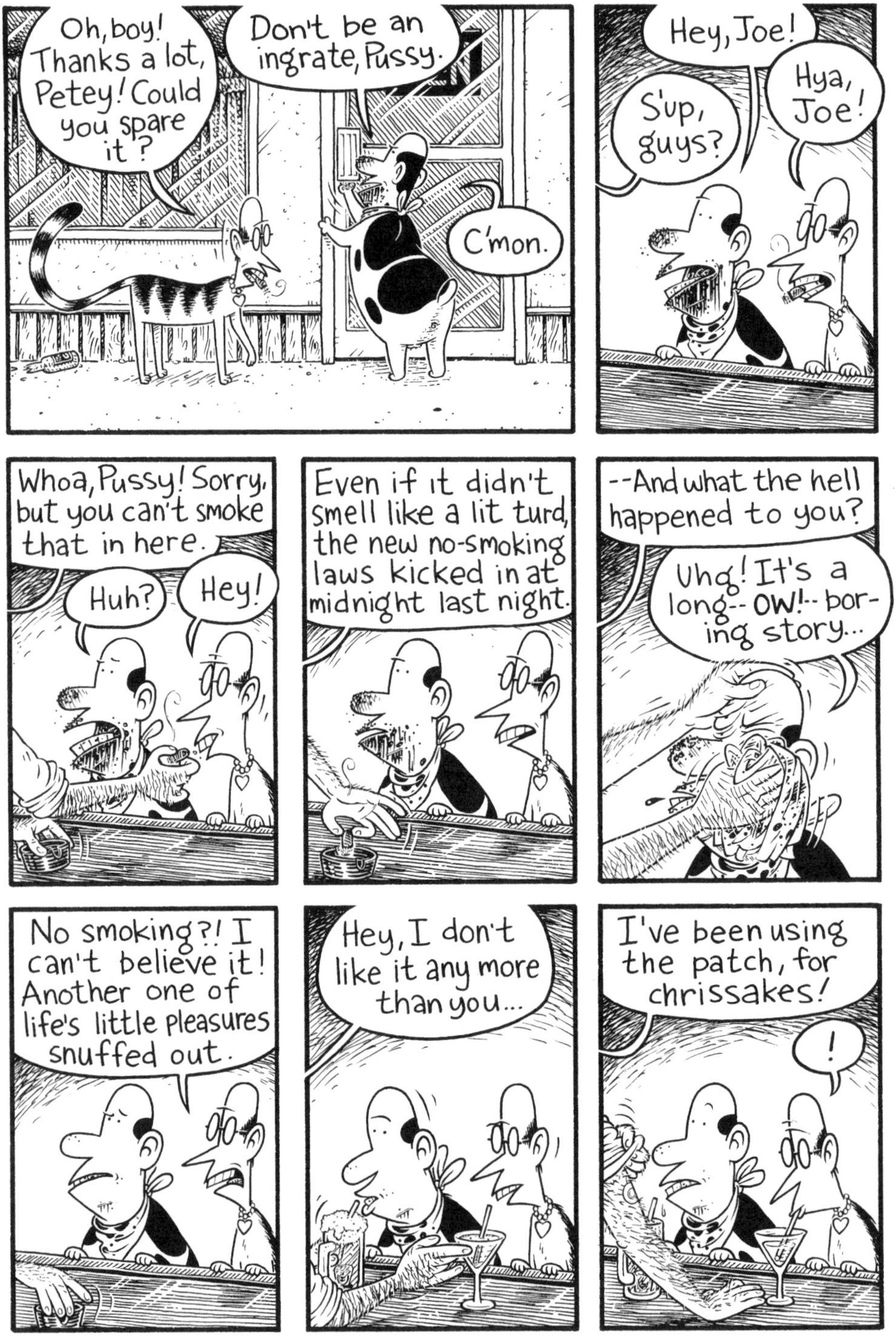
Oh, boy! Thanks a lot, Petey! Could you spare it?
Don't be an ingrate, Pussy.
C'mon.
Hey, Joe!
S'up, guys?
Hya, Joe!
Whoa, Pussy! Sorry, but you can't smoke that in here.
Huh?
Hey!
Even if it didn't smell like a lit turd, the new no-smoking laws kicked in at midnight last night.
--And what the hell happened to you?
Uhg! It's a long--OW!--boring story...
No smoking?! I can't believe it! Another one of life's little pleasures snuffed out.
Hey, I don't like it any more than you...
I've been using the patch, for chrissakes!
!

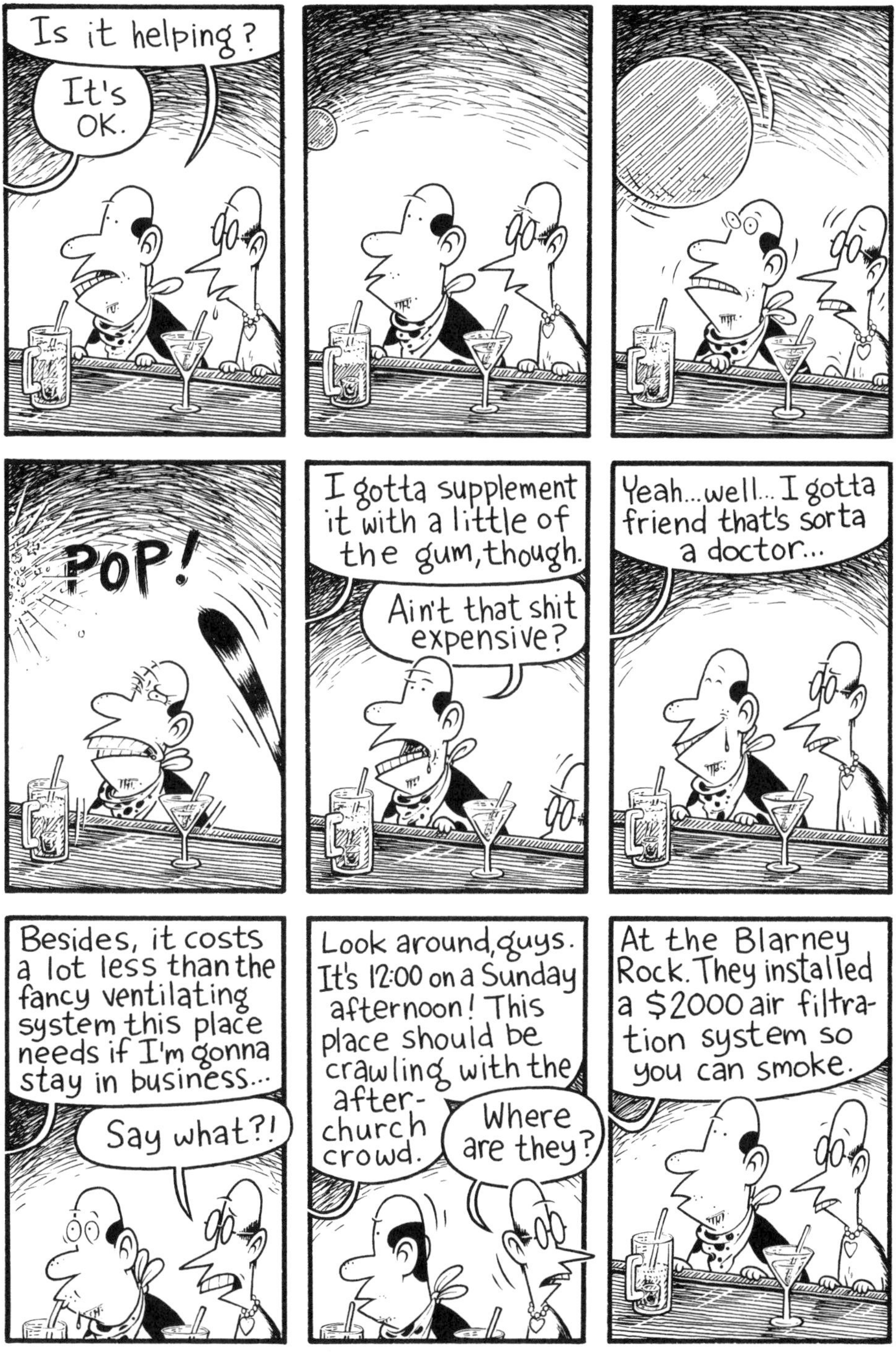
Is it helping?
It's OK.
POP!
I gotta supplement it with a little of the gum, though.
Ain't that shit expensive?
Yeah...well... I gotta friend that's sorta a doctor...
Besides, it costs a lot less than the fancy ventilating system this place needs if I'm gonna stay in business...
Say what?!
Look around, guys. It's 12:00 on a Sunday afternoon! This place should be crawling with the after-church crowd.
Where are they?
At the Blarney Rock. They installed a $2000 air filtration system so you can smoke.

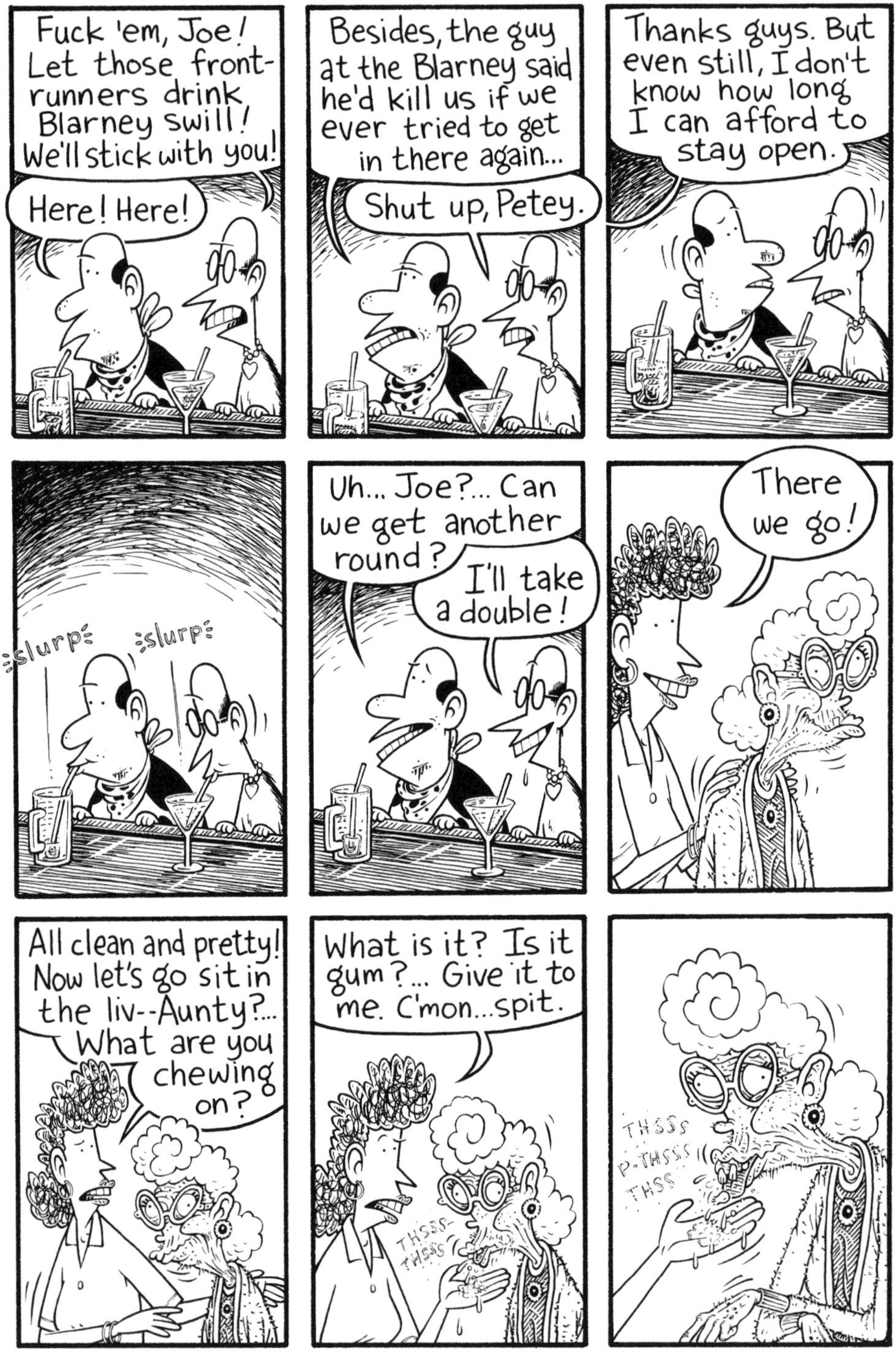
Fuck 'em, Joe! Let those front-runners drink Blarney swill! We'll stick with you!
Here! Here!
Besides, the guy at the Blarney said he'd kill us if we ever tried to get in there again...
Shut up, Petey.
Thanks guys. But even still, I don't know how long I can afford to stay open.
slurp
slurp
Uh... Joe?... Can we get another round?
I'll take a double!
There we go!
All clean and pretty! Now let's go sit in the liv--Aunty?...
What are you chewing on?
What is it? Is it gum?... Give it to me. C'mon...spit.
THSSS-
THSSS
THSSS
P-THSSS
THSS

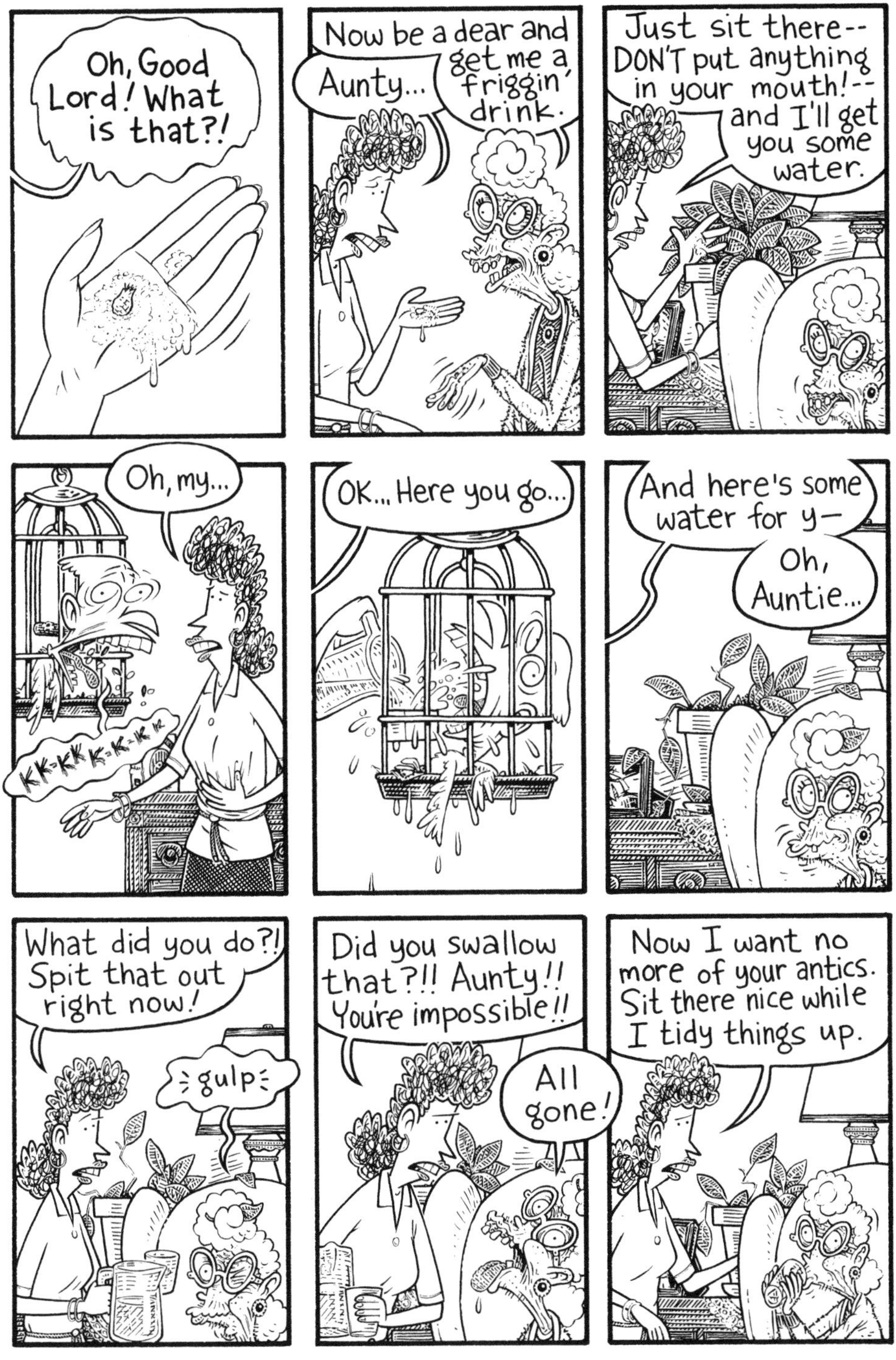
Oh, Good Lord! What is that?!
Aunty...
Now be a dear and get me a friggin' drink.
Just sit there-- DON'T put anything in your mouth!-- and I'll get you some water.
Oh, my...
KK-KK-K-K-K
OK... Here you go...
And here's some water for y—
Oh, Auntie...
What did you do?! Spit that out right now!
gulp
Did you swallow that?!! Aunty!! You're impossible!!
All gone!
Now I want no more of your antics. Sit there nice while I tidy things up.

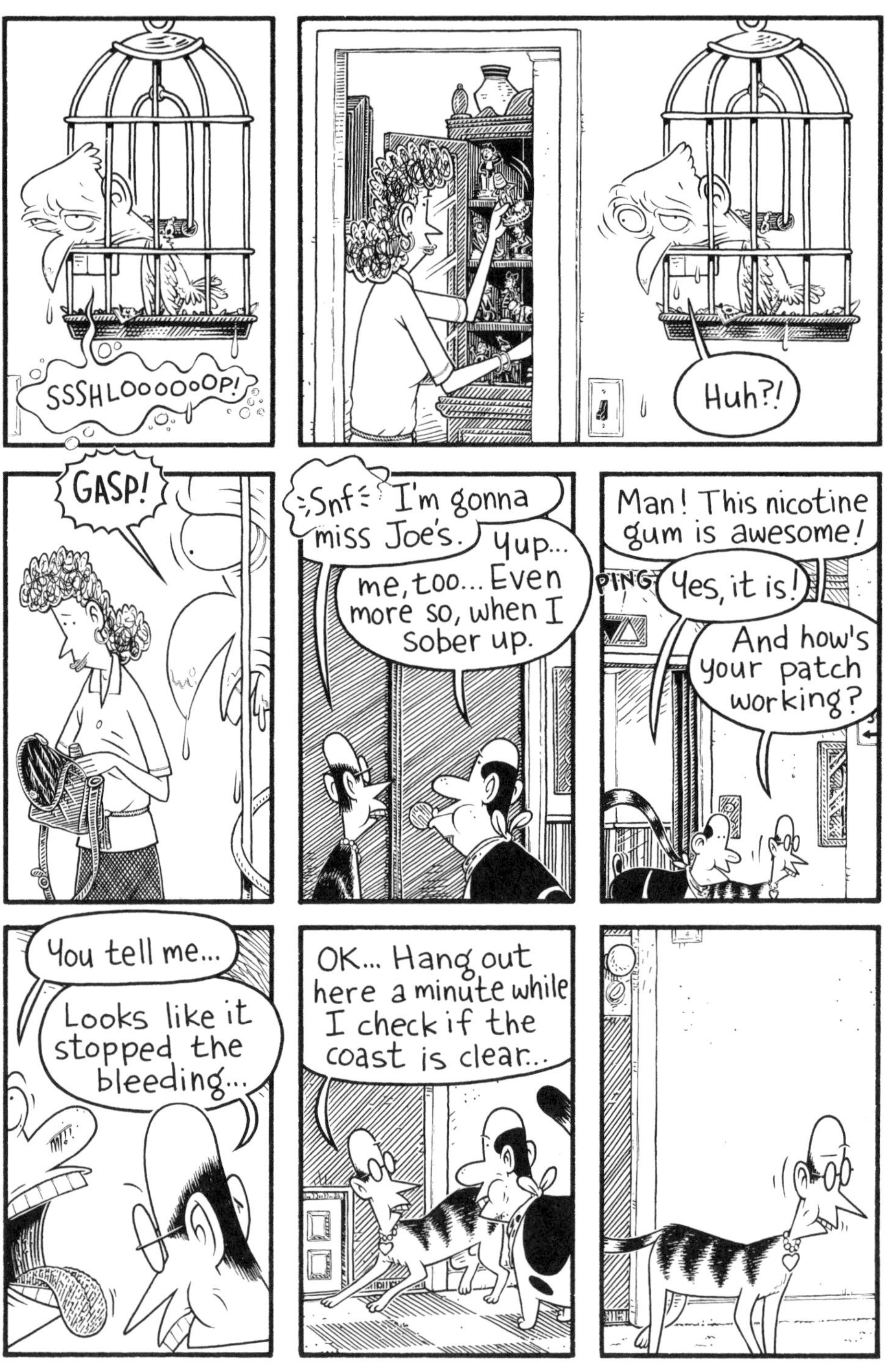
SSSHLOOOOOOOP!
Huh?!
GASP!
Snf I'm gonna miss Joe's.
Yup... me, too... Even more so, when I sober up.
Man! This nicotine gum is awesome!
PING
Yes, it is!
And how's your patch working?
You tell me...
Looks like it stopped the bleeding...
OK... Hang out here a minute while I check if the coast is clear...

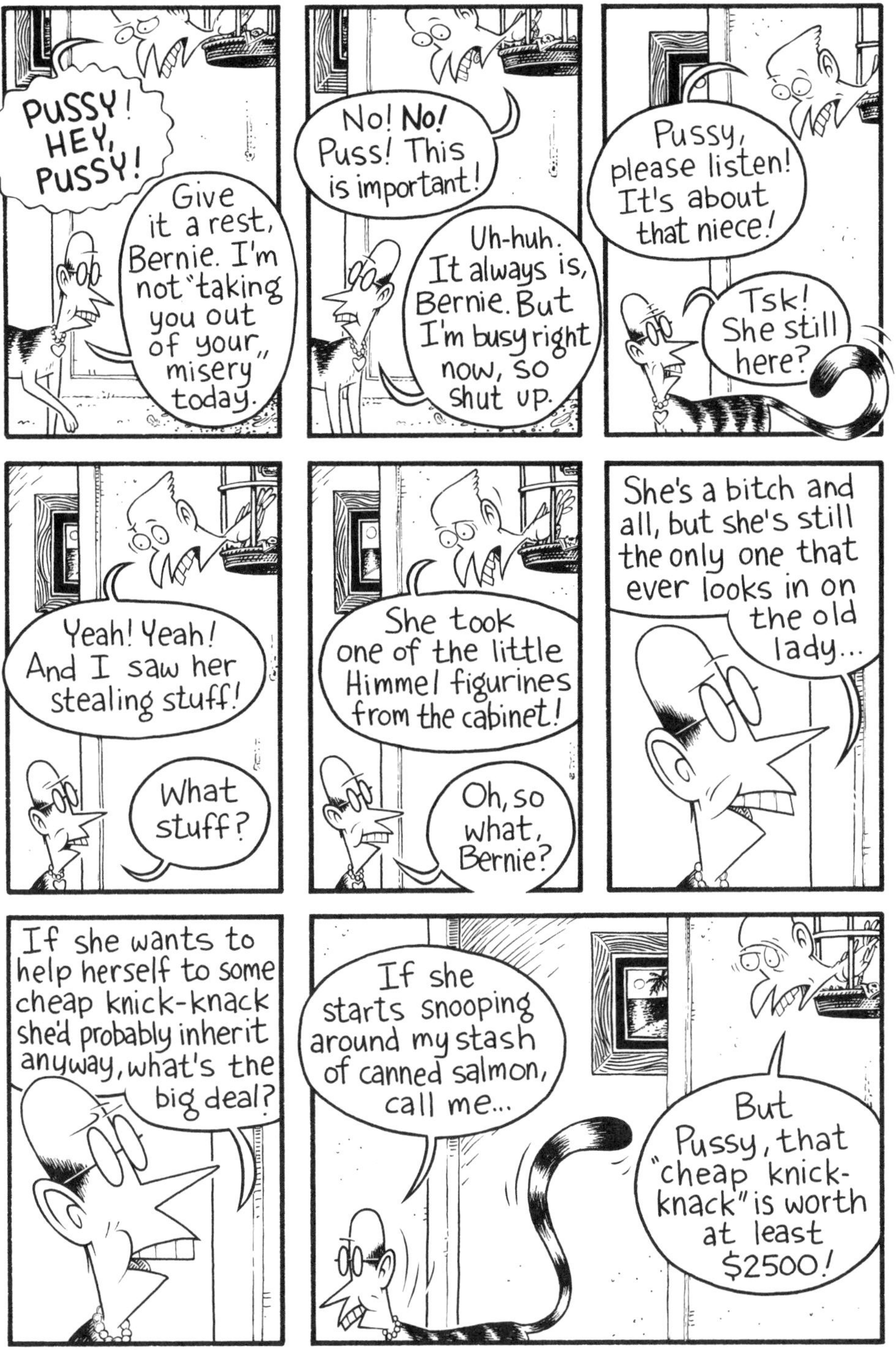
PUSSY! HEY, PUSSY!
Give it a rest, Bernie. I'm not "taking you out of your misery" today.
No! No! Puss! This is important!
Uh-huh. It always is, Bernie. But I'm busy right now, so shut up.
Pussy, please listen! It's about that niece!
Tsk! She still here?
Yeah! Yeah! And I saw her stealing stuff!
What stuff?
She took one of the little Himmel figurines from the cabinet!
Oh, so what, Bernie?
She's a bitch and all, but she's still the only one that ever looks in on the old lady...
If she wants to help herself to some cheap knick-knack she'd probably inherit anyway, what's the big deal?
If she starts snooping around my stash of canned salmon, call me...
But Pussy, that "cheap knick-knack" is worth at least $2500!

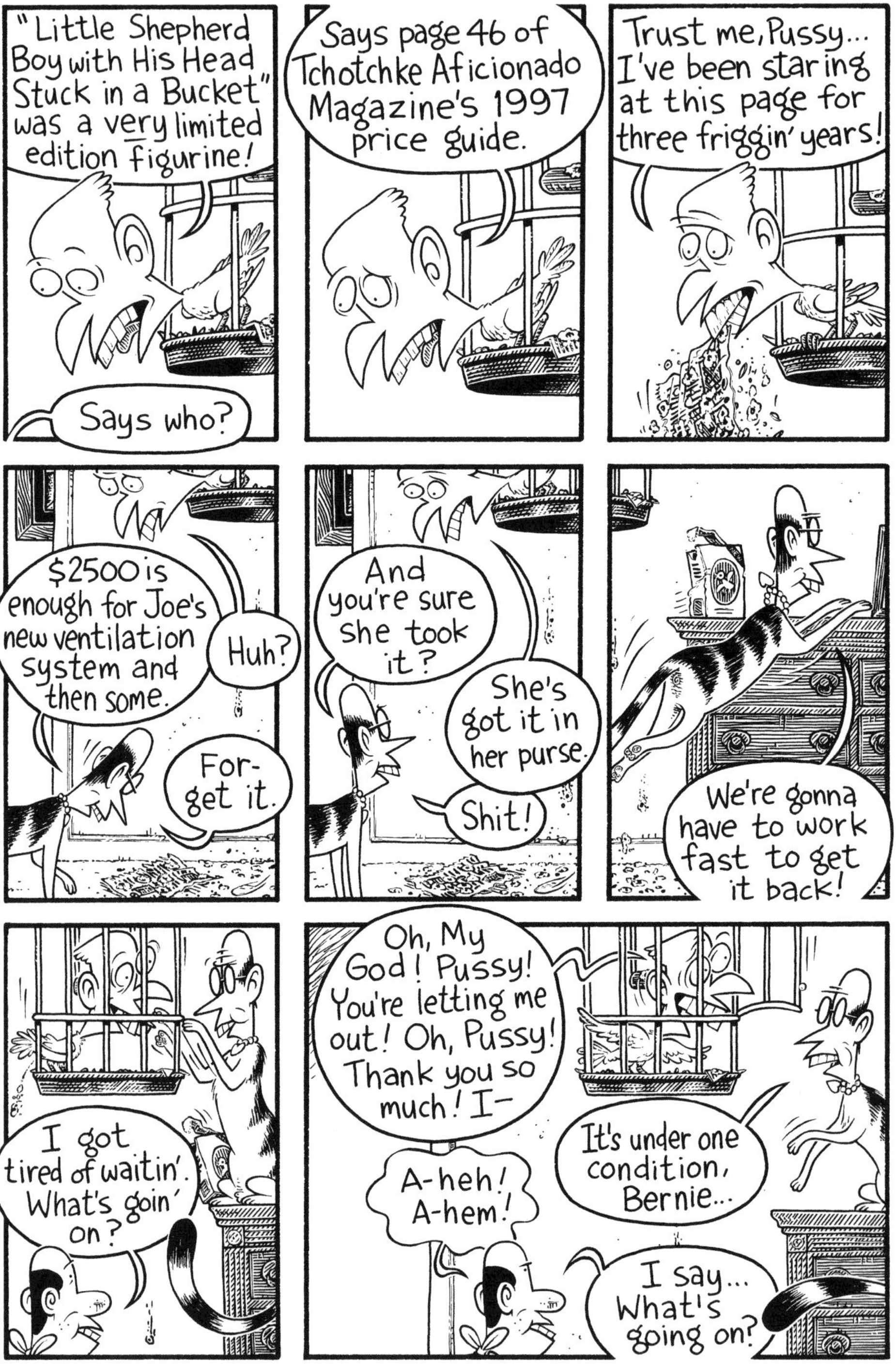
"Little Shepherd Boy with His Head Stuck in a Bucket" was a very limited edition figurine!
Says who?
Says page 46 of Tchotchke Aficionado Magazine's 1997 price guide.
Trust me, Pussy... I've been staring at this page for three friggin' years!
$2500 is enough for Joe's new ventilation system and then some.
Huh?
For-get it.
And you're sure she took it?
She's got it in her purse.
Shit!
We're gonna have to work fast to get it back!
I got tired of waitin'. What's goin' on?
Oh, My God! Pussy! You're letting me out! Oh, Pussy! Thank you so much! I—
It's under one condition, Bernie...
A-heh! A-hem!
I say... What's going on?

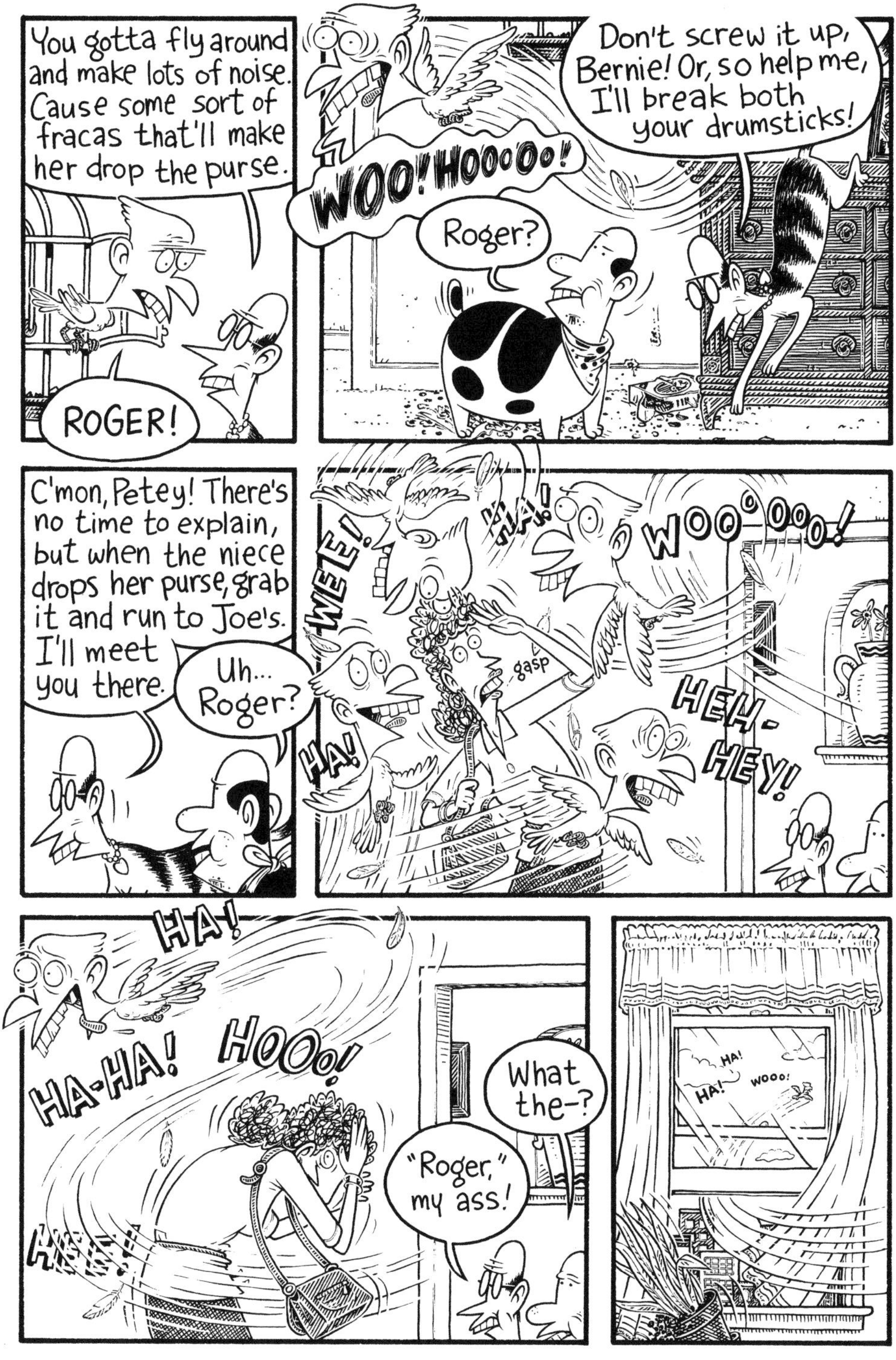
You gotta fly around and make lots of noise. Cause some sort of fracas that'll make her drop the purse.
ROGER!
Don't screw it up, Bernie! Or, so help me, I'll break both your drumsticks!
WOO! HOOoOo!
Roger?
C'mon, Petey! There's no time to explain, but when the niece drops her purse, grab it and run to Joe's. I'll meet you there.
Uh... Roger?
WEE!
HA!
WOOoOOO!
gasp
HA!
HEH-HEY!
HA!
HA-HA!
HOOo!
What the-?
"Roger," my ass!
HA!
HA!
WOOO!

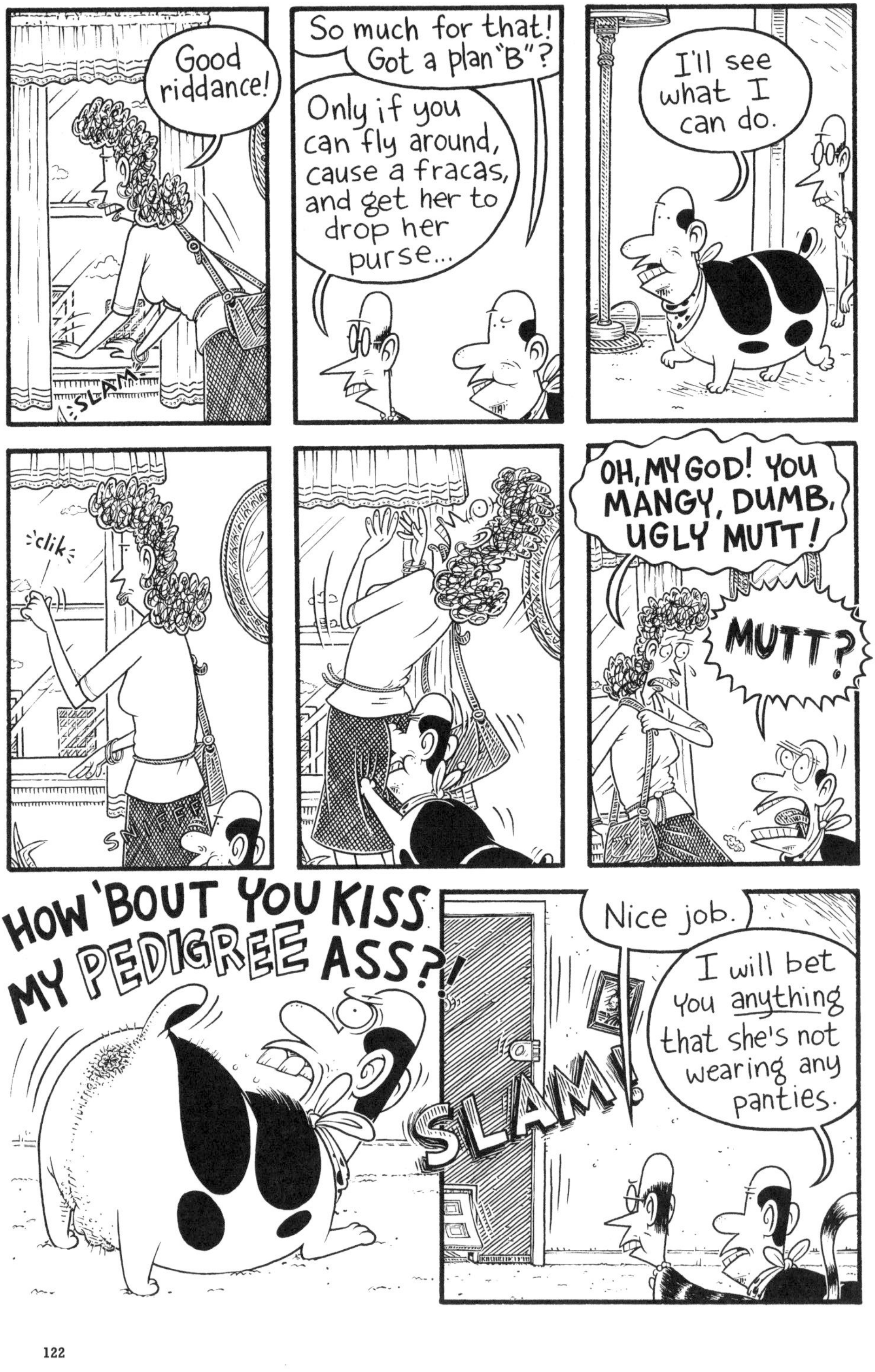
Good riddance!
SLAM
So much for that! Got a plan "B"?
Only if you can fly around, cause a fracas, and get her to drop her purse...
I'll see what I can do.
clik
SNIFFF
OH, MY GOD! YOU MANGY, DUMB, UGLY MUTT!
MUTT?
HOW 'BOUT YOU KISS MY PEDIGREE ASS?!
SLAM!
Nice job.
I will bet you anything that she's not wearing any panties.

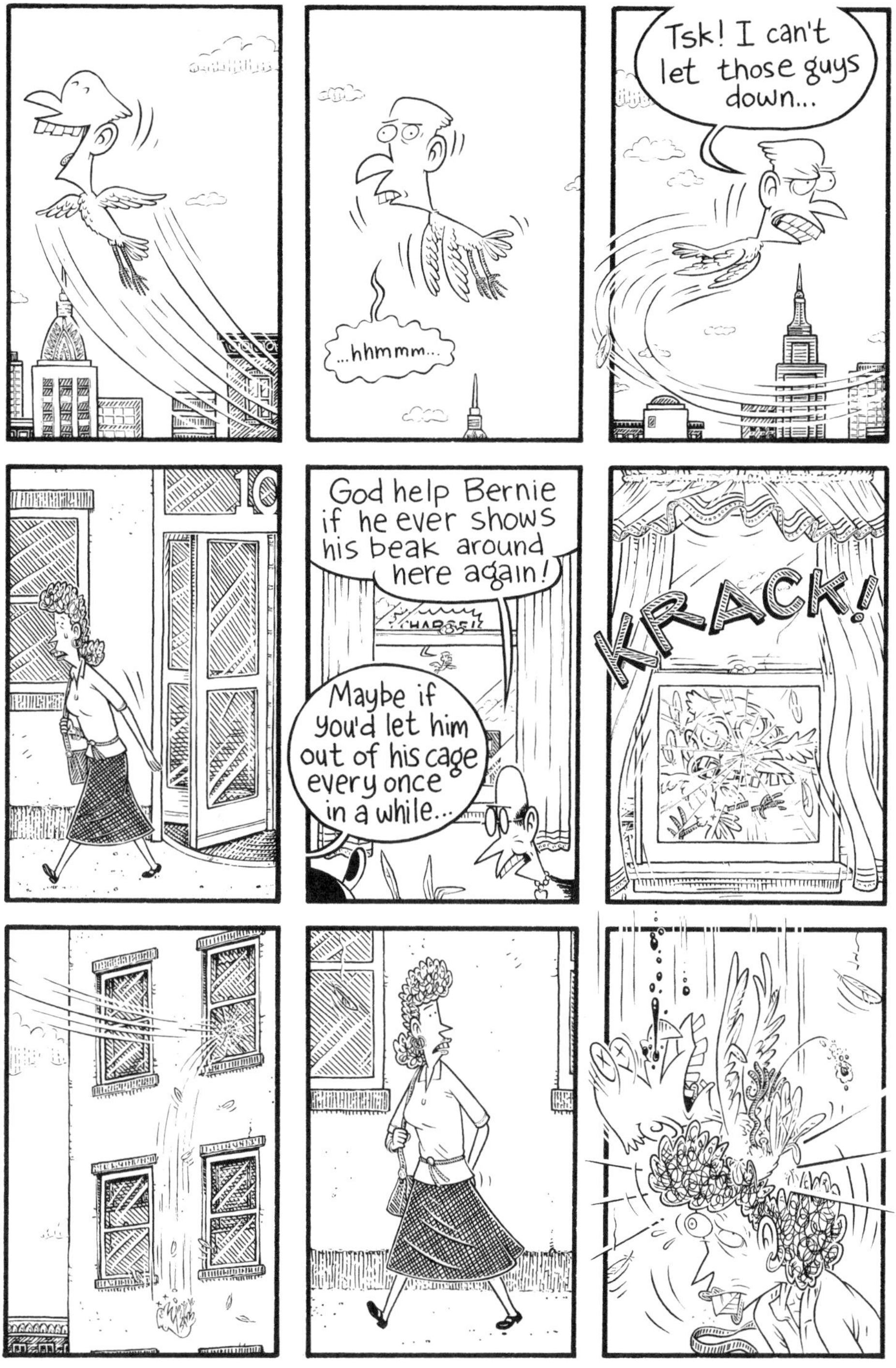
Tsk! I can't let those guys down...
...hhmmm...
God help Bernie if he ever shows his beak around here again!
Maybe if you'd let him out of his cage every once in a while...
KRACK!

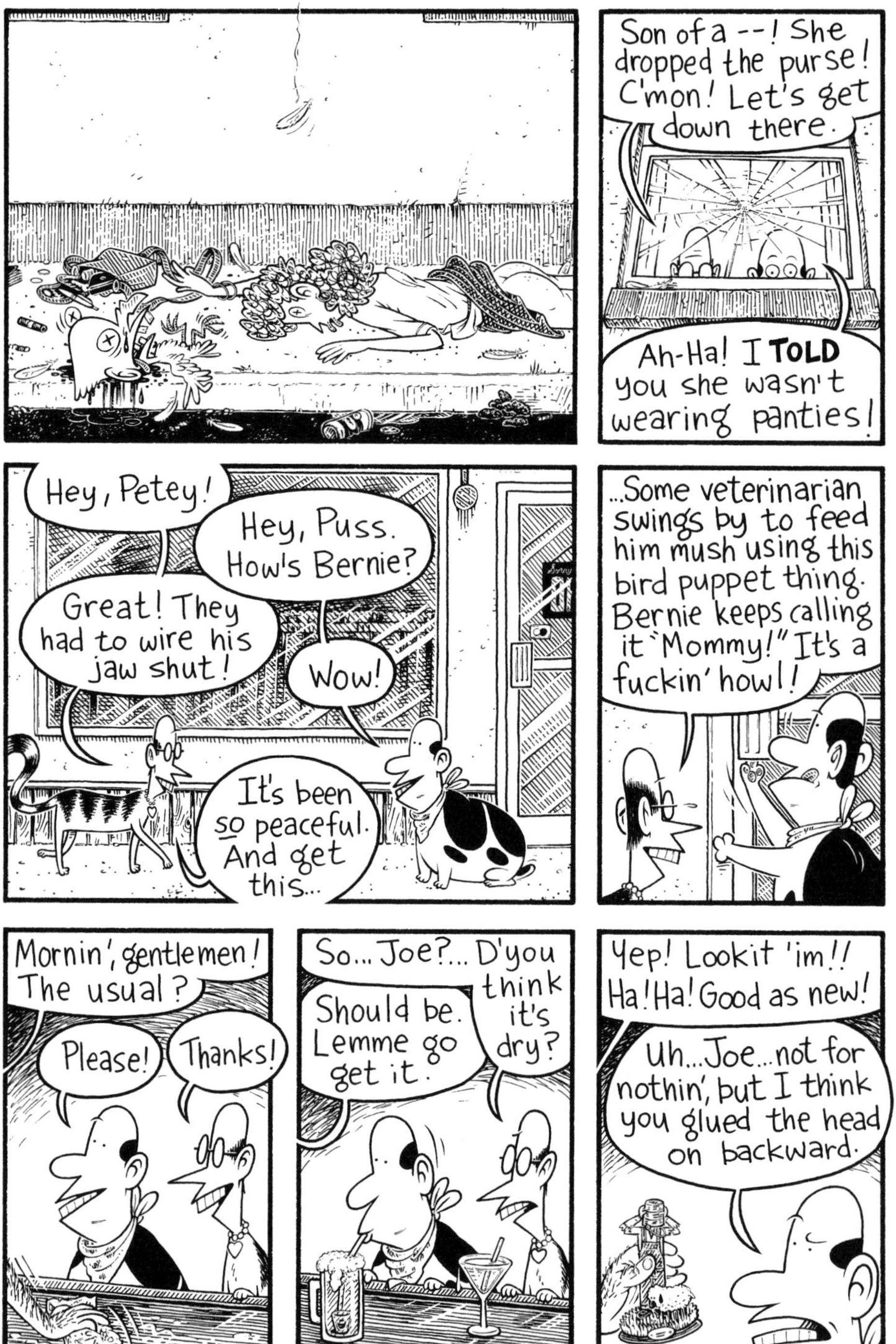
Son of a --! She dropped the purse! C'mon! Let's get down there.
Ah-Ha! I TOLD you she wasn't wearing panties!
Hey, Petey!
Hey, Puss. How's Bernie?
Great! They had to wire his jaw shut!
Wow!
It's been so peaceful. And get this...
...Some veterinarian swings by to feed him mush using this bird puppet thing. Bernie keeps calling it "Mommy!" It's a fuckin' howl!
Mornin', gentlemen! The usual?
Please!
Thanks!
So... Joe?... D'you think it's dry?
Should be. Lemme go get it.
Yep! Lookit 'im!! Ha! Ha! Good as new!
Uh...Joe...not for nothin', but I think you glued the head on backward.

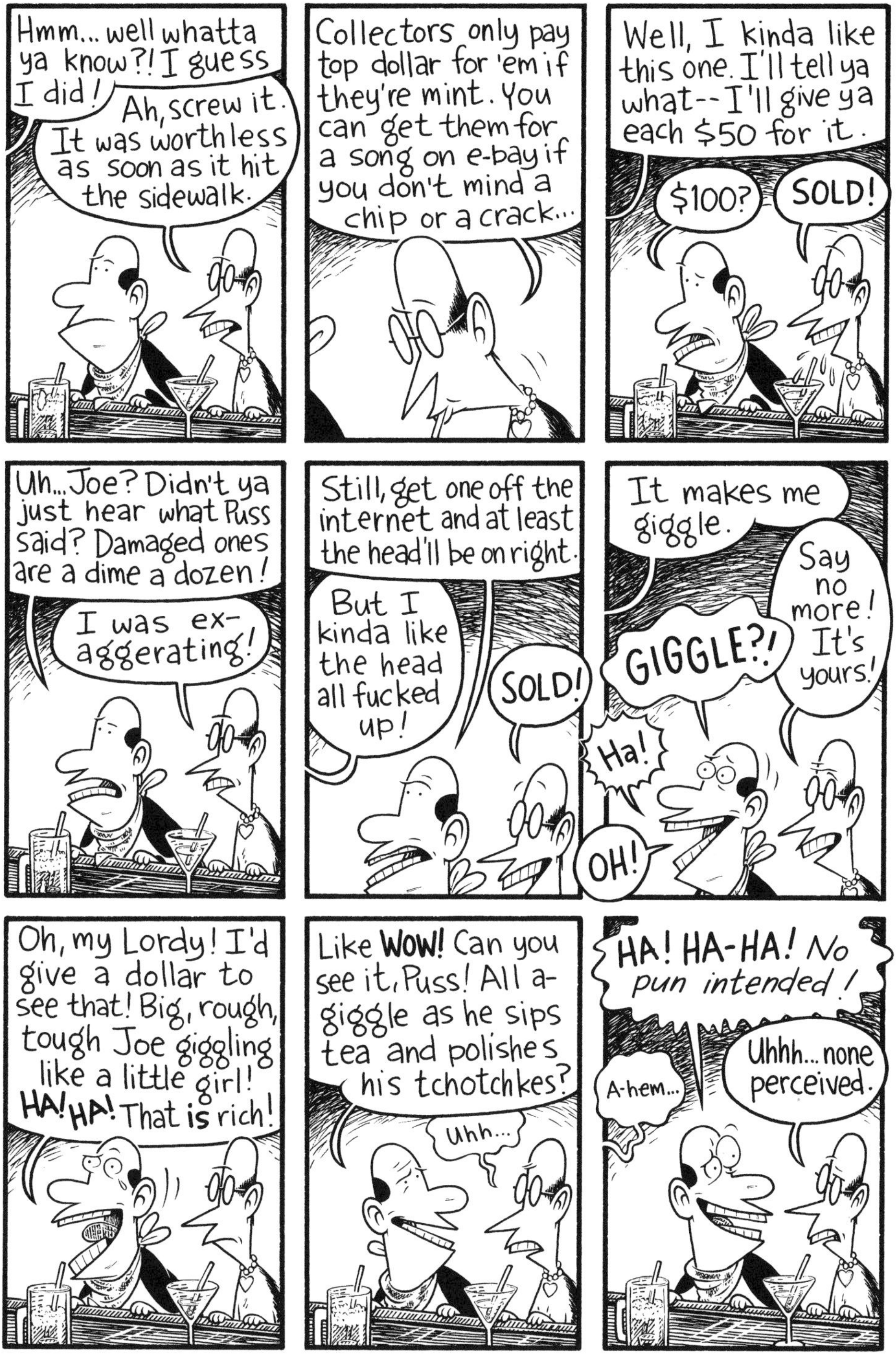
Hmm... well whatta ya know?! I guess I did!
Ah, screw it. It was worthless as soon as it hit the sidewalk.
Collectors only pay top dollar for 'em if they're mint. You can get them for a song on e-bay if you don't mind a chip or a crack...
Well, I kinda like this one. I'll tell ya what-- I'll give ya each $50 for it.
$100?
SOLD!
Uh...Joe? Didn't ya just hear what Puss said? Damaged ones are a dime a dozen!
I was ex-aggerating!
Still, get one off the internet and at least the head'll be on right.
But I kinda like the head all fucked up!
SOLD!
It makes me giggle.
GIGGLE?!
Say no more! It's yours!
Ha!
OH!
Oh, my Lordy! I'd give a dollar to see that! Big, rough, tough Joe giggling like a little girl! HA! HA! That is rich!
Like WOW! Can you see it, Puss! All a-giggle as he sips tea and polishes his tchotchkes?
Uhh...
HA! HA-HA! No pun intended!
A-hem...
Uhhh...none perceived.

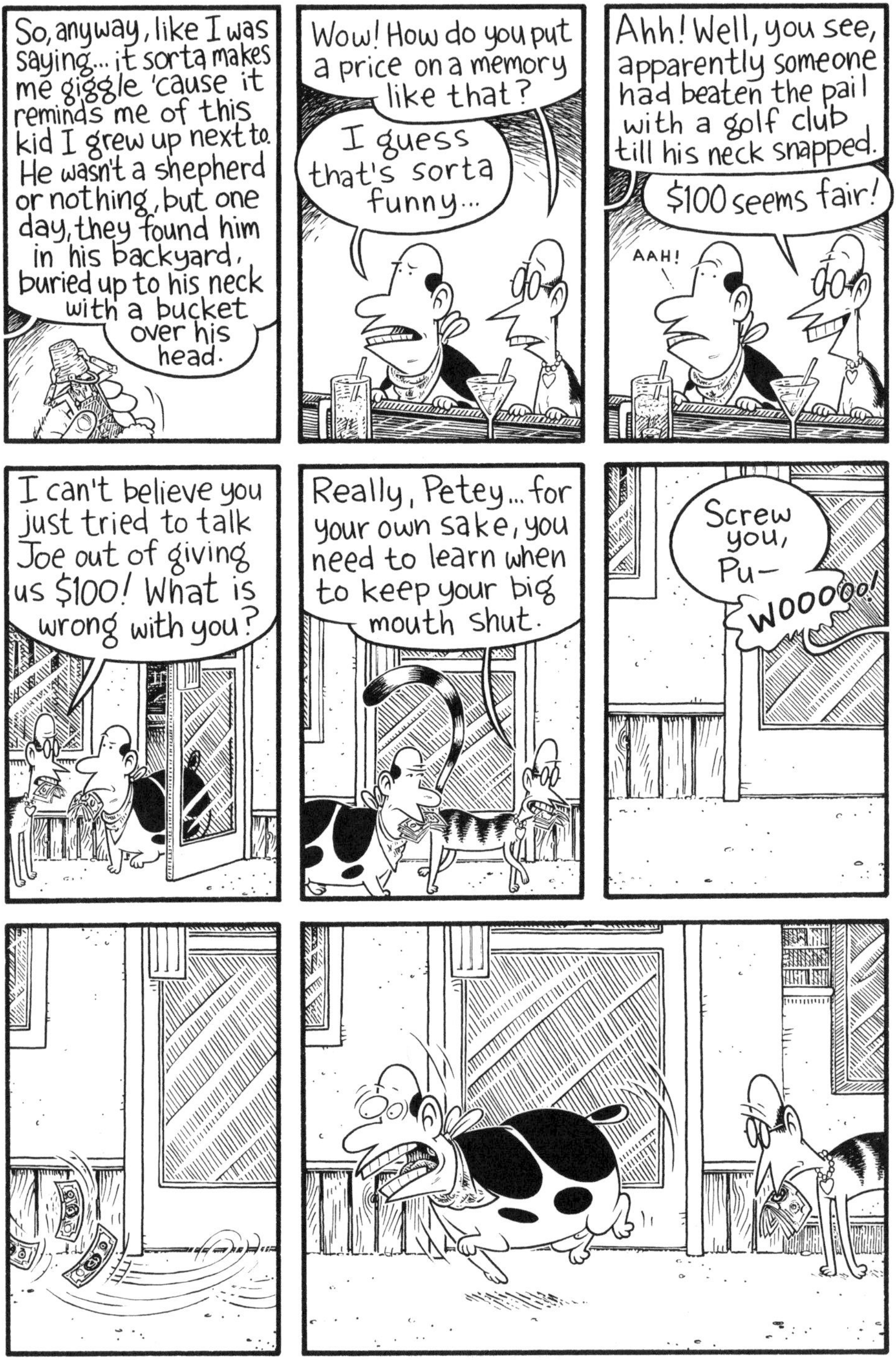
So, anyway, like I was saying... it sorta makes me giggle 'cause it reminds me of this kid I grew up next to. He wasn't a shepherd or nothing, but one day, they found him in his backyard, buried up to his neck with a bucket over his head.
Wow! How do you put a price on a memory like that?
I guess that's sorta funny...
Ahh! Well, you see, apparently someone had beaten the pail with a golf club till his neck snapped.
$100 seems fair!
AAH!
I can't believe you just tried to talk Joe out of giving us $100! What is wrong with you?
Really, Petey... for your own sake, you need to learn when to keep your big mouth shut.
Screw you, Pu–
WOOOOO!